Robin Wood's

CORES

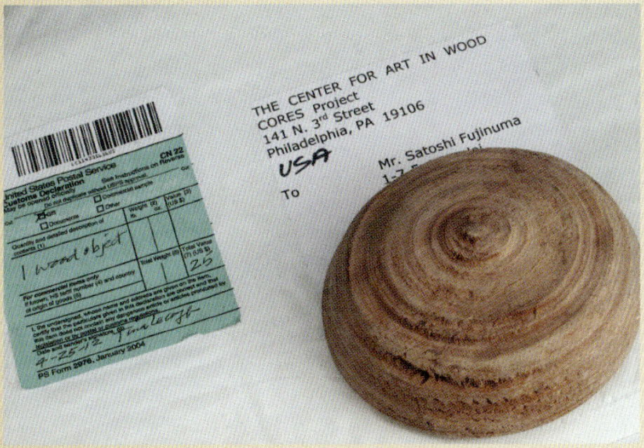

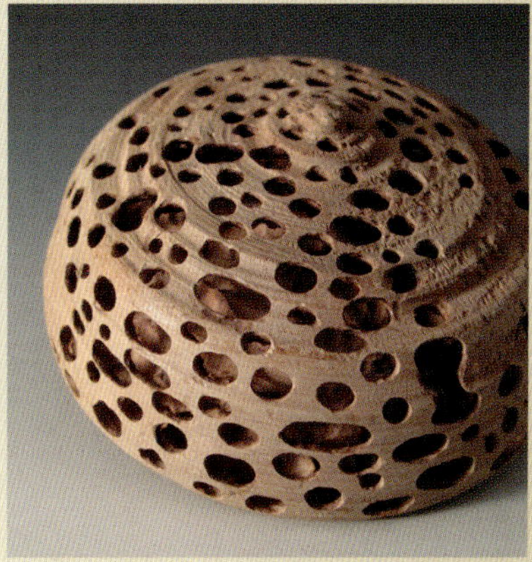

RECYCLED

Schiffer Publishing Ltd
4880 Lower Valley Road · Atglen, PA 19310

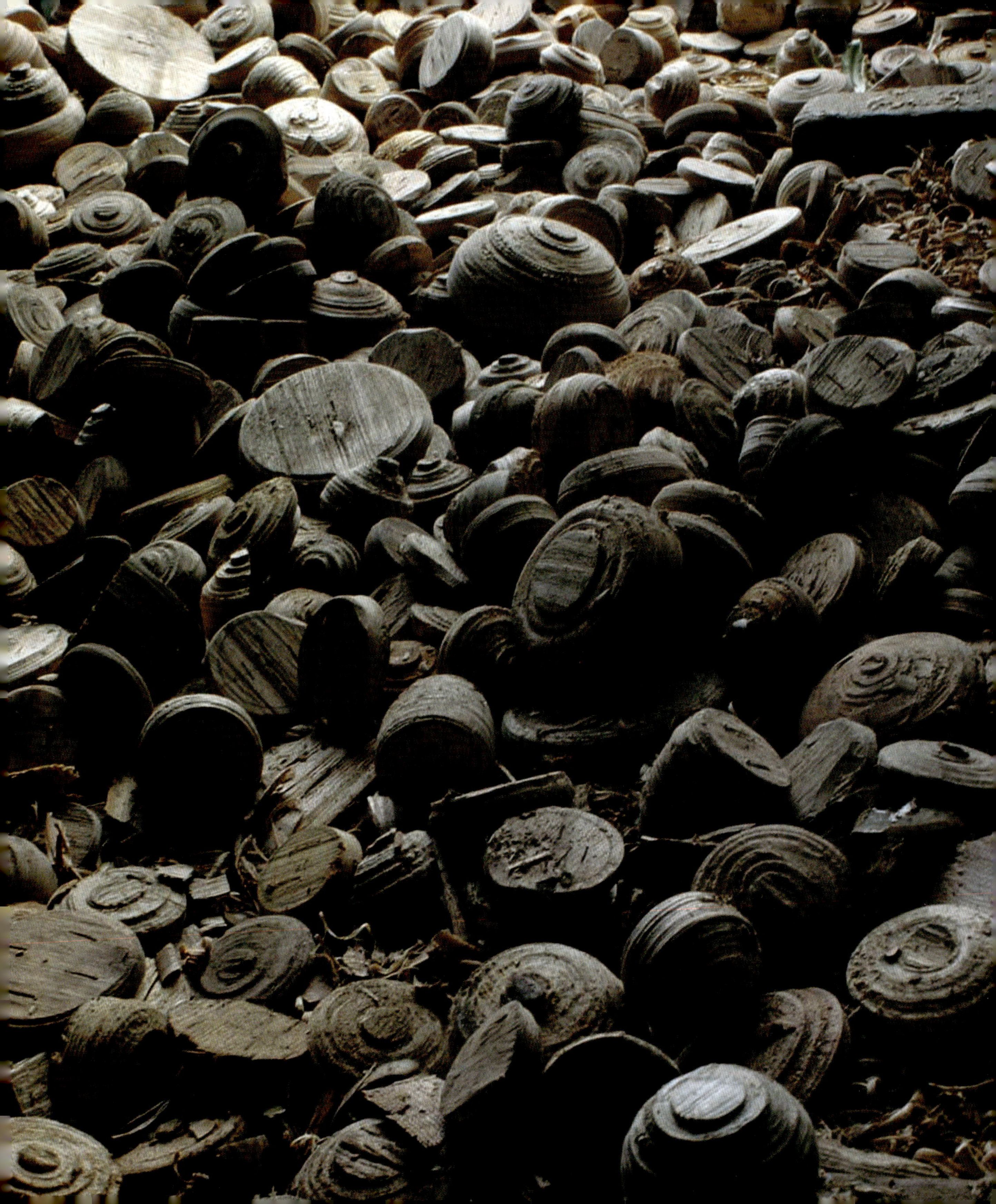

Contents

Introduction

Initially, they were chunks of roughly rounded wood that had tumbled out of bowls turned in an ancient technique. Then, at the hands of more than two score modern artists, they became the objects in an exhibition by The Center for Art in Wood.

The Center is pleased to produce this documentation of ***Robin Wood's CORES Recycled,*** the exhibition that occurred from November 2, 2012, through February 16, 2013.

Robin Wood of the United Kingdom is an accomplished pole turner and author, known for his historical and functional objects that help keep the tradition of pole turning alive and in front of the public. The leg-powered process Robin uses results in thousands of solid, round chunks—cores—that get broken out of the center of the bowl at the last moment.

The CORES exhibition—and attendant fundraiser—was inspired by Wood's installation in the Center's ***Challenge VII: dysFUNctional*** exhibition in 2008, which included a video. As Wood described it at the time: "These cores are the waste product of traditional turning on a foot-powered lathe. Such cores have been found in rubbish pits for more than 2,000 years. Archaeologists reconstruct turners' activity from the waste cores, so here is a record for the last couple of years. Archaeologists name the different shapes. I just throw them on the floor and wonder if they will ever be studied in the same way. This short film shows how bowls are turned on the pole lathe; in the end, the cores fall into a pile on the workshop floor."

The cores, of various woods, are unique in color, size, and shape, depending on the interior shape and diameter of Robin's bowls. They range from 2" x 2" to 3" x 4". Many are hand-sized; a few are the size of two hands. Robin donated 100 cores to the Center to be used for this exhibit. The Center sent out a core each to select artists who agreed to rework it into a new piece of art. Sales of the resulting work benefit the Center's programming.

In addition to the artists' finished objects for this exhibition, the images here include photographs to illustrate the artists' processes and previous works to give the reader a glimpse of context.

Included in these pages is an extract of ***Craft, Industry and Everyday Life: Wood and Woodworking in Anglo-Scandinavian and Medieval York***, a major archaeological study of medieval pole-lathe turnings and other industries by Carole A. Morris.

Also here is Wood's essay responding to the artists' submissions for the exhibit and a commentary by Albert LeCoff, the executive director of The Center for Art in Wood.

By Judson Randall, editor

From Waste Wood to Wood Art

By Albert LeCoff
Co-Founder and Executive Director
The Center for Art in Wood

Long a participant in the Center's exhibitions, Robin Wood has become both the spiritual and actual fount of a major recent exhibition: *Robin Wood's CORES Recycled*. A British wood-turner, he has fostered the tradition of English "bodgers," a centuries-old class of makers. Bodgers went into the woods and set up pole lathes using the limber tree branches overhead. For their wood source, they cut only the trees that they could turn into products that day, thereby preserving future supplies of raw material. These pole lathes, guided by eye and powered by foot, made turning an early physical fitness regimen. Robin passionately carries on this tradition, and has painstakingly researched and written articles and books to document historic processes and wood bowls and spoons.

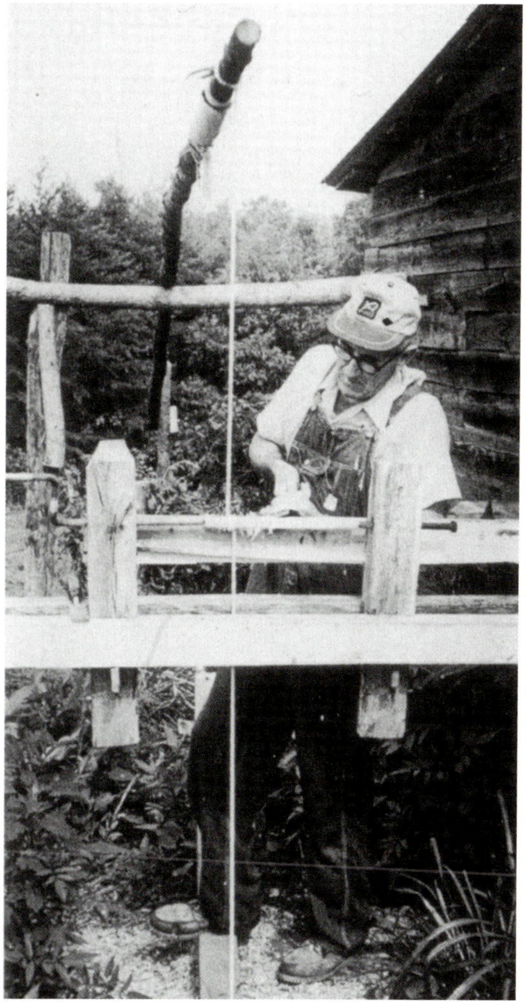

In 2000, my wife,Tina, and I saw Robin at work at a wood turning conference in France. As we watched, he set up his pole lathe under a huge spreading shade tree, using the overhead branches to harness power between the springy branch and his foot-powered treadle.

Deceptively simple, it was easy to transport from England for this special event. Supple branches, a few homemade tools, and Robin's strong leg made shavings fly onto the carpet of green grass. It was a perfect, hypnotic summer day, complete with the euphoric scent of nearby fields of Sweet Pea flowers, raised as a commercial seed crop. We brought a small stack of Robin Wood's bowls home to the United States for daily use.

In 2001, Robin submitted *Star Bowls* to the Center's exhibition entitled *Challenge VI—Roots: Insights & Inspirations in Contemporary Turned Objects*. The photo he sent the jurors showed tall piles of *Star Bowls*, stacked upside-down inside each other, on a knoll adjacent to a stone wall.

In 2008, for the Center's *Challenge VII: dysFUNctional* exhibition, Robin submitted a video testament to his stone wood shop and his practice of turning bowls. The video, captured by Nicola Wood, his videographer and wife, documented the trail of hundreds of cores that accumulate at the door of his shop. For each bowl, at the last moment, Robin knocks the core out of the center of a bowl while it's still chucked on the lathe. These cores recall the remnants that archeologists eventually found in forests and in the village of York. For the exhibition, Robin shipped the Center the video of himself, turning a bowl and releasing the center core, as well as a large box of cores. The video played on a white wall with the heap of cores laid against the wall. Entitled *Cor Blimey*, the installation documented the process that results in the piles that accumulate outside Robin's shop. The video created a mesmerizing record of the pole-turning process. *Cor Blimey*, including the cores, is now part of the Center's Museum Collection.

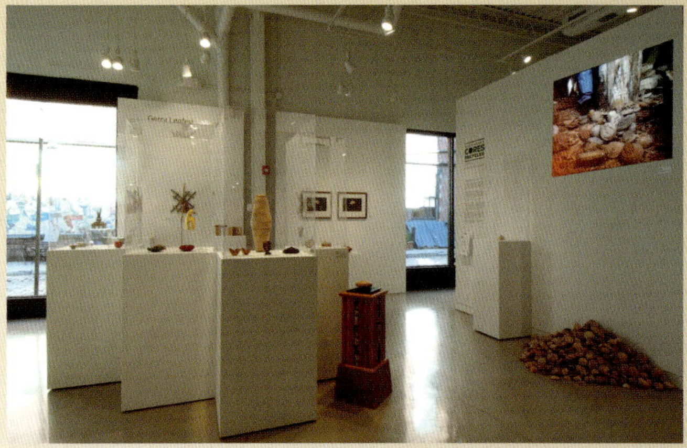

Fast forward to 2012. Somehow, a redundant stash of cores came to mind as a supply of raw materials—a pile of things to recycle. What would happen if we challenged artists to make something from these hand-sized cores? What new small treasures would result? Robin liked the idea, too, and the Center announced Robin's donation of cores for the challenge and as a fundraiser to support the Center's nonprofit programming.

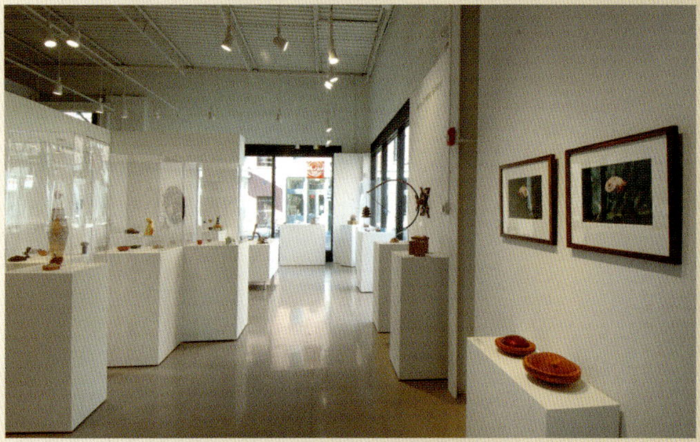

We invited Robin Wood and established and emerging artists to participate, including turners, furniture makers, and sculptors. We sent cores out internationally to the willing artists, and left Robin to select one from his own piles. We asked the artists to return photographs of their original core and their recycled core, along with their final object for the exhibition.

Forty-nine artists returned amazing variations of cores to the Center, surpassing our wildest expectations.

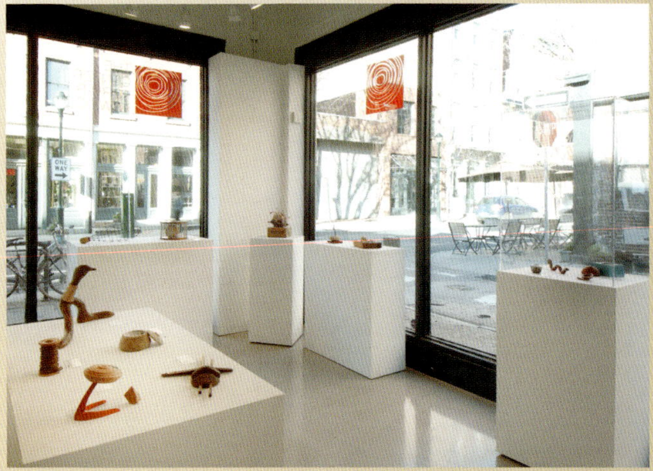

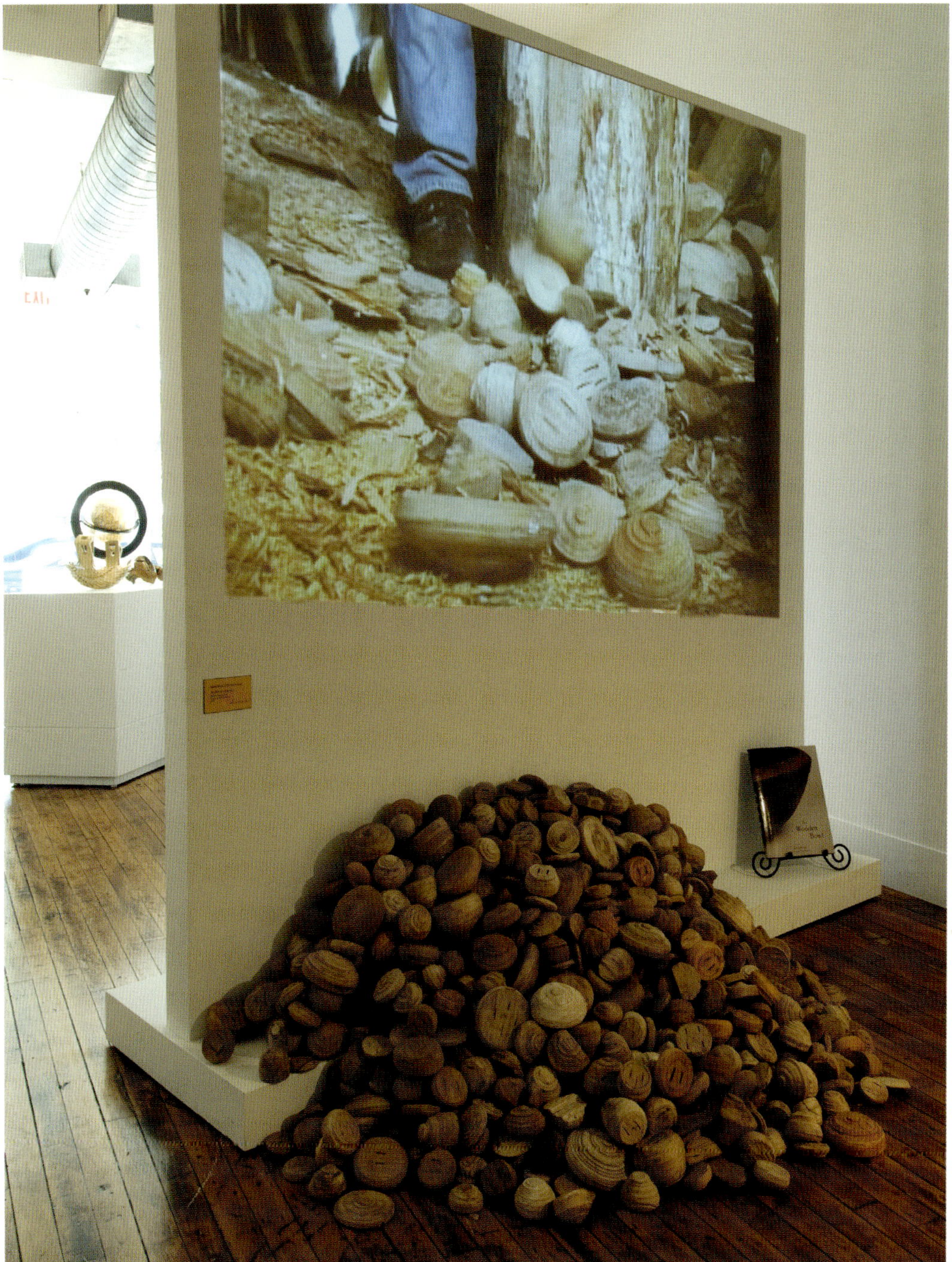

»

Neil Turner exposed the natural character hidden in the rough material. He created texture on it with a Dremel tool.

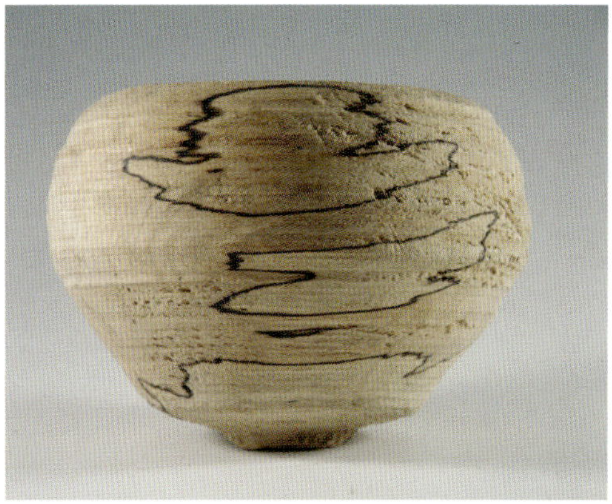

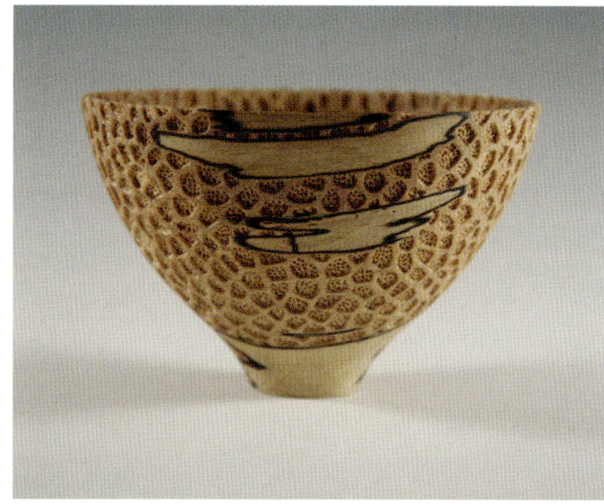

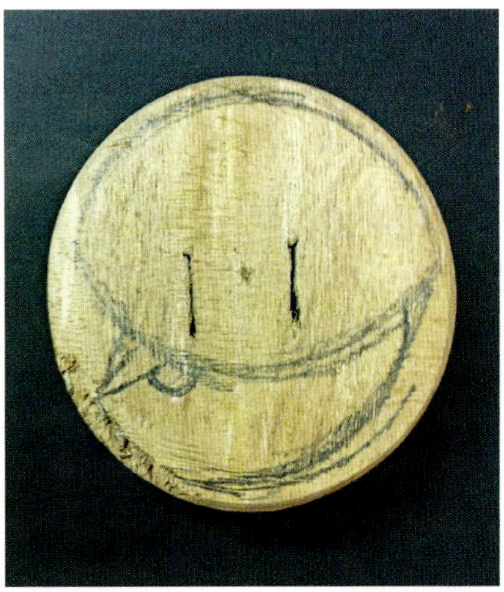

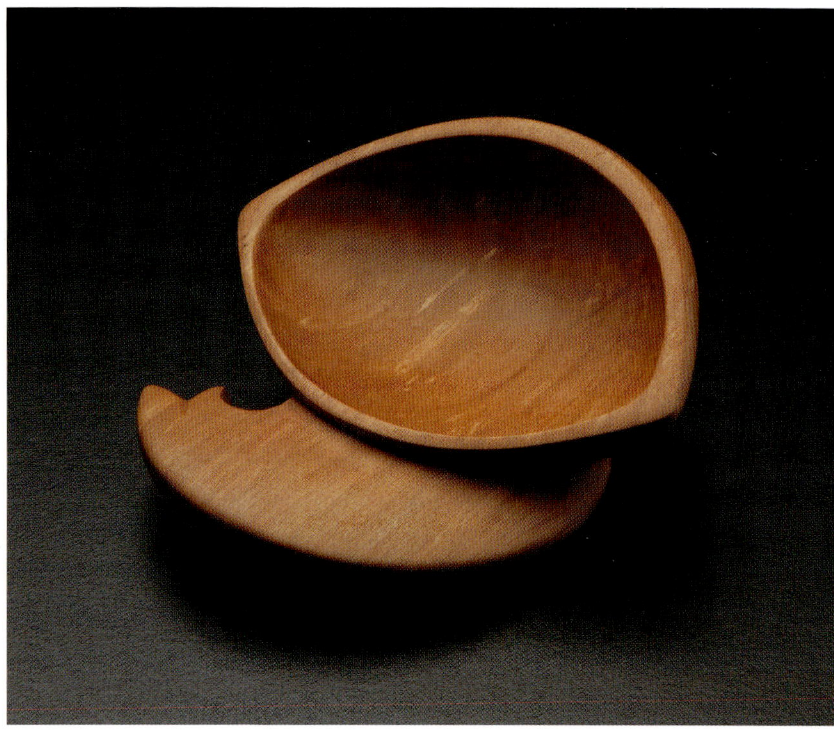

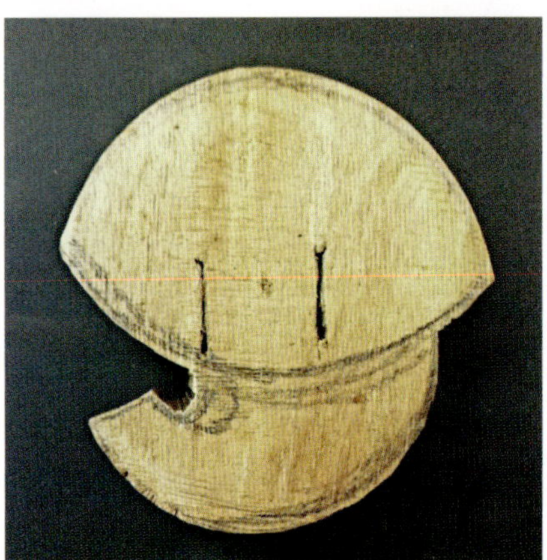

«

Norm Sartorius carefully planned out his spoon, adhering to his aim that "carved from unique and unusual woods my spoons are sculptures and my sculptures are spoons."

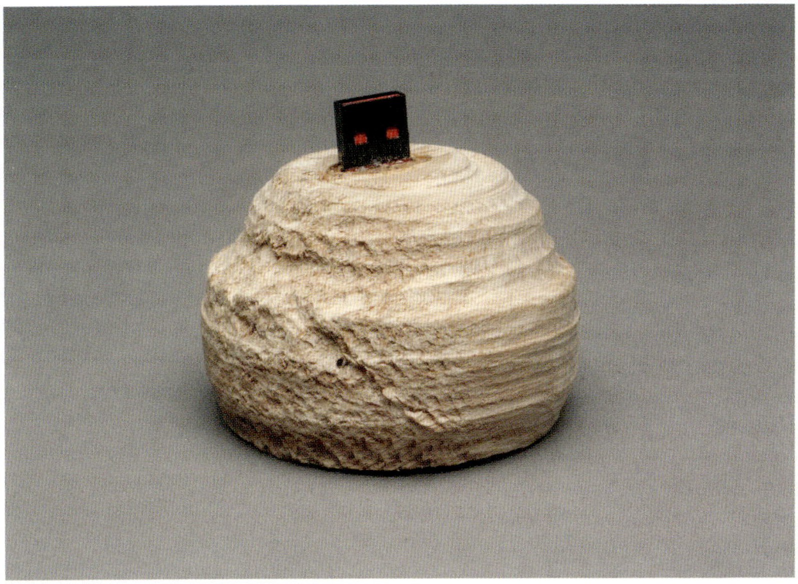

«

Robin Wood embedded a computer chip into his core. It included a presentation and offer to send the buyer one of his bowls intended for daily use.

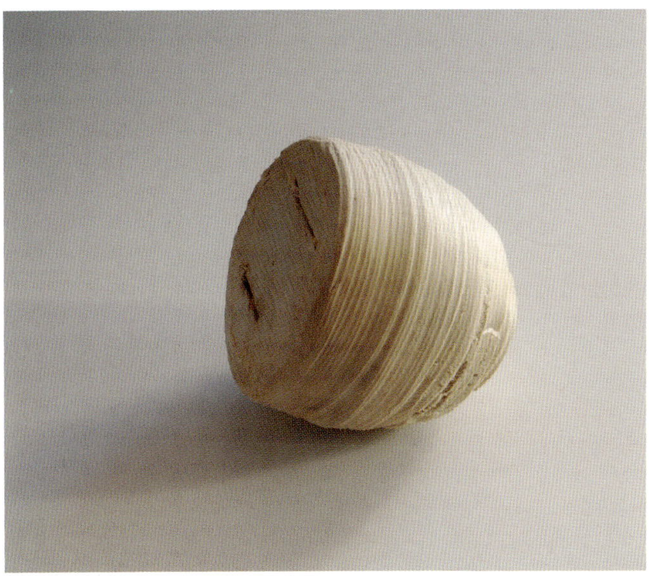

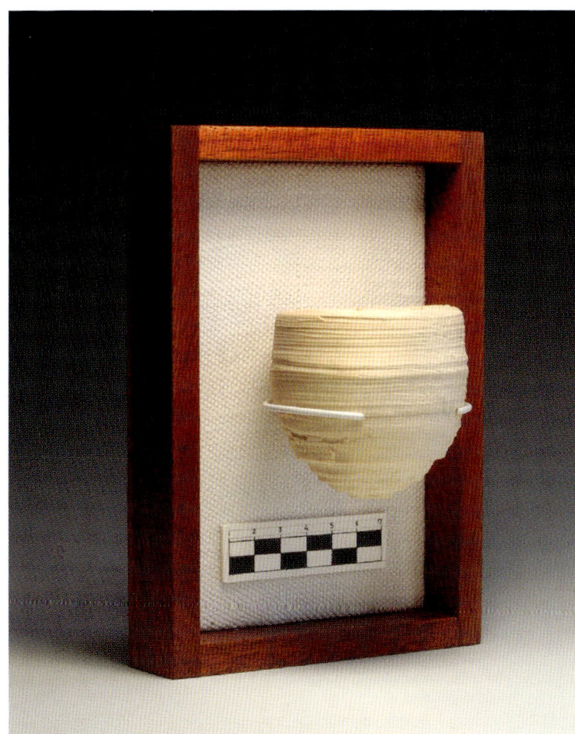

»

Yoav Liberman presented his core as an archeological specimen, complete with scale.

»

Randall Rosenthal's match book is typical of his *trompe l'oeil* creations but in an uncharacteristically small scale.

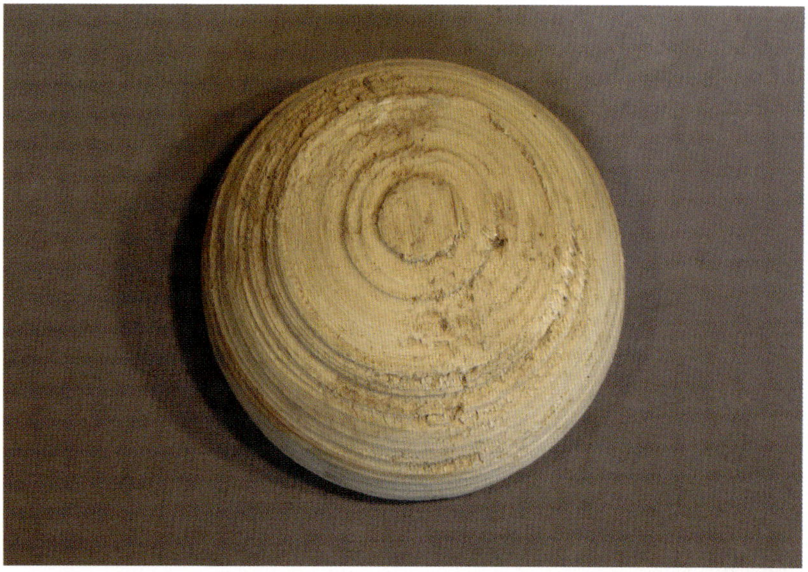

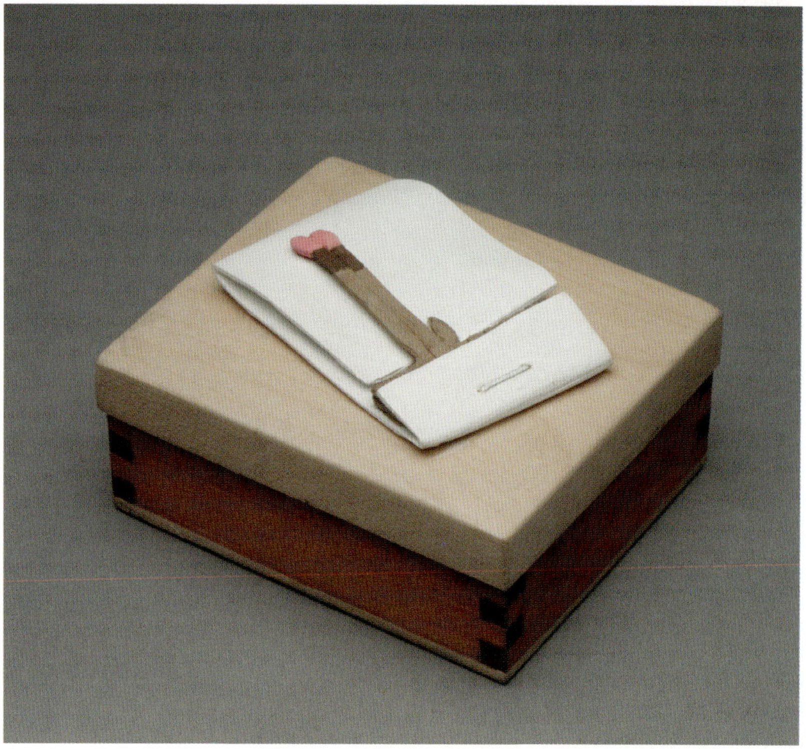

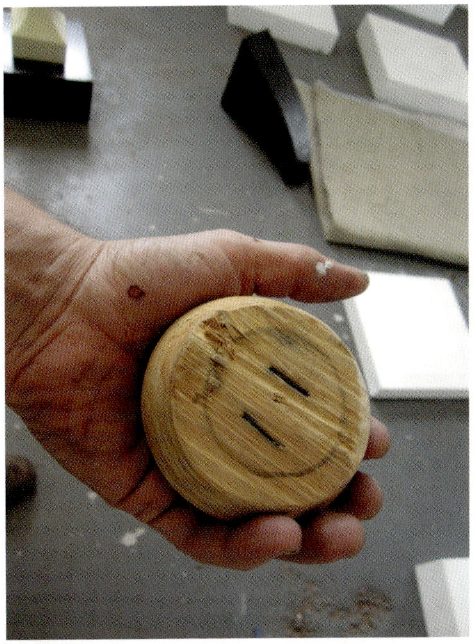

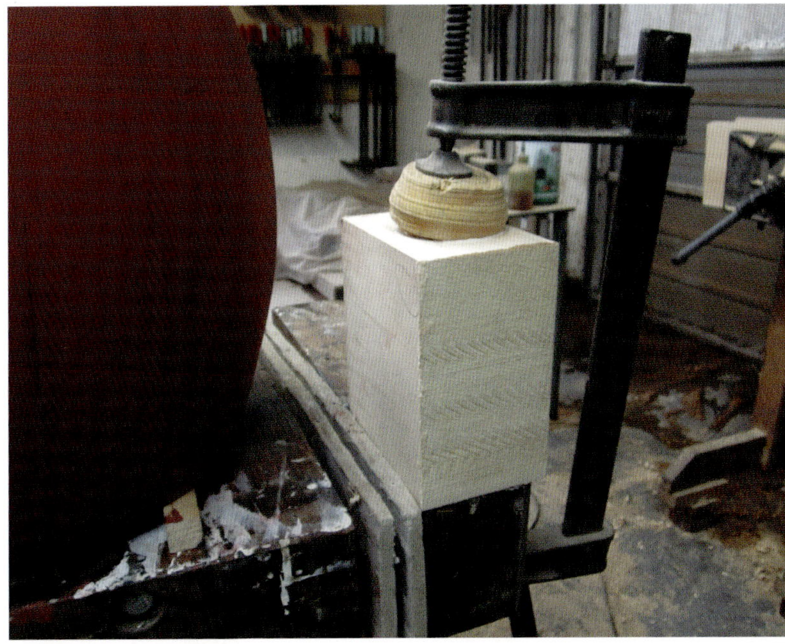

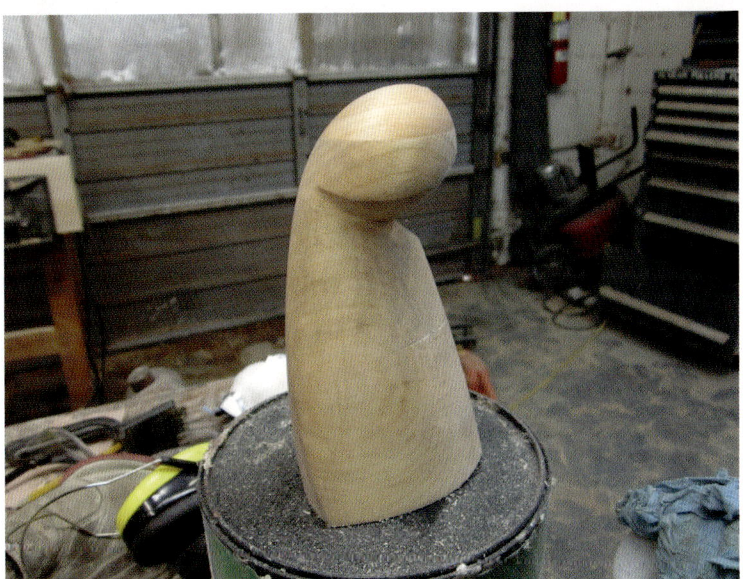

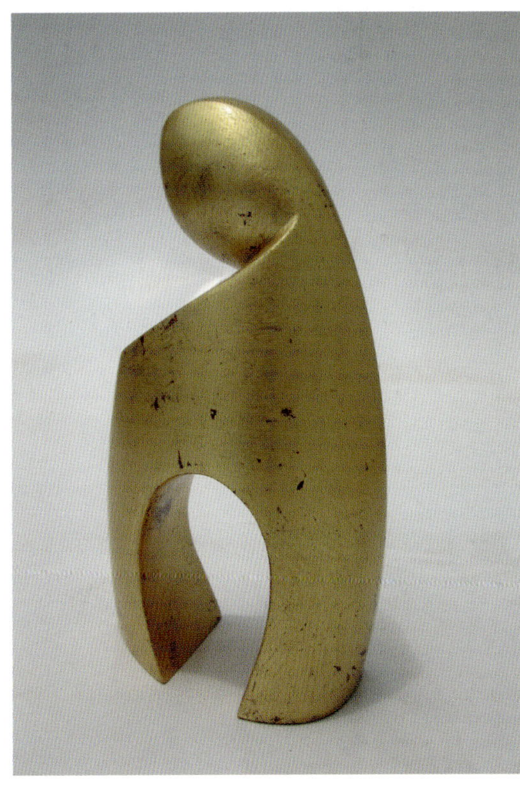

»

Joël Urutty created a maquette that recalls his larger-than-life figures, yet incorporated a fresh hollow center.

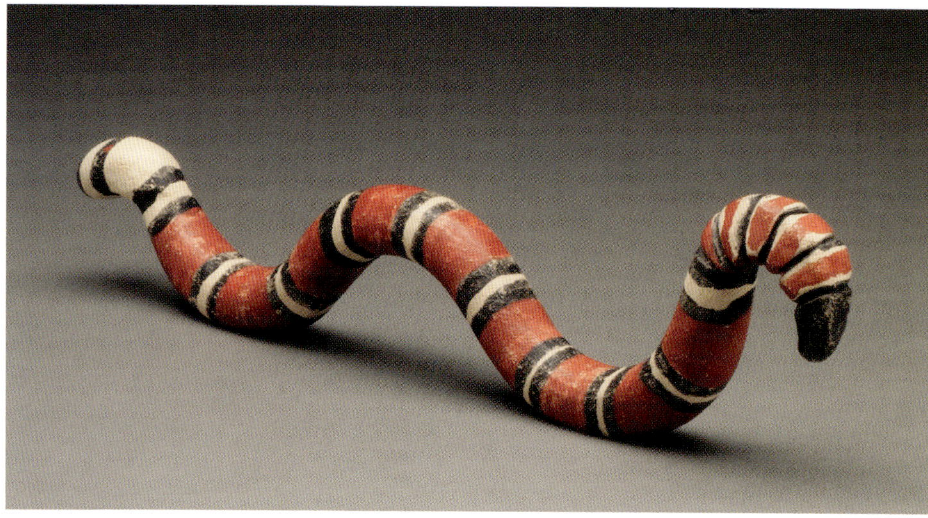

Beth Ireland completely deconstructed her core and fabricated and colored a critter.

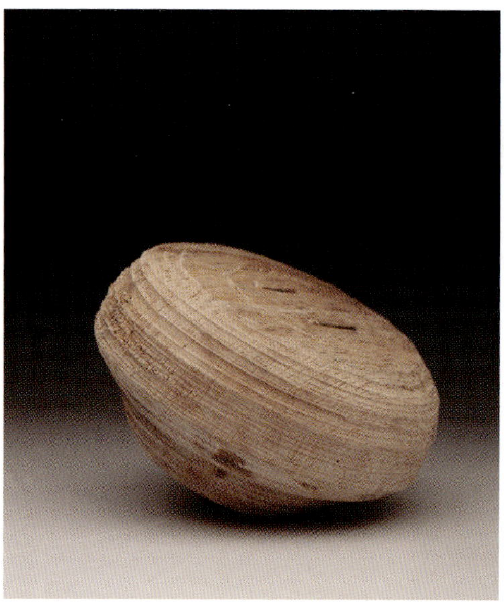

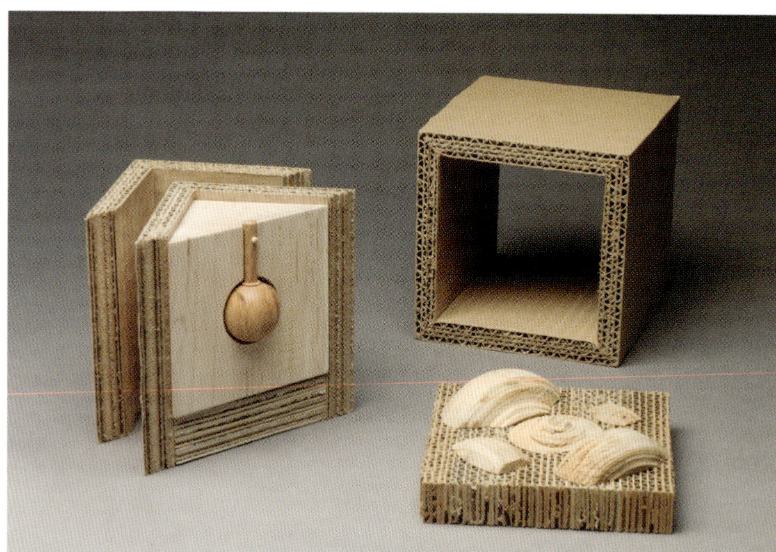

Chris Weiland captured his core in a corrugated, triangulated box—it is displayed open or closed.

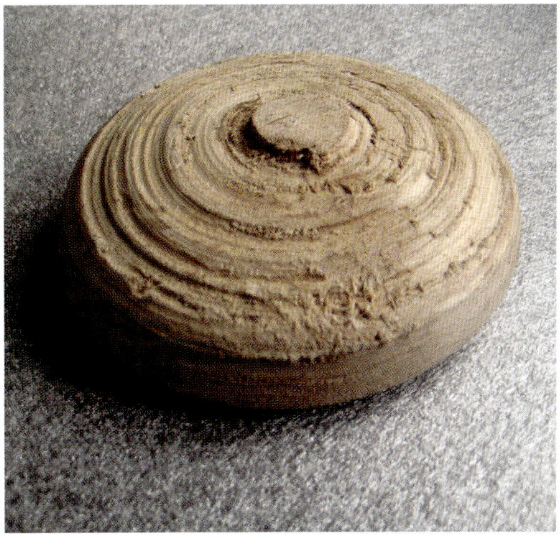

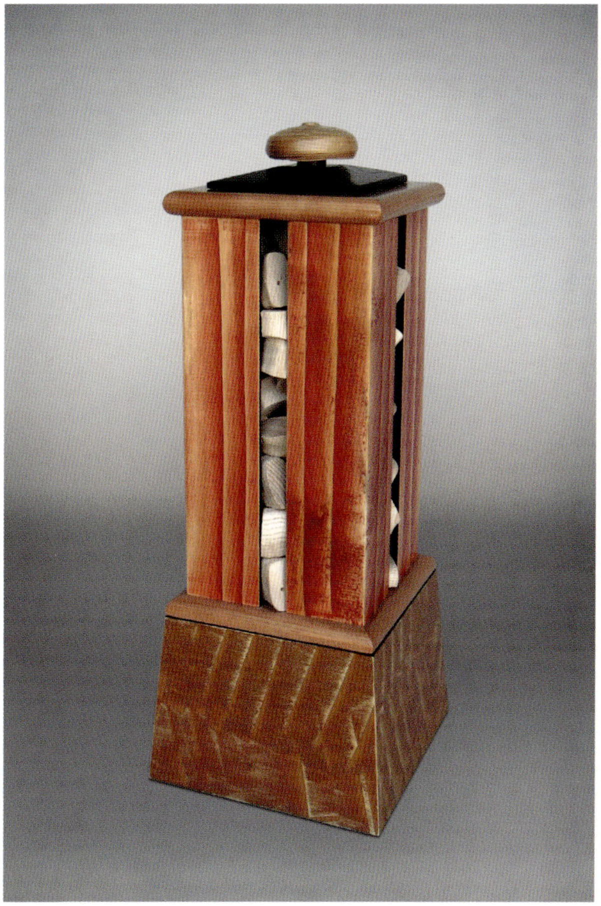

»

Brad Smith trapped his own scraps into a tower typical of his found-object furniture, topped by his core.

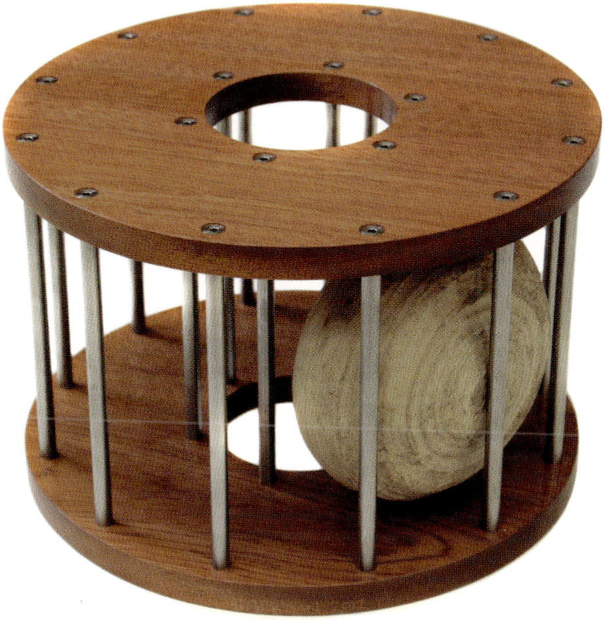

«

Peter Harrison created a rolling armature and permanently trapped his core.

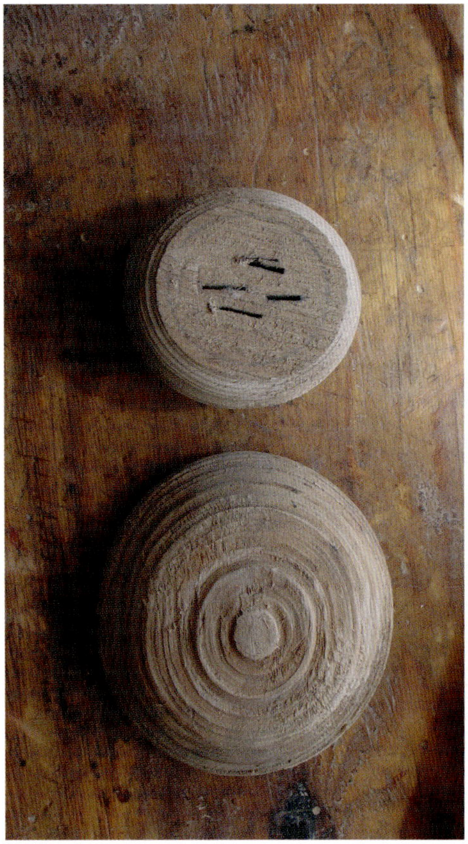

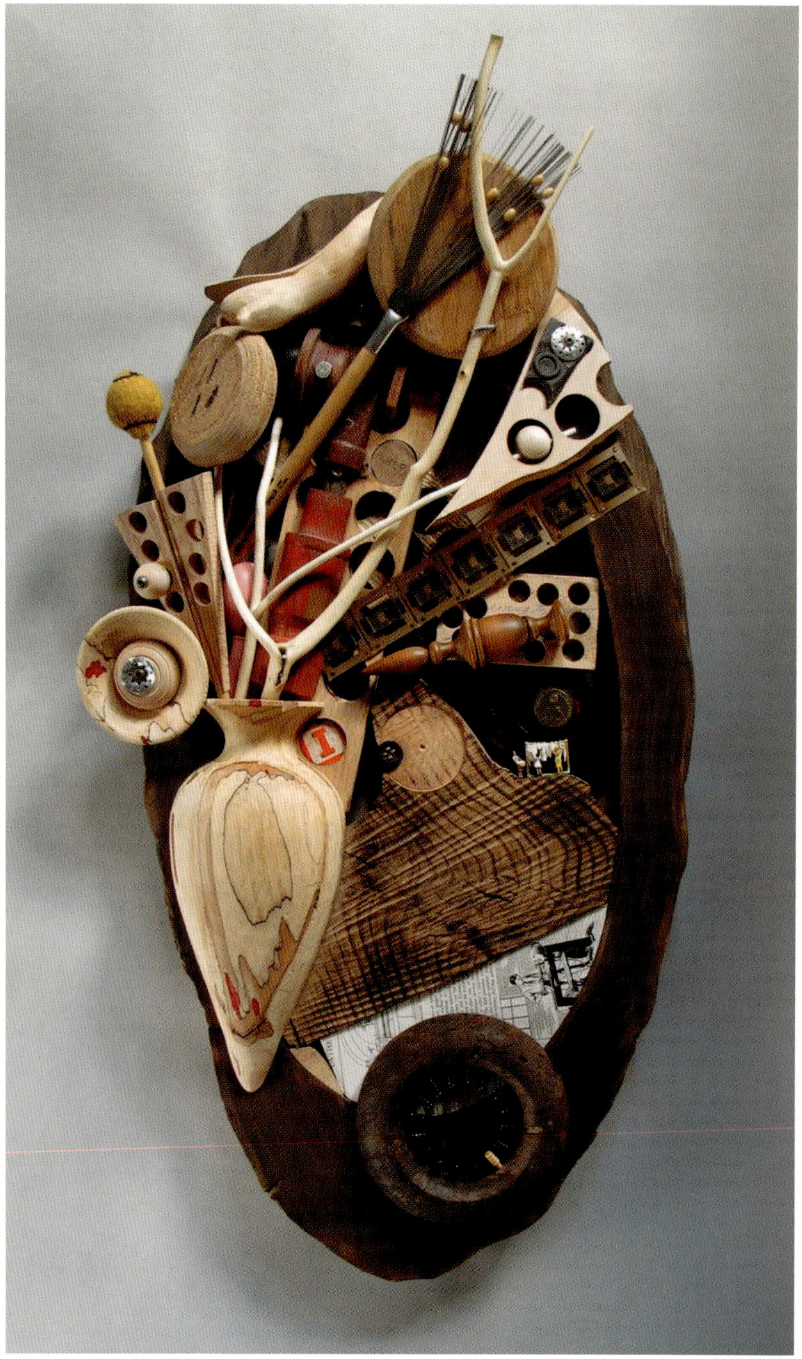

»

Michelle Holzapfel similarly thought of her own varied scraps. She froze them in time on a tall wall piece incorporating her cores.

What a wonderful, stimulating artistic experiment—the CORES project. Robin Wood sharing his bounty of artifacts led to artists imagining and then applying their skills—and best of all—their humor. What a great way to recycle artistic talent as well as wood.

15

"The Craft of Lathe-turning, Lathe-Turned Vessels and Manufacturing Waste"

Extract from *Craft, Industry and Everyday Life: Wood and Woodworking in Anglo-Scandinavian and Medieval York*

By Carole A. Morris

Any Anglo-Scandinavian or medieval household, whatever its place in the social order, would have had a large range of wooden vessels and utensils for storing, preparing, presenting and consuming food and drink, and for many other domestic purposes.

....[The pole lathe] is a composite device constructed from parts which can be fixed together and taken apart again. In Anglo Scandinavian York this would have been an important property in a device which may often have had to be transported to different sources of raw material in woodland and set up in situ there.

Any pole-lathe has four essential attributes. Firstly, two metal centre points which are fixed into the stocks and point towards each other along a horizontal axis, to serve as pivots on which the material being turned can be rotated. In the case of spindle-turning, a single piece is worked between the points. In face-turning, a separate mandrel is fixed rigidly, either to the base of a vessel (the spur centre), or to the open end (the cup centre). This entire assembly then rotates on the metal points. The second essential attribute is a means of rotating the work on the metal points. A rope or thong is fixed above the lathe to the end of a pole. This can either be a sapling in situ or, more often, a cut pole fixed at the other end and supported by a fulcrum. ... The thong is looped around the single piece of wood or mandrel and passes through the bed to a treadle or stirrup below. The arrangement of the thong around the mandrel is such that when the treadle is depressed with the foot, the edge of the worked material nearest the turner moves downwards (the cutting stroke). This bends the pole which keeps the thong taut.

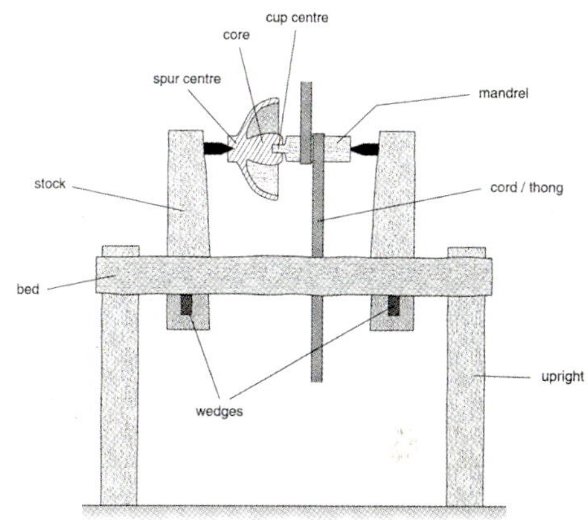

Fig.995 *Side view of a pole-lathe*

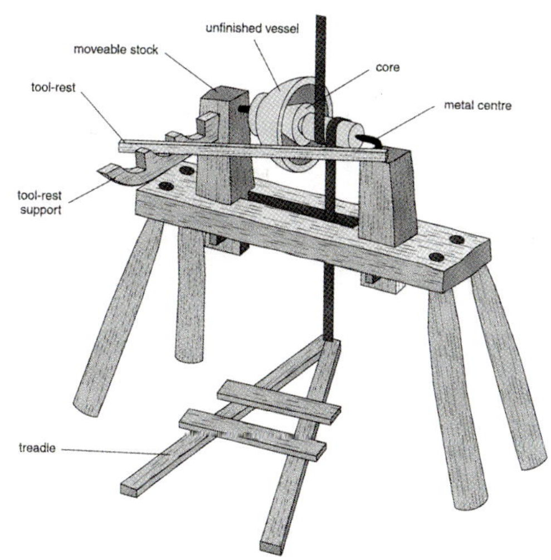

Fig.986 *Oblique view of a pole-lathe*

When the treadle is allowed to rise, pulled up by the pole, the worked material is rotated in the opposite direction (the return stroke). The overall action of the material on the lathe is therefore reciprocating.

Thirdly, the lathe must be rigid, whether it is set up temporarily in woodland or as a permanent fixture in a workshop. Finally, it is essential that the lathe possesses a rest on which to support the cutting tool. During the cutting stroke, the downward force on the working end of the turner's gouge or chisel as it removes wood is very great, and the tool could not be held firmly in the turner's hands alone. A tool-rest is necessary to act as a fulcrum for the tool, and needs to be as close to the work as possible. On the return stroke, the cutting tool is withdrawn slightly from the work.

There are several sources of evidence which suggest that medieval bowl-turners (including those in York) used green, unseasoned timber for their bowls, unlike some of the recent pole-lathe bowl-turners who used large roughouts of air-dried timber. Many turned wooden bowls found in excavations are not perfectly circular, but oval, with their longer axis along the grain. When bowls are turned green, they always become slightly oval as they dry out and their rim edge also has a tendency to curve slightly in profile.

Marks in base waste, end waste and cores indicate the types of centre attachments used at the end of the mandrels and as pivot points for face-turning and spindle-turning on the lathes in 9th-11th century York. Only three types seem to have been used: mandrel hole, multiple metal plate and single metal point centres. Cores from other British sites show that at least six types of centre attachments were in use, some with restricted distributions, and these and the corresponding marks made in the cores are illustrated schematically in Fig.992. Mandrel hole, metal plates, bar and plate, metal pins and multiple metal points (Fig.992a-e) were all used in face-turning when the mandrel had to be firmly fixed to either spur or cup centre, whereas a single metal point (Fig.992f) is a pivot point mark and occurs on all spindle-turned waste products and occasionally on face-turned base waste. The very small square, lozenge-shaped, triangular and rectangular marks are related to spindle-turning using a bow-powered lathe (Fig.992g-i).

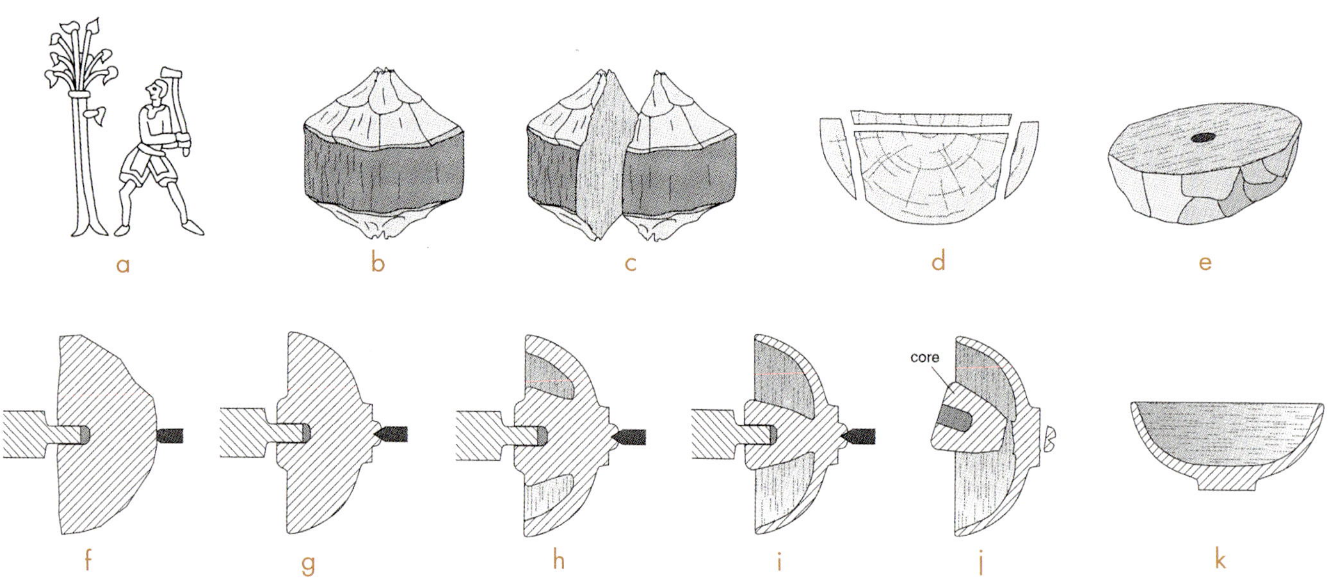

Fig.990 *Stages of preparation of a face-turned bowl from tree to finished product.*

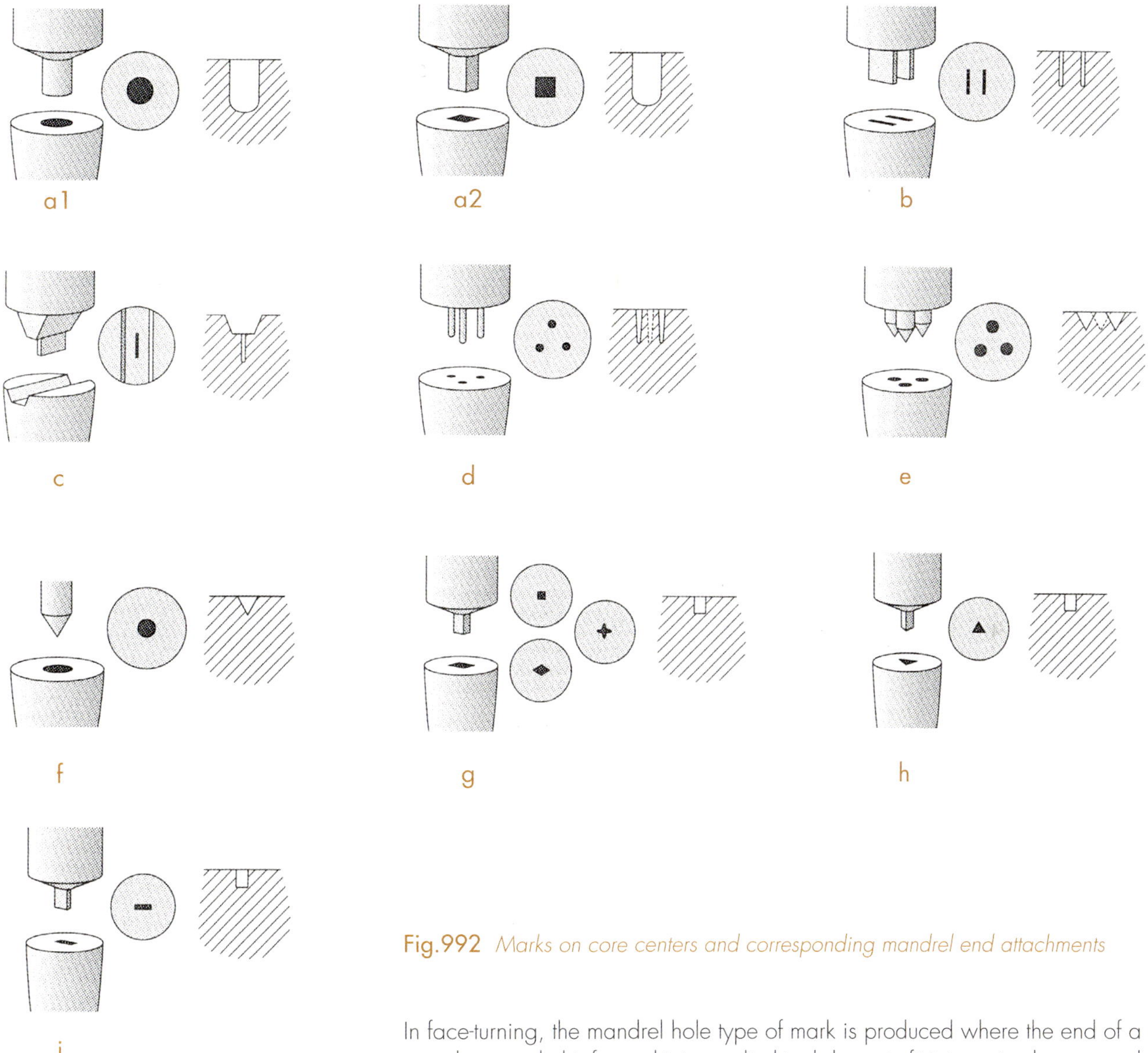

Fig.992 *Marks on core centers and corresponding mandrel end attachments*

In face-turning, the mandrel hole type of mark is produced where the end of a wooden mandrel is formed into a cylindrical shape to fit into a circular augered hole in the roughout bowl centre or base and all nine basic outlines are found in AngloScandinavian York, although it is accepted that the difference between some of them is very arbitrary. Different shapes could have been the result of making different sizes of vessel, of face-turning or spindle turning, of a repeated process, of using the same tool etc. Important facts emerge from some of the matrices which may help to explain this variation in shape.

Many of the face-turned cores have truncated shapes with wide rather than pointed bases, and were produced when the turner reduced the risk that the core would break before his work was finished by leaving a wide base. He needed to remove less wood than for a bowl with a conical or curved conical core and the method was therefore economical of time. However, whereas in general the latter cores could either be parted off the lathe or snapped off easily at their points, the truncated cores needed extra effort and skill to remove them cleanly after the assembly had been removed from the lathe. Some truncated cores have 'feet' where they were not removed with an absolutely straight cut and brought some of the underlying wood with them, leaving a deeper scar in the internal base of the vessel

Most of the cores with feet came from [c.975-later 11th century]. There are 184 face-turned cores from Coppergate, only 31 of which have narrowed or pointed bases, showing that the Anglo Scandinavian turners preferred to leave wide core bases when face-turning. The same table shows that of 112 spindle-turned cores, only three are truncated, turners preferring to create either narrowed or pointed cores when spindle-turning. This choice is also connected to the nature of the wood and its grain direction, since it is much more difficult to remove a core with a wide base if cutting across the grain, which would be the case if the vessel were spindle-turned. In addition, many spindle-turned vessels had very narrow or even globular profiles, which would also have hindered the removal of a core with a wide base, as described above. Thus, most truncated cores were face-turned and most narrow and pointed cores were spindle-turned.

There seem to have been two basic groups of spindle-turned core shapes. One was the conical and curved conical group (62 cores), which varied in size from tiny cores such as [one that] is only 35mm [1.38″] in diameter and 26mm [1.02″] long, to long cores such as [one that] is 89mm [3.50″] long and 47mm [1.85″] in diameter. The cores in this group most probably came from vessels with rounded profiles, but varying in size. The second group is of narrow cylindrical, cylindrical and conical, and irregular cores, some of them over 75mm [2.95″] long, which were almost exclusively spindle-turned, and probably came from narrow and sometimes deep, straight-sided or globular vessels.

Fig.1003 *The basic core outline shapes:*
(a) curved conical
(b) conical
(c) cylindrical
(d) cylindrical and conical
(e) S-shaped
(f) truncated curved conical
(g) truncated conical
(h) truncated S-shaped
(i) irregular

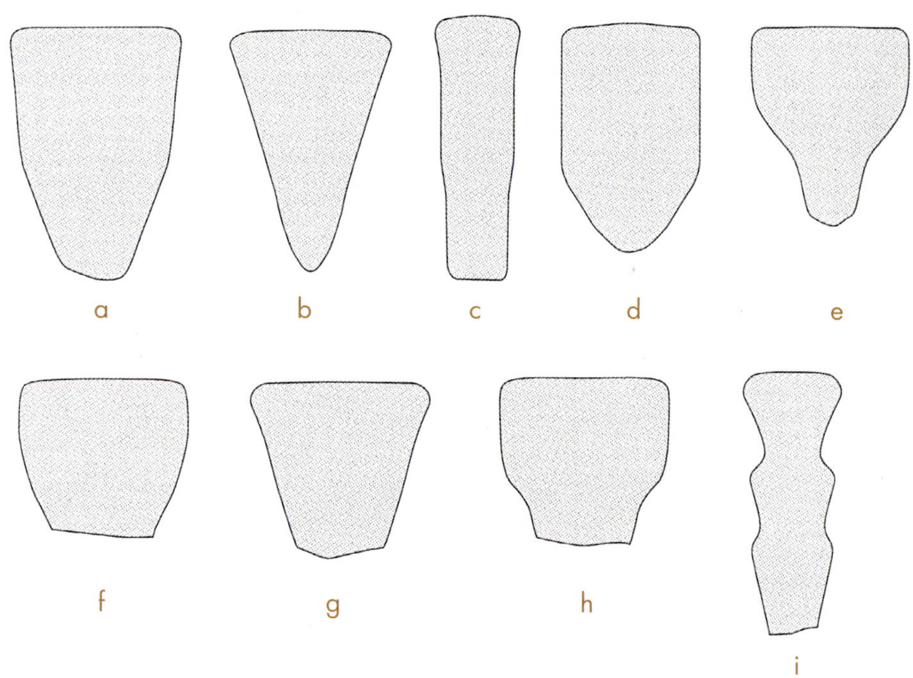

	Mid 9th-late 9th/Early 10th Century	A/S	Late 9th/ Early 10th Century–c.930/5	c.930/5–c.975	c.975	c.975–Early/Mid 11th Century	Mid-later 11th Century	Mid-later 11th Century	Later 11th–16th Century	?	Total
Conical			1	11	2	8		1		1	24
Truncated Conical		1		2	1	40	4	3	2	1	54
Curved Conical		1	1	13	6	33		2	3	1	60
Truncated Curved Conical	1	1		20	3	50		4	2	2	83
S-shaped				2	1	4					7
Truncated S-shaped				2	1	15				1	19
Irregular				8		5			1		14
Cylindrical				10		7					17
Cylindrical and Conical				4	1	10				1	16
Shape Unknown				1		4					5
Total	1	3	2	73	15	176	4	10	8	7	299

Table 197 *The incidence of each core shape produced at different periods at 16-22 Coppergate*

Table 197 shows which shapes were produced at different periods. All but 37 of the 301 cores found on the Coppergate and 22 Piccadilly sites were firmly dated to between c.930 and the mid 11th century, and these 264 cores include all nine shapes. Five of the other 37 were undated and five more were Anglo-Scandinavian but not attributable to any particular period. The overwhelming conclusion is that although there was lathe-turning from the earliest Anglo-Scandinavian occupation of the area in the mid-late 9th century, lathe-turning on a commercial scale was carried out on or near Coppergate mainly from c.930 to the early-mid 11th century; since all nine core shapes are represented, a wide range of vessels must have been produced. The deposits dated to [mid-later 11th century] are limited in extent, ... so the fourteen cores from these deposits suggest that lathe-turning may have continued in the mid-late 11th century. In addition, there are no late 11th-16th century deposits surviving in the street frontage areas where the majority of cores were found, so the nine cores dated to [later 11th-16th century] may also represent a continuation of lathe-turning in the area.

Table 197 also shows that 222 out of the 301 cores were of only four types—conical, curved conical and their truncated versions. These four shapes, however, have been found in layers dating to [mid 9th to later 11th-16th century], and must have been produced from the earliest Anglo-Scandinavian settlement in the area right through to the medieval period.

Morris, Carole A. ***Craft, Industry and Everyday Life: Wood and Woodworking in Anglo-Scandinavian and Medieval York.*** York: England. Council for British Archeology, 2000.

Robin Wood's CORES Recycled – A Reaction

By Robin Wood

I should start by saying I have over the years disposed of maybe 15,000 cores; they are a by-product of my bowl turning. They are tactile objects with a lot of character and to me they also encapsulate much embodied history. Lots of people say "you could make something from that." I ask them what they would make from it and offer it to them, but I have never found anything I really wanted to make with them myself other than a great big pile of them as a picture of all the bowls they belonged to.

When Albert LeCoff suggested the "cores recycled" idea, I pictured folk getting this little gnarly bit of wood and surely no one could make much out of that. Well, I clearly underestimated the creativity of my fellow wood artists. The finished pieces vary hugely, but I love the thought that has gone into them. I particularly loved the ones that really feel as if the artists have understood the value of the original piece. Some others feel as if the artist really wanted to make something different or wished they had a different piece of wood and they have only used the core because that was the deal. I can understand, as I have struggled to fit my work to a preconceived exhibition brief too. The fact that all of the work was donated as a fundraiser for The Center for Art in Wood gives a lovely warm feeling, and I feel privileged to have been part of all that wonderful giving.

When I look through the pieces of work, they seem to fall into various groups. I guess the obvious route is to take the lump of wood and carve, texture, turn, and paint to create a tiny sculptural object. There are many of these, and I find them all very satisfying. I can understand the technical difficulty of working on something so small, of avoiding the splits around the mandrel spike holes, and of working with the inevitable tearout that you get on the original core.

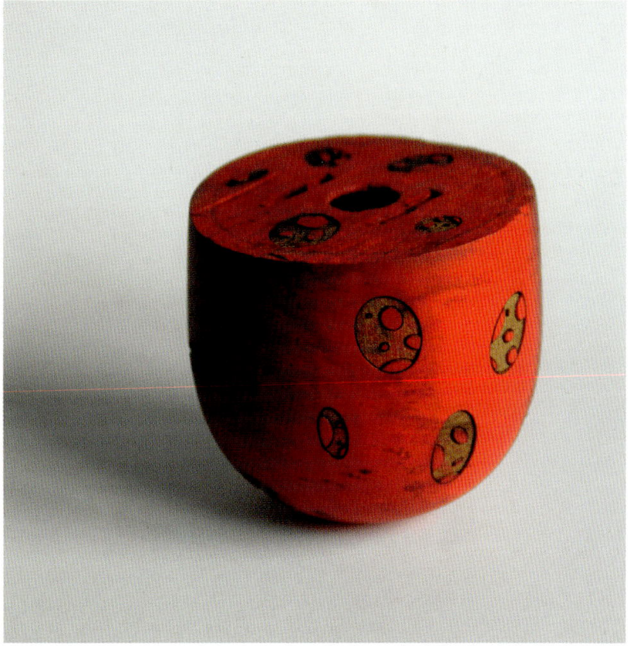

»

Jerome Blanc's *Wood's Candy* is a delightful example; I like that it keeps the texture and mandrel marks on the top showing through the paint and the balance of smooth paint cut through to bare wood.

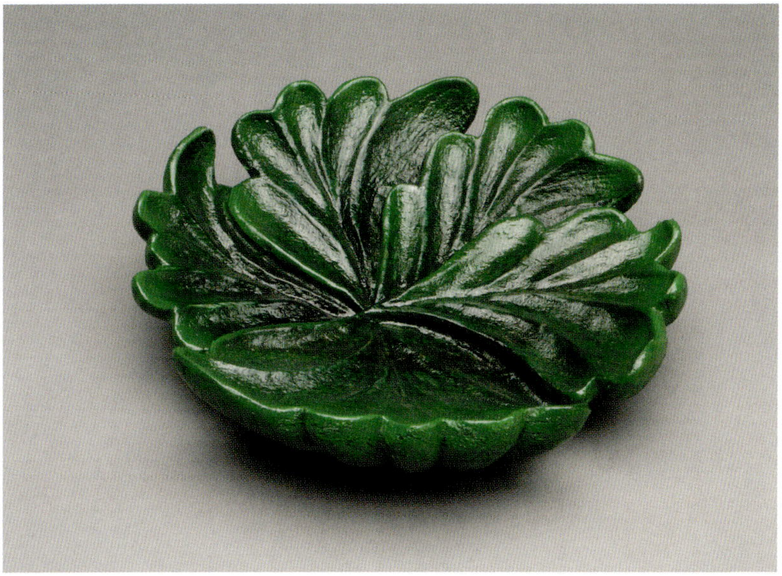

«

Ron Fleming's *Fern Platter* appealed too. It is a total transformation of the wood but has transformed it into something equally organic; it feels like a liverwort splashed with water by a stream.

»

Satoshi Fujinuma took the carving route but left the surface of the core intact, hollowing away like a woodworm. I love this piece. It values the texture of the original, but by taking away, it adds so much. Just boring holes would have been fun but to completely undercut the surface is great. It is technically difficult and reminds me of the Chinese carvings where folk carve a ball inside a ball inside a ball.

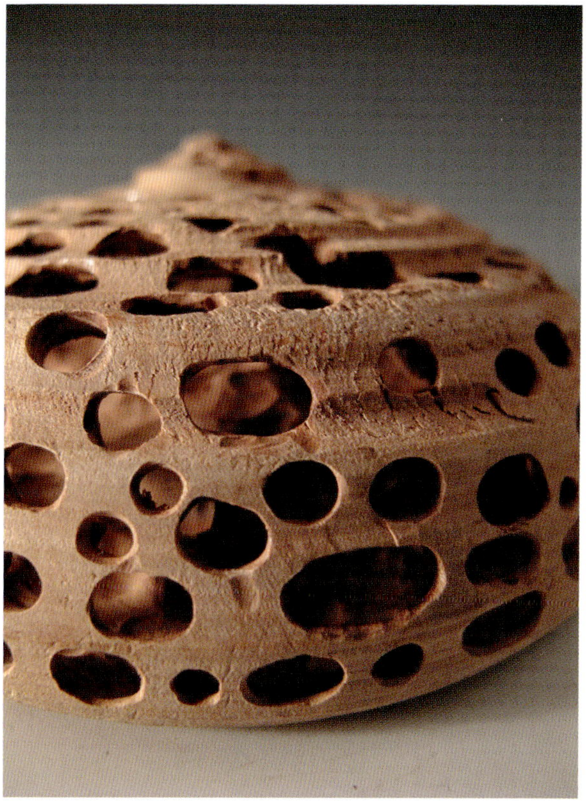

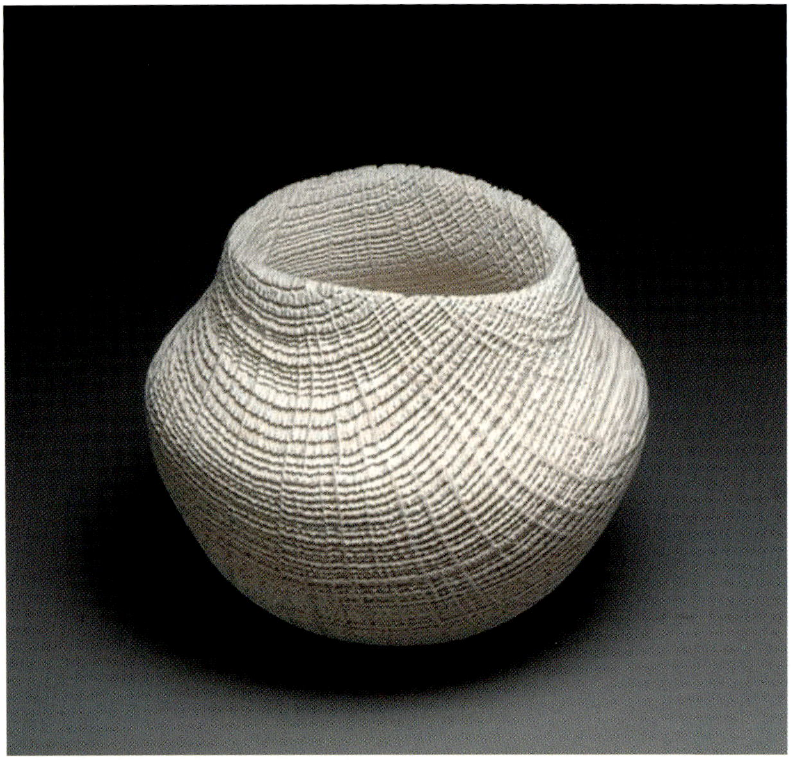

«

Michael Peterson started with a very unusual core, I very rarely turn oak, and I suspect that this was the bowl I made for Sherwood Forest from a 500-year-old tree. I love what he has done with it—a tiny vessel with texturing that beautifully brings out the medullary rays that are a particular feature of this wood.

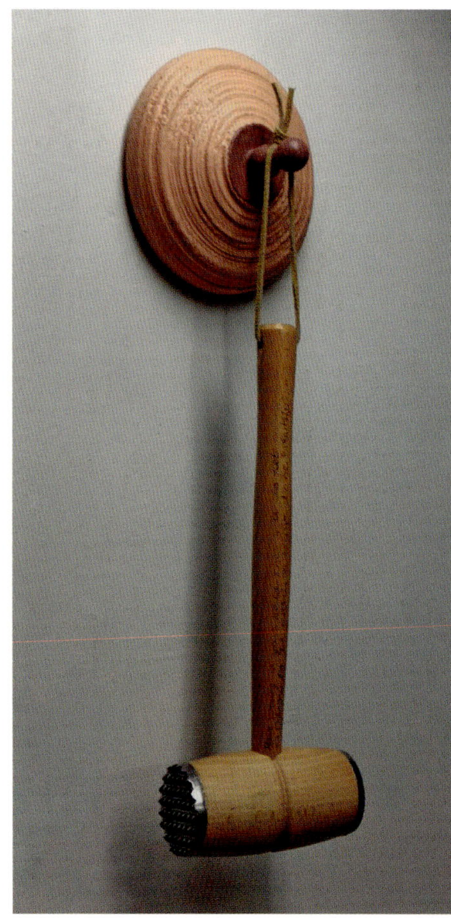

»

Among the other turners, carvers, and texturers, Hilary Pfiefer gets a mention for making something beautiful and useful and most of all for using a William Morris quote. The leaflet I sent out with bowls used to say "rather choose rough work than smooth work ... Never imagine there is a reason to be proud of anything that may be accomplished by patience and sand-paper." (John Ruskin)

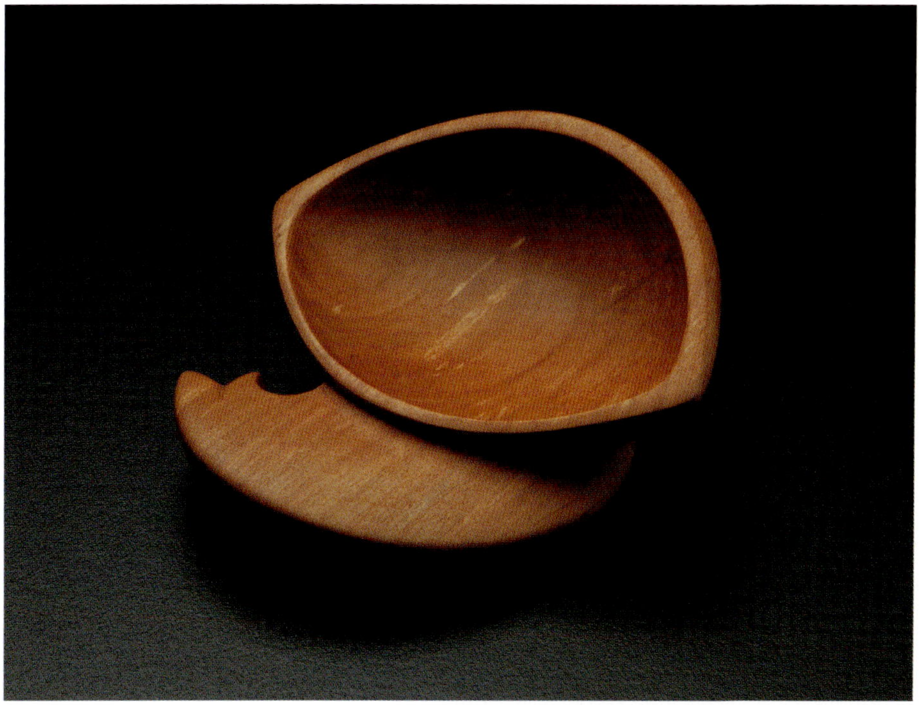

«

Norm Sartorius somehow managed to get a spoon out of a core, beautifully finished. It's labelled as plum but I have not turned plum for many years; it is most likely pear and looking at the color I am pretty sure it's a core from the big pear tree that I used to turn the star bowls for the Center's *Challenge VI* show in 2000; it must have been hanging around the workshop a while.

»

The form and the depth of the surface treatment of Michael Scarborough's *Akai Maru (Red Circle)* are delightful, and having spent time woodworking in Japan, I have an affinity for this sort of work and enjoy the cross-pollination of ideas. Whilst it is tiny, it is something that would work on a large scale equally well.

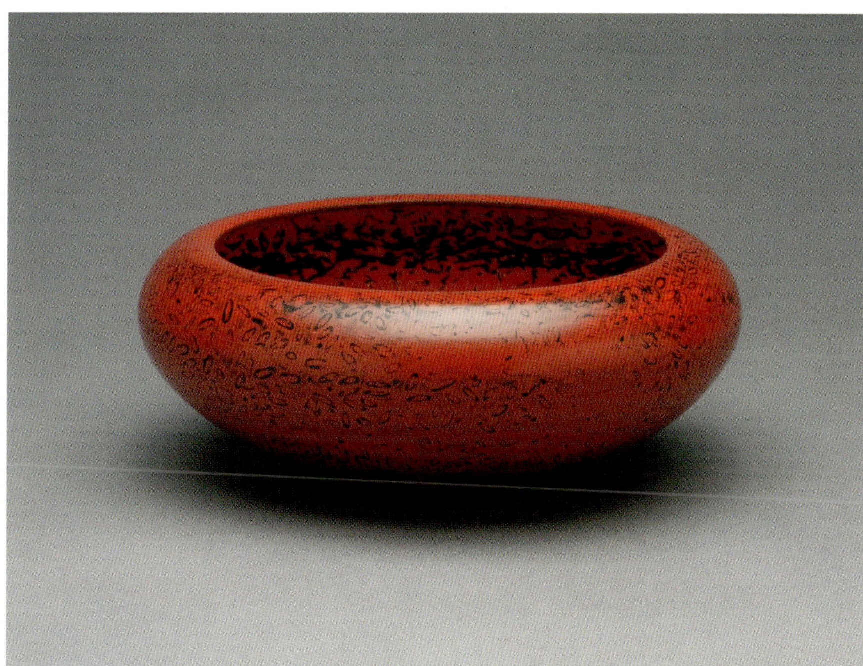

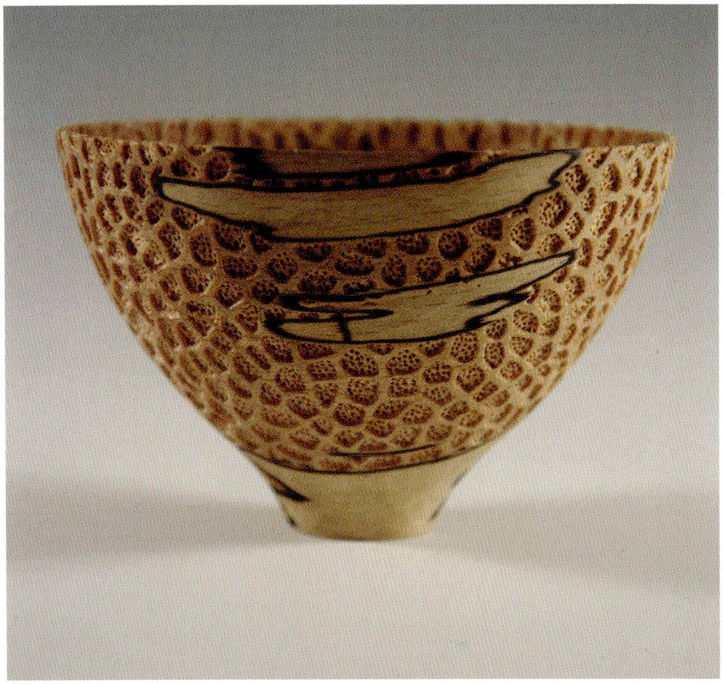

«

Neil Turner's *Coral Core* was the first piece I saw a photo of and I was blown away. It is still one of my favorite pieces. I love the turning; it's a very sweet form and the texturing is perfect, too, but leaving the spalted areas as highlights just works so well for me.

All these pieces are unique and special, but it helps me to discuss them by grouping them, so the next set include artists who didn't do much with the core but added to it or presented it in some way. I like to think these folks liked their core so much they didn't want to cut it, turn it, carve it, or sand it. In some of the pieces, the core is set on a podium alone, and in others, it is subtly placed amongst a group of related objects and textures. I find these pieces work well.

»

Doug Haslam's *Adamski Call Home!* clearly is telling some sort of story. Who is Adamski? Google helps with insights into the life of bonkers UFO man George Adamski, so just the title gives me enough info to get the insight into the artwork that I am after. I find this piece well executed. It sits like a mini lectern at a jaunty angle, and I like it all the more since I have thought of cores as many things over the years but UFOs is a new one for me. Just taking that slice out and finishing the surfaces allows us to see the interior and three dimensions rather than just the surface, too.

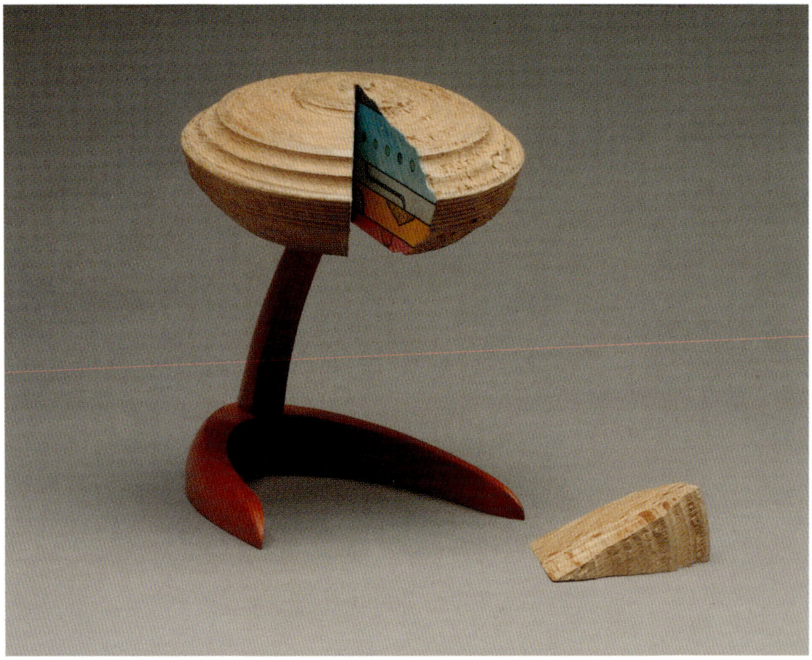

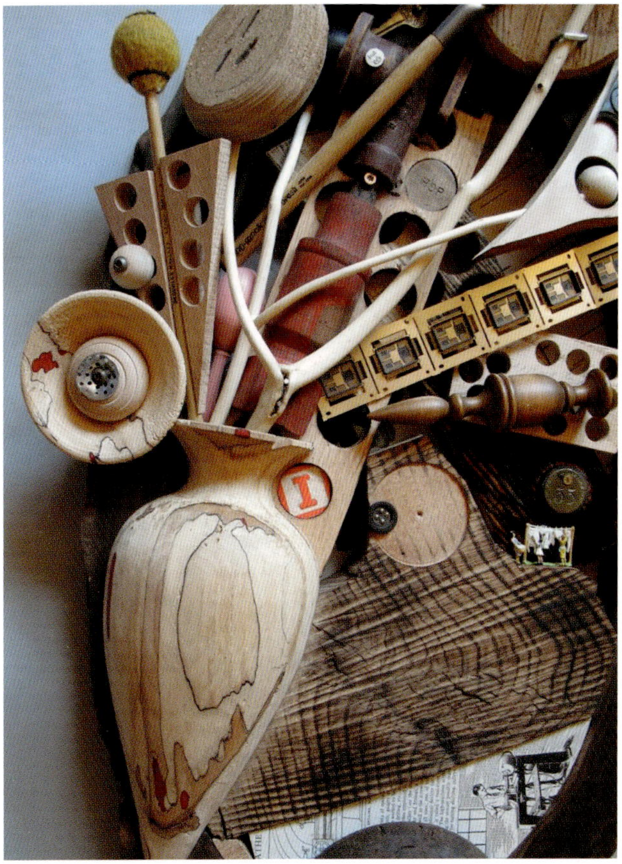

«

I love Michelle Holzapfel's ***Cores Collage Arranged by the Laws of Chance.*** For a start, it is a fascinating collection of objects, all I suspect with back stories that we don't know, but which she explains in her statement. At a glance it could be a nod to those amazing carved creations of Grinling Gibbons with their piled masses of woodiness. But then when I read the title it makes me think of all the wooden bowls I see around people's homes stuffed with bizarre collections of random objects. Was it really arranged by chance? I imagine Michelle adding olives to a pizza with a random scatter and then moving a few around to get a better distribution. However it was done and whatever the thought process, it is interesting and works as a piece of art for me

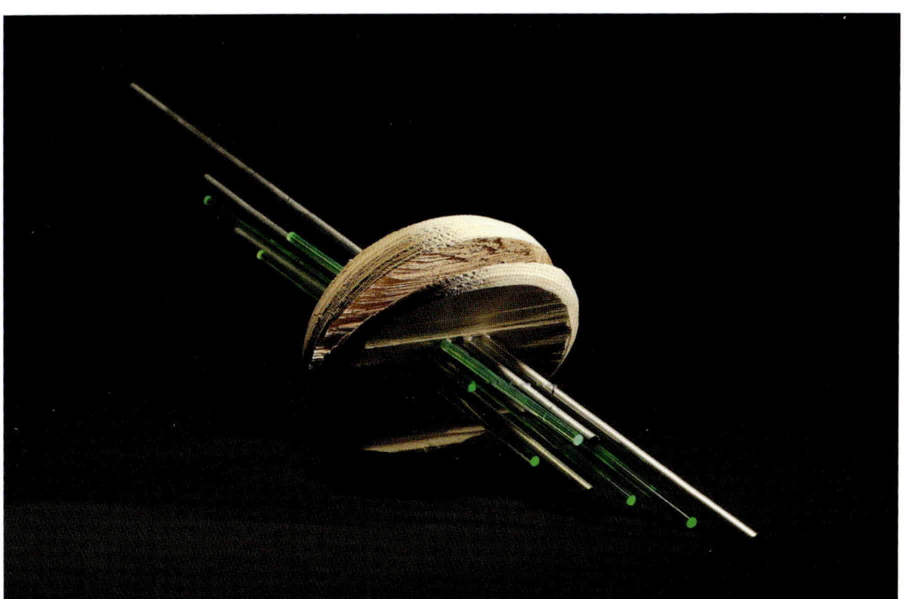

«

Richard Hooper plays with the word title in ***Reactor Core;*** we Brits like wordplay and I guess it shares that with my original piece ***Cor Blimey***. I like it on many levels; I like that it uses the original rough core, split open and contrasted against hard shiny smooth rods. I like that any reference to nuclear raises emotions in anyone and that always helps art. I like the wordplay and most of all I love the stunning photograph.

»

One of my favorite pieces is *Round and Round* by Michael de Forest; here we have all the rough gnarly exterior of the weathered and split core but it's hollowed out and made into a lidded vessel with a surprise inside. The milk paint feels like a good natural medium to add to a core, too.

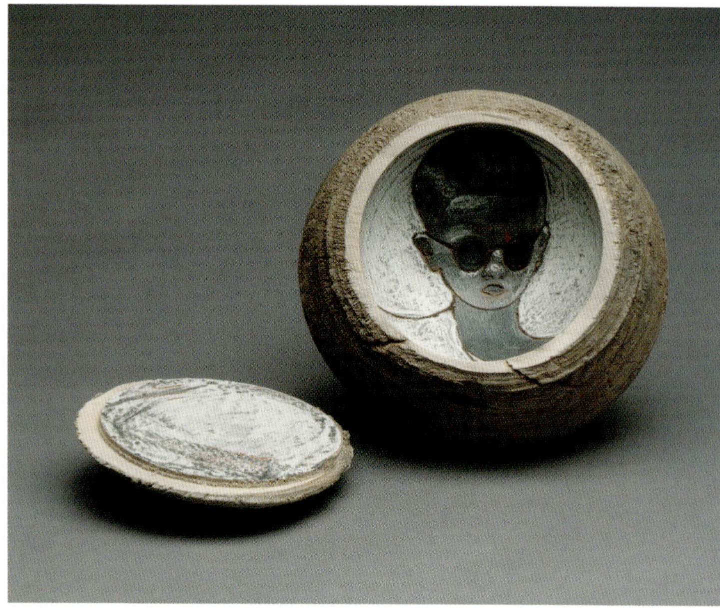

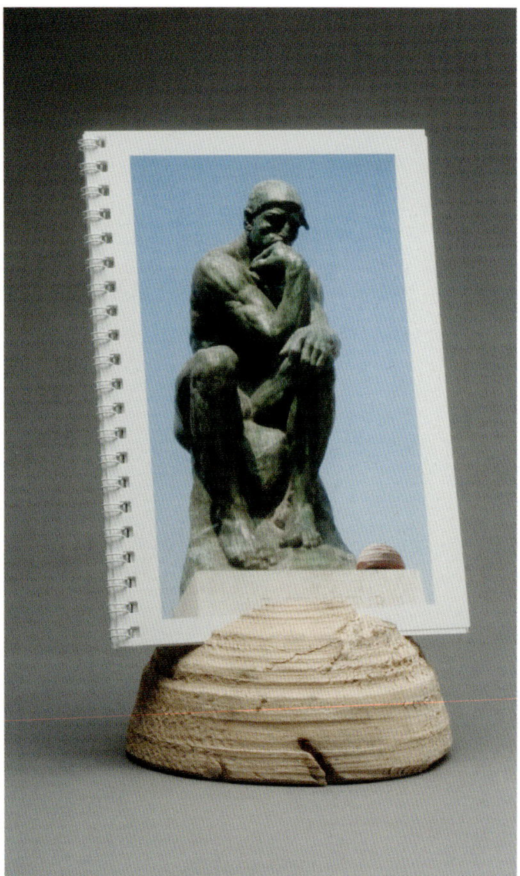

«

Max Krimmel's *CORE Dreams* is another favorite. So very simple. The one use I have made of cores in the past is as Christmas presents. I drill a couple of holes, poke some holly in, cut an angled slot, and slide in a card with a note. This piece is added to greatly by choosing Rodin's *The Thinker* as the subject. If we are going to do "Art," then in today's world it's the thought that is important. Rodin, of course, predates conceptual art and was from a strong craft/sculpture/drawing/modelling tradition. Such a simple piece that can raise so many questions, like Duchamp's readymades or Ai Weiwei's work, it's not about the execution. It doesn't even matter whether any of these ideas were in Krimmel's mind, his piece sparked ideas for me, though I would be interested to know what his core dreams were.

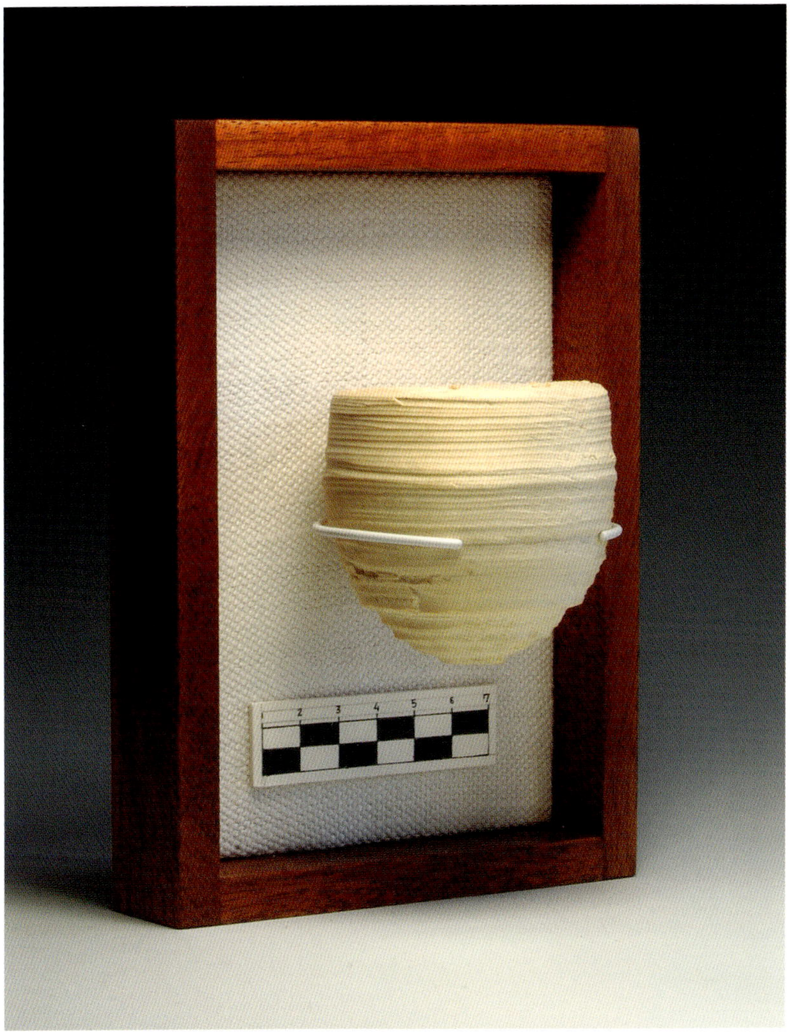

«

In *Artifact,* Yoav Liberman tells us he aims to present the core as an archaeological specimen; it also feels reminiscent of Victorian insect displays in museum cabinets pinned hovering above a white board. Context is vital for our understanding of objects, and I feel the way the various artists have presented these little altered cores is a very interesting study in context. At the end of the day, they will all probably be presented in the gallery on a white podium, printed in a glossy book, and taken to new homes where they will be given treasured positions with space and light. The same object thrown in a bowl of knickknacks or on a table at a car boot fair would not speak to us in the same way. Context validates objects, but for the artist then finding beauty and meaning where others don't see it is the real thrill.

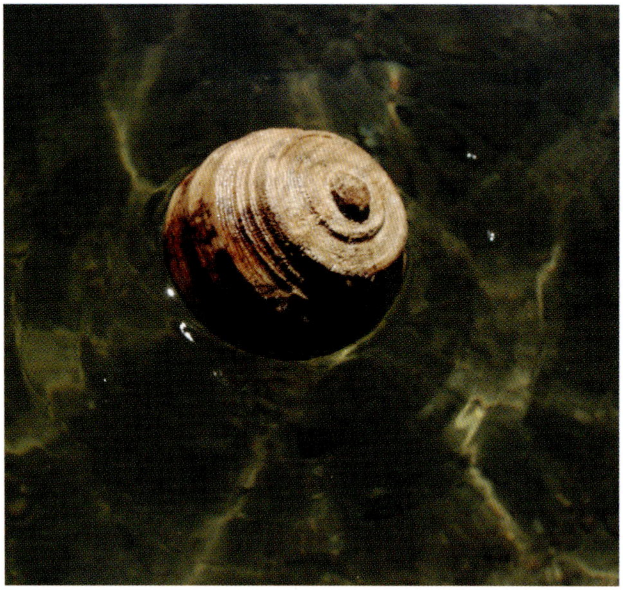

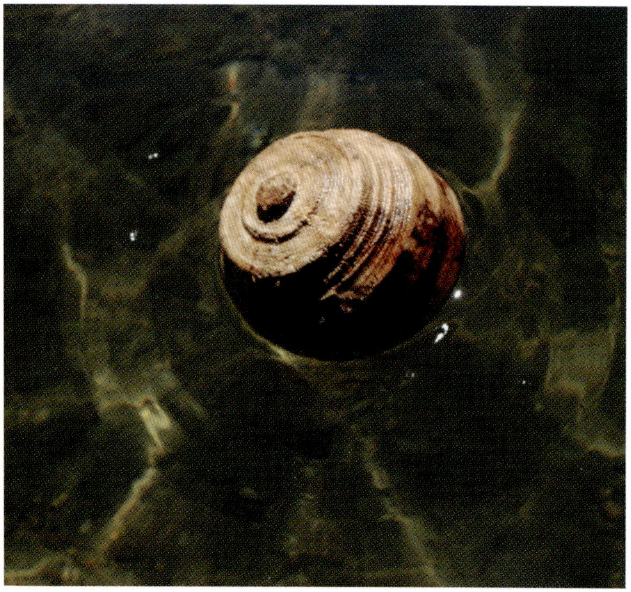

Gord Peteran gets the prize for laziest artist of the lot. His core is completely unaltered in the best Duchamp tradition. It is merely presented in a new way to create a new piece of art. It is my favorite piece in the exhibition. I think artists were asked to supply before and after images; Peteran doesn't even take a second shot; he simply flips the original. This creates a book-matched pair that has a long tradition in woodwork and always looks good. I always find the rough textures of my work look good in natural settings, and in the water the core looks very beautiful, the light dances. What does the piece say? I like to think it says, here's a great little thing, I don't know what to do with it, but I like it just as it is. I feel much the same way, which is why I never burn them and always have a thousand or so kicking about the workshop.

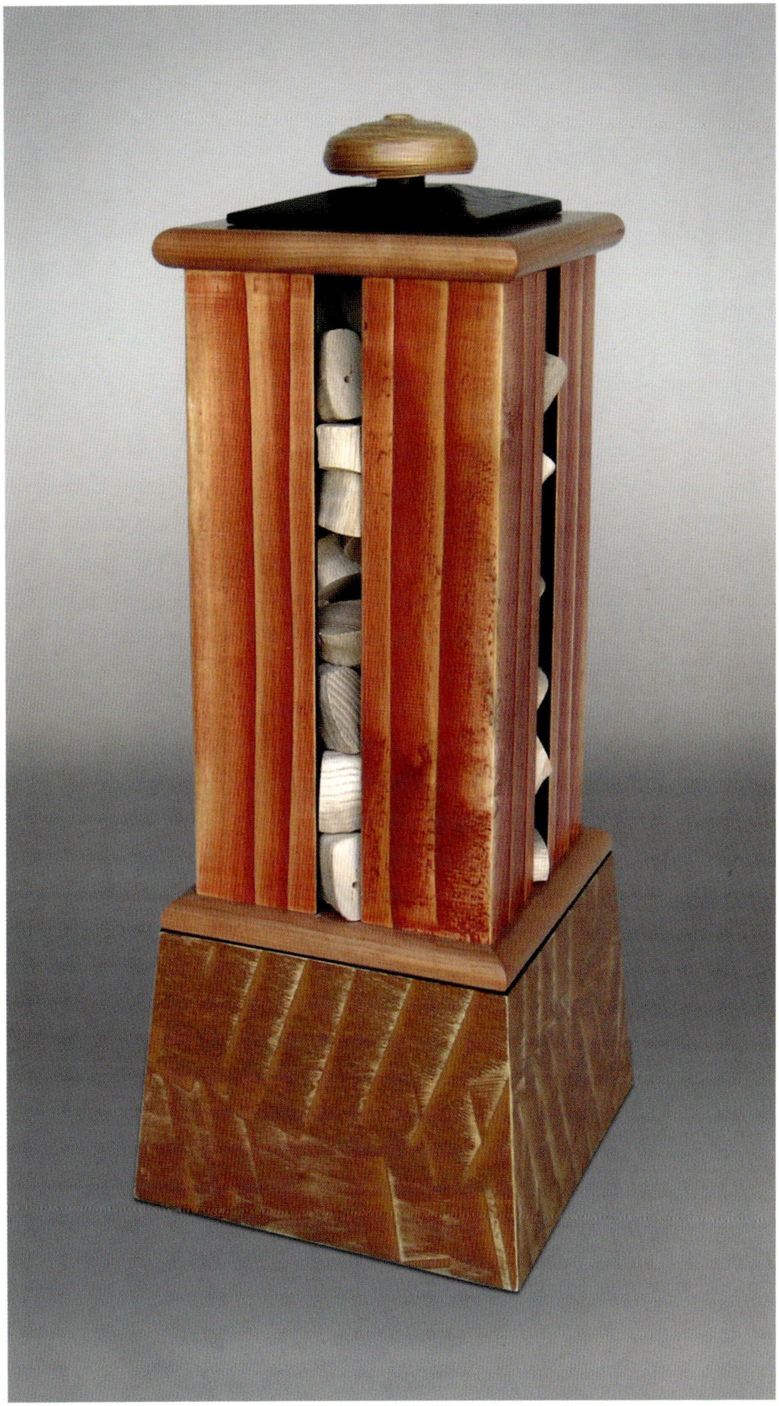

«

Brad Smith's *165 Heels* almost fits into the category of "you didn't really want the core" as it sits unaltered atop a little cabinet. But inside the cabinet are 165 heels: what is that about? Are they a similar discarded by-product? They definitely feel related, and the other thing that appeals is the texture at the base of the cabinet. I don't know how this texture was made but it is very reminiscent of the wonderful texture created by the Japanese adze or chouna, a tool I adore. The whole piece has rather a Japanese feel, so with that and its unanswered questions about the heels, I like it.

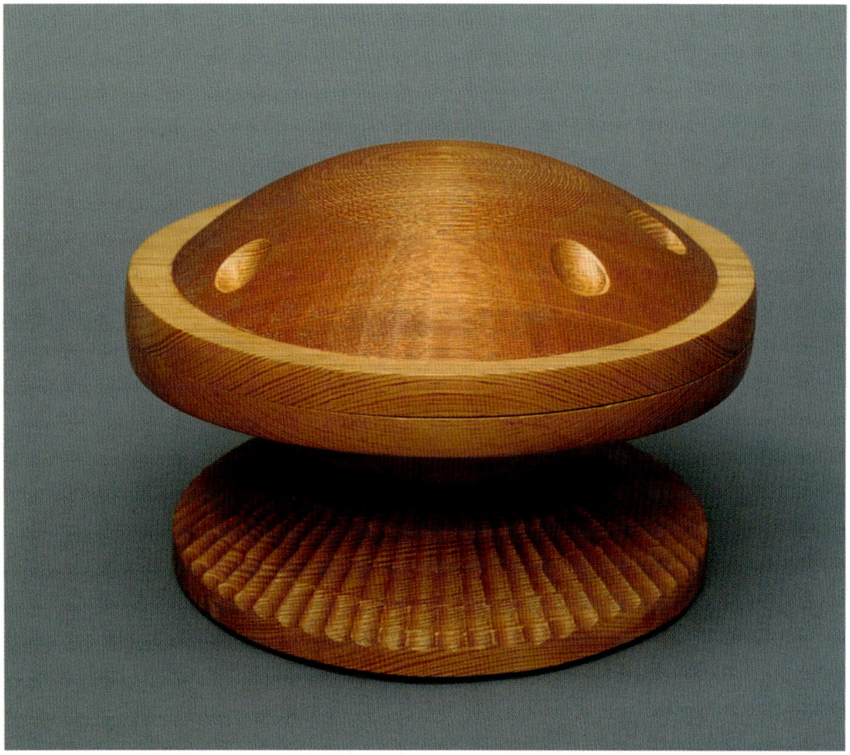

«

Hiyami Arakawa made *Capsule Hermetica, a container for an object of rarefied distinction*. I love the story of how this piece came about, as the core was picked up mistaken for a portable hard drive. That is fun since I turned my own core into a flash drive. For me the following piece of writing is art enough and the physical work just adds to it: "I imagined this ovoid chunk of densely packed fiber as an organic hard drive of sorts, a repository of knowledge, history, fact, mythology … an 'artifactoid' if you will." I wish I could have written those words.

»

I had planned to write about the other pieces that are sliced, manipulated, transformed in other ways but have run out of room. The imagination, ingenuity, and spirit of the wood art world seem to be well and I am grateful to all of the artists for engaging with the project in such a thoughtful and generous manner. I have enjoyed the results immensely.

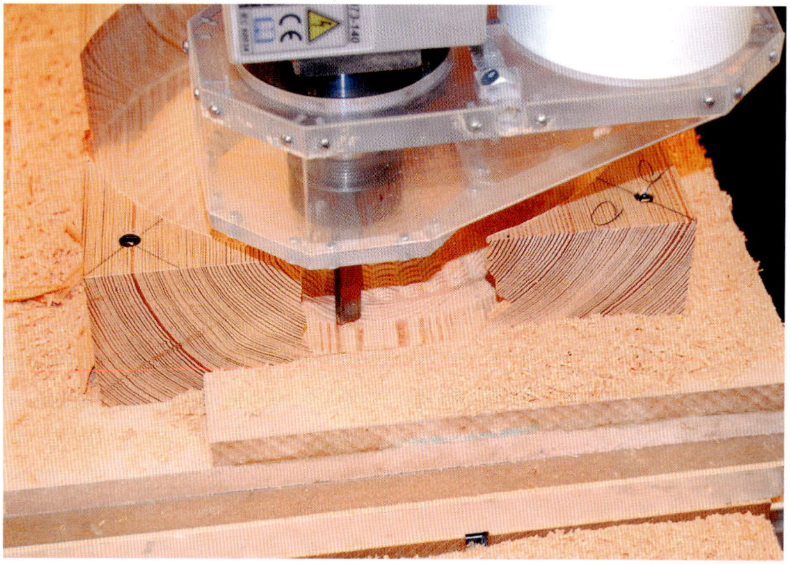

Artists' Works

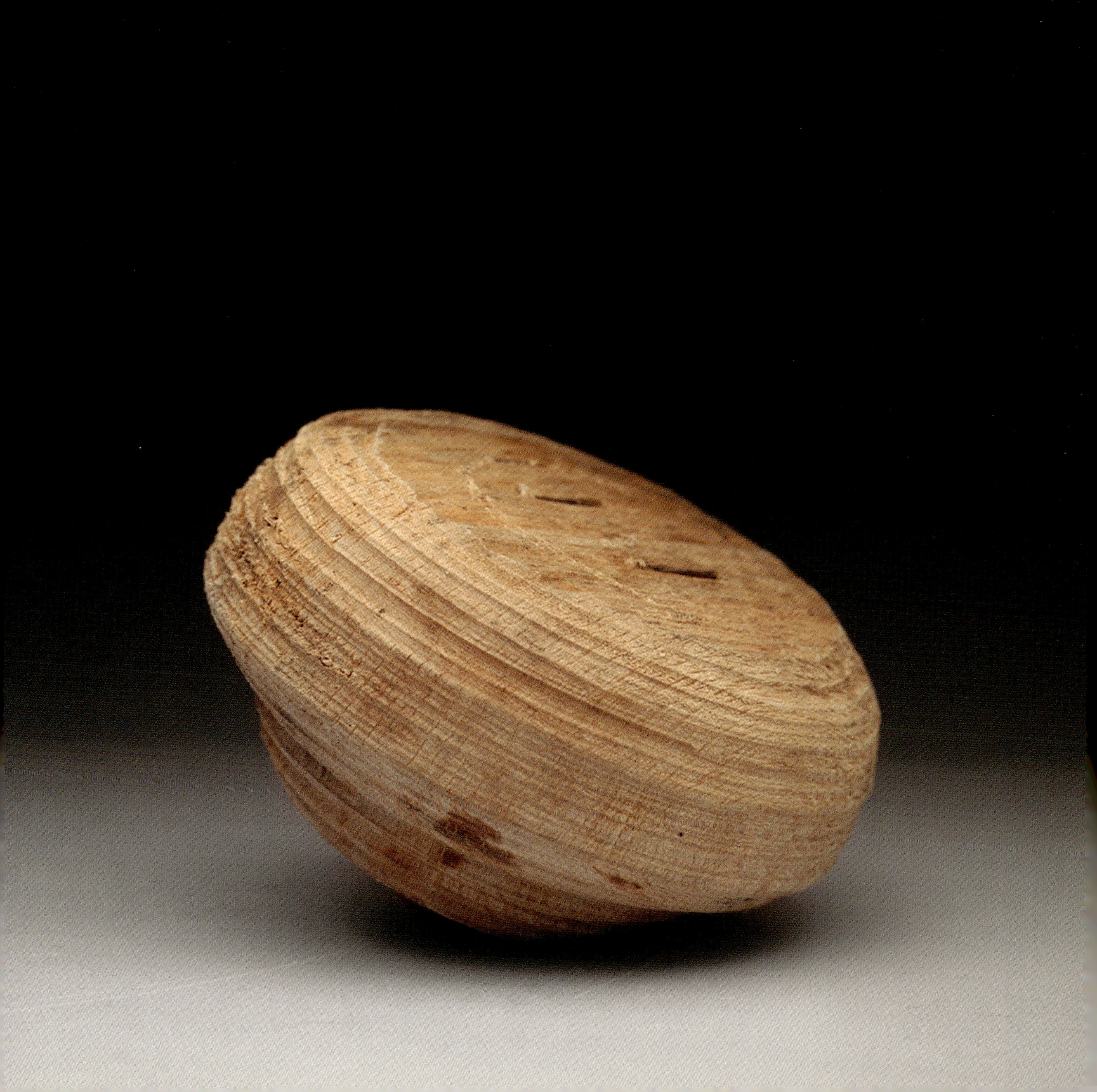

Hayami Arakawa

UNITED STATES

Capsule Hermetica, a container for an object of rarefied distinction, 2012
Core, pine, brass, auto lacquer | 5 ¼" x Dia. 9"
Photo by Hayami Arakawa

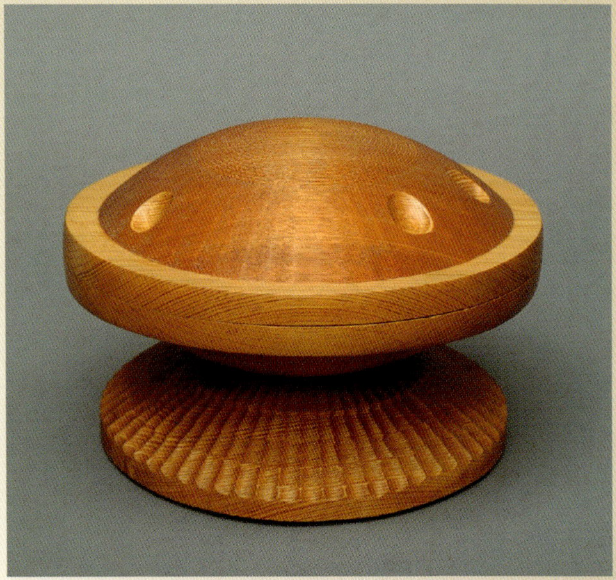

Upon receiving my core sample in the mail, I imagined the object as a primal hockey puck, so I pushed the oak core around the grass with a hockey stick, fishing for inspiration. I continued this interactive sport method by flipping the core around with a lacrosse stick followed by a round of bowling with scrap pieces of wood as pins. This method of interactive inspiration, while fun, ended up being fruitless and arguably misguided.

The core sat passively for weeks next to my computer. One day I was rushing to work and grabbed the core sample by accident, it being the approximate size and weight of my external hard drive. Getting to work I could only laugh at my blunder. The laugh was in part at my silly mishandling and in larger part panic, because I knew I would be totally improvising a lecture in thirty minutes. Surviving that teaching day, on my drive home I imagined this ovoid chunk of densely packed fiber as an organic hard drive of sorts, a repository of knowledge, history, fact, mythology ... an "artifactoid" if you will.

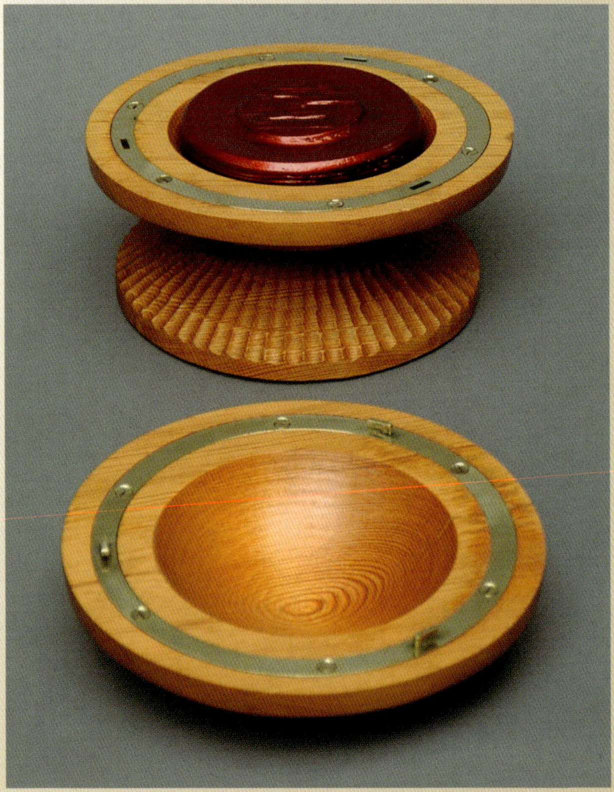

I started to design a protective case for this precious keeper of human knowledge, imagining that it would be found decades, centuries, or millennia later. Possibly pondered over by some advanced race or perhaps by some curious kid digging through the dirt looking for something to play with. The core's surface should be protected as well; ten coats of auto lacquer should suffice and the color red would indicate its importance potential. Inspired by the proximity to a computer, I decided to design and fabricate the container using the CAD/CAM machinery at MIT. I chose pine to construct with because of its resistance to rotting and its ease of machinability.

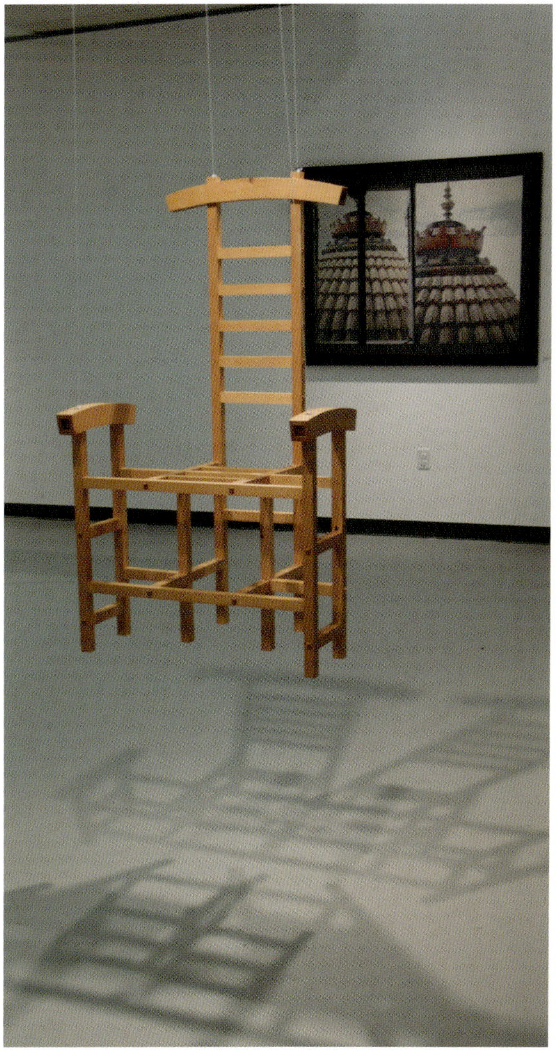

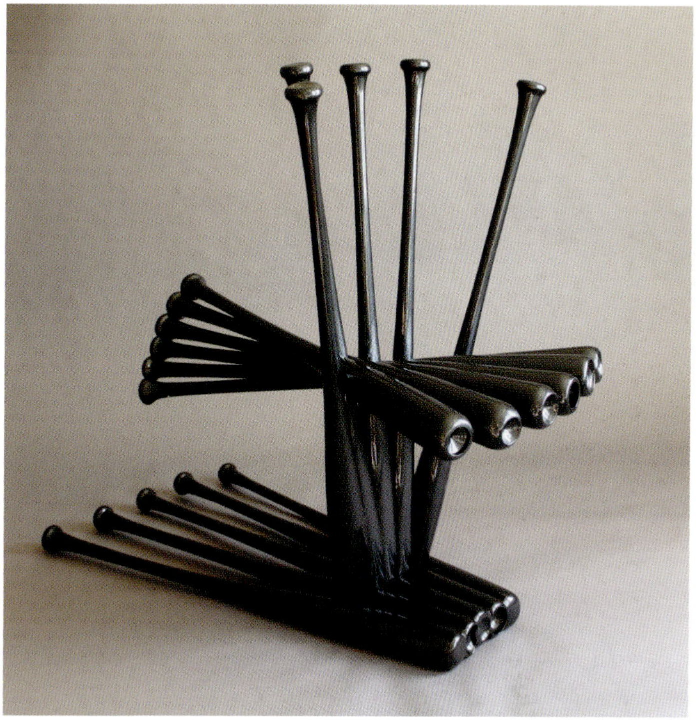

Twilight Hitters Chair, 2010

Recycled maple wood bats, silver speckled dark grey auto lacquer

35" x 28" x 42"

Gizo (Hollow) Chair, 2004

Recycled Alaskan yellow cedar from a thousand-year-old forest that had been dead for one hundred years

47" x 28" x 21"

Michael Bauermeister

UNITED STATES

Expanded Core, 2012
Core, sycamore | 17" x Dia. 6"
Photo by Michael Bauermeister

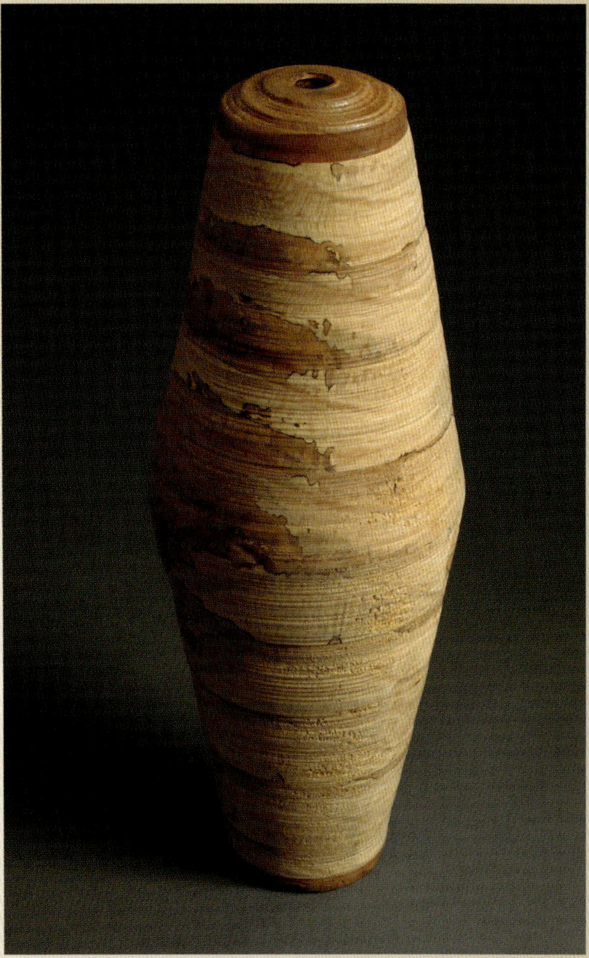

The piece I made for the CORES project was a tall wood vessel. But most of the vessels I make are much taller! I make wooden vessels because I have to make something, and I've come to the conclusion that it doesn't much matter what. These sculptural forms offer the viewer a place to start, the iconic and comfortable bowl and container, and from there, I'm free to explore any idea or mood I can imagine. Since my background is as a cabinetmaker, I usually build a vessel up out of several pieces of wood, which is then carved, turned, and sometimes painted before being lacquered and polished. I like to work in a scale not usually associated with wood bowls, forcing the viewer to see them in a new light.

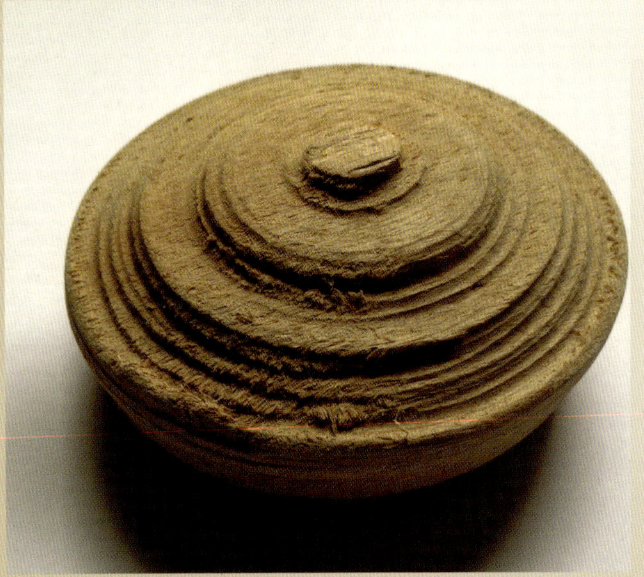

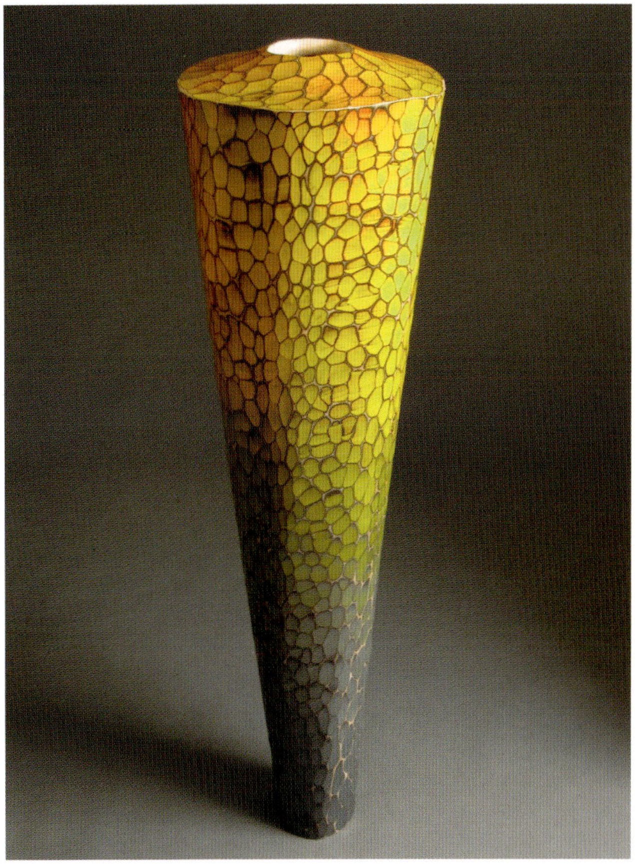

Citri, 2010

Linden, tinted lacquer | 50" x Dia. 14"

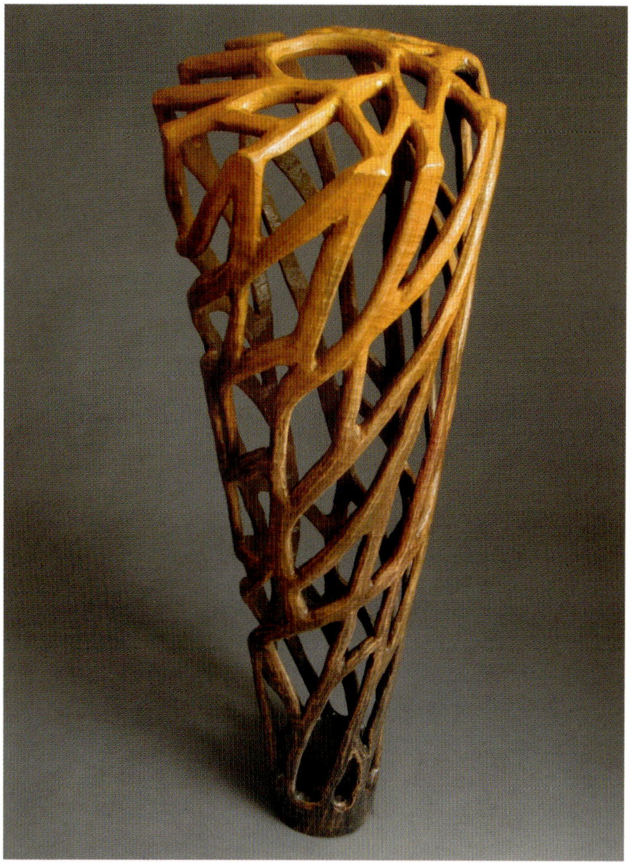

Winter Lace, 2010

Oak | 48" x 13" x 13"

Derek Bencomo

UNITED STATES

Harmonica, 2012
Core (maple), pigment | 4" x 4 ½" x 4 ¼"

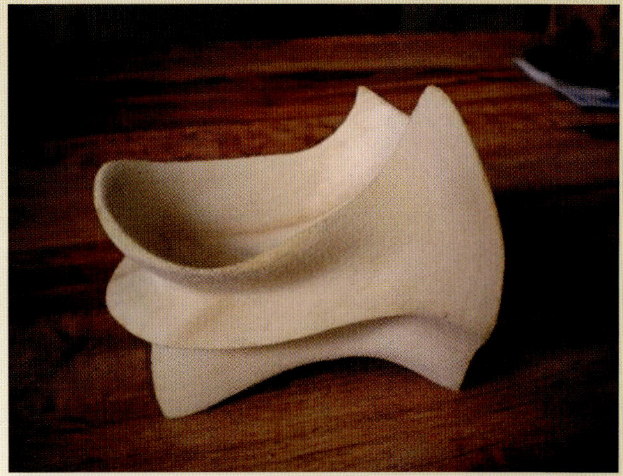

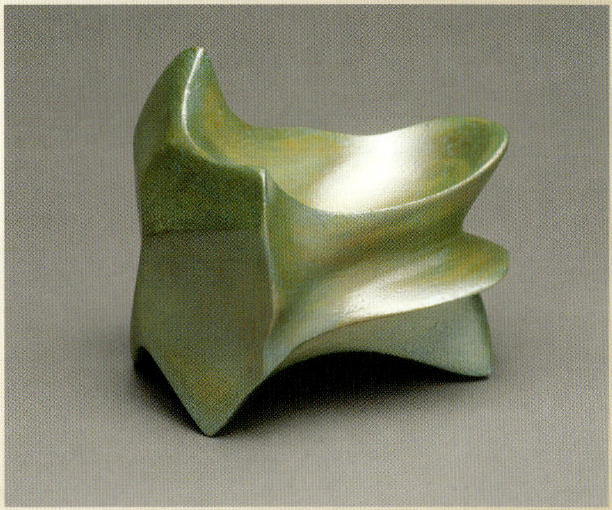

This is my twenty-fifth year working as an artist, which has put a new spin on what I want to say.

In my early six or seven years, I turned out hundreds of bowls, platters, and vases. One thing that I noticed was that my scrap pile of waste wood was bigger than my "good wood" pile. All the unusual and best grained wood was in the scrap pile, just because I wanted or needed to have good wood for bowls. So in order to use the good grain in my pieces, I stopped cutting away the so-called bad wood and started to mount logs and odd-shaped pieces on my lathe, carving the free-form pieces into my bowls. My signature style was starting to be born.

By chance, in 2009, I had contacted The Center for Art in Wood to get some information for an artist friend of mine who was from Australia. The director from the Center told me that an artist had dropped out of their fellowship program that was to take place in about three weeks and offered the fellowship to me. So I spent my summer in Philadelphia at Moore College of Art and Design. The first time I worked on art in fourteen months, I spent days and nights working away, creating old work as well as new work.

Back on Maui in 2010, I moved off the beach to upcountry with a new outlook on life.

I started doing pure sculpture. In 2012, I had a crazy idea to create fifty pieces out of fifty different woods to celebrate my life turning fifty. I ended up making over ninety pieces! This was the most that I ever made in any year over my years as an artist. Now I am into my twenty-fifth year as an artist. Time to celebrate this year with a few new surprises, and time to get serious and to push myself and my art to a whole new level. So blessed and thankful that I am.

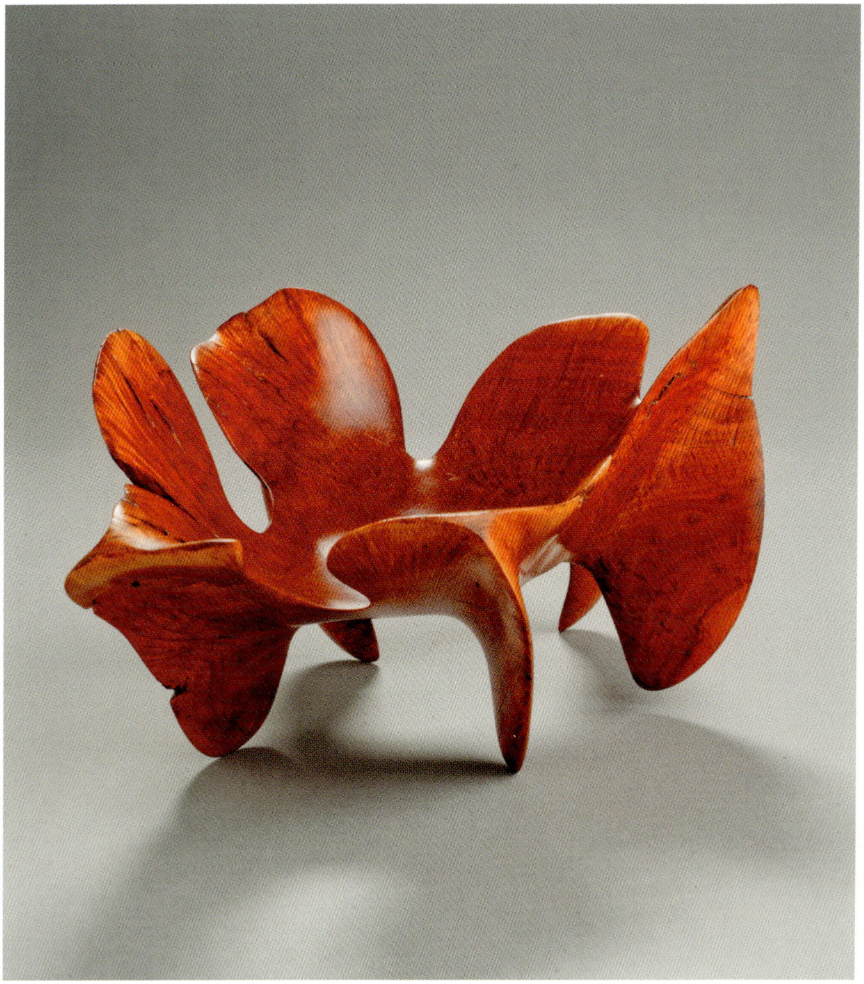

Ocean Harmony, 2000

Milo | 8" x 14 ½" x 9"
Collection of Paul Greenbaum
Photo by Tony Novak-Clifford

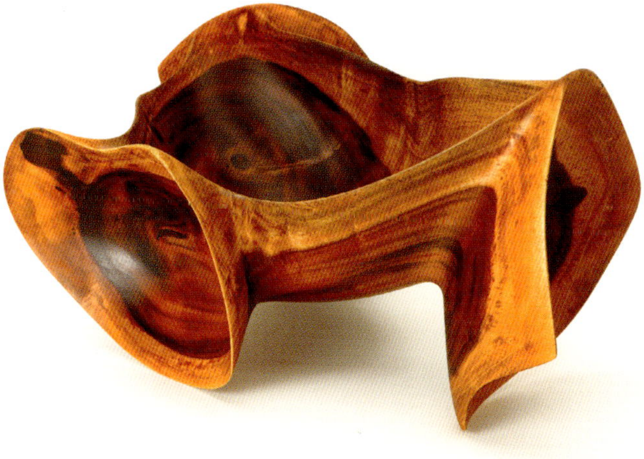

Vessels that Dance, 2012

Manzanita burl | 5" x 8" x 7"
Collection of Ron Gerton
Photo by Tony Novak-Clifford

Garry Knox Bennett

UNITED STATES

Core #3 – Nailed it!. 2012
Core, steel | 6 ¾" x 4 ¾" x 4 ½"

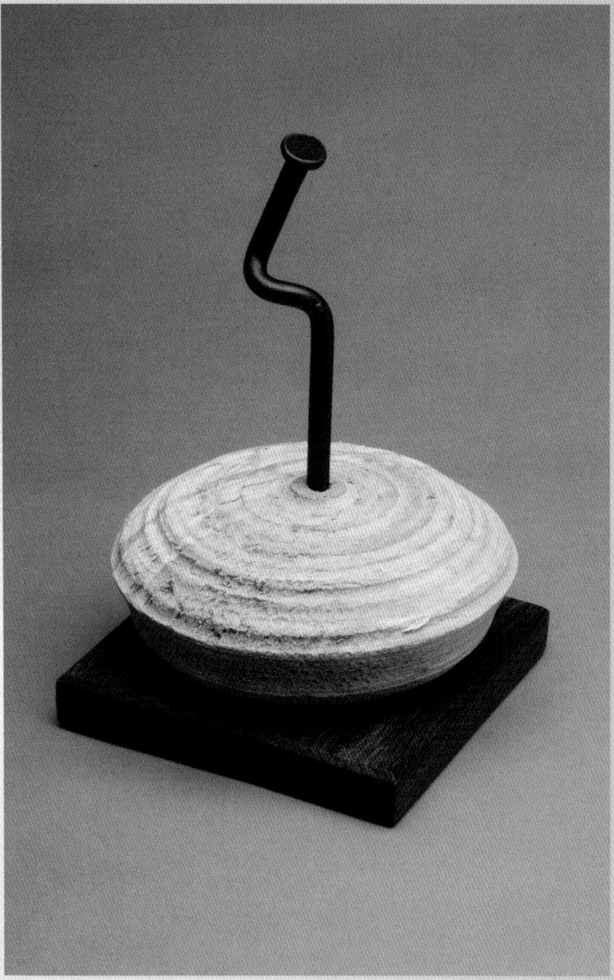

I love challenge and will intentionally try to set up situations that keep pushing me forward. I enjoy taking one element and letting it re-emerge in subsequent pieces until I feel that any issues I may perceive have been resolved.

Pulling together all of the visual and material components (surface, color, texture, etc.) that go into my work creates excitement for me and serves as a continuing challenge. I follow the same process with my painting, jewelry, and sculptural work.

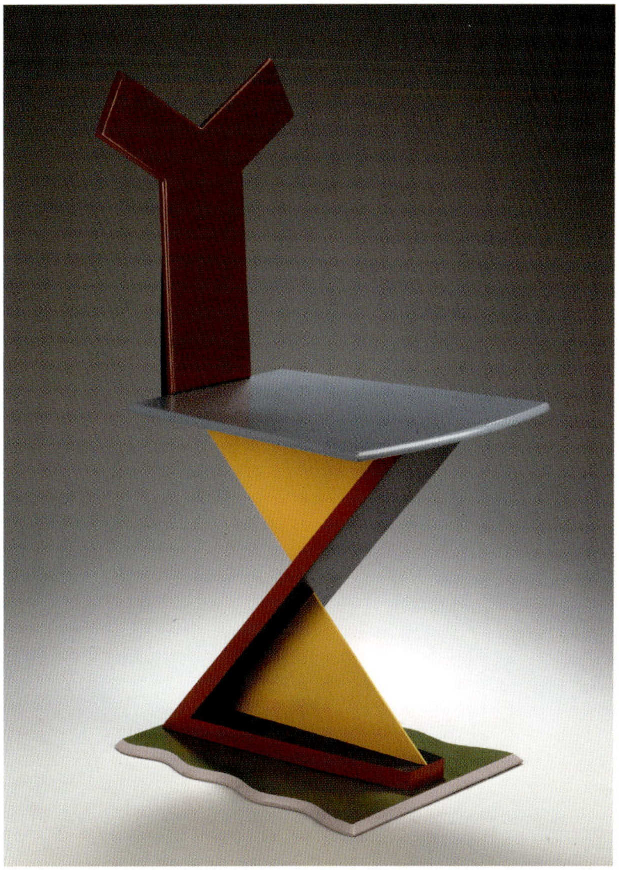

GerritRietveld series #14: "XYZ Chair," 2003

Lacquered wood, aluminum 33 1/2" x 15" x 18"
Photo by M. Lee Fatherree

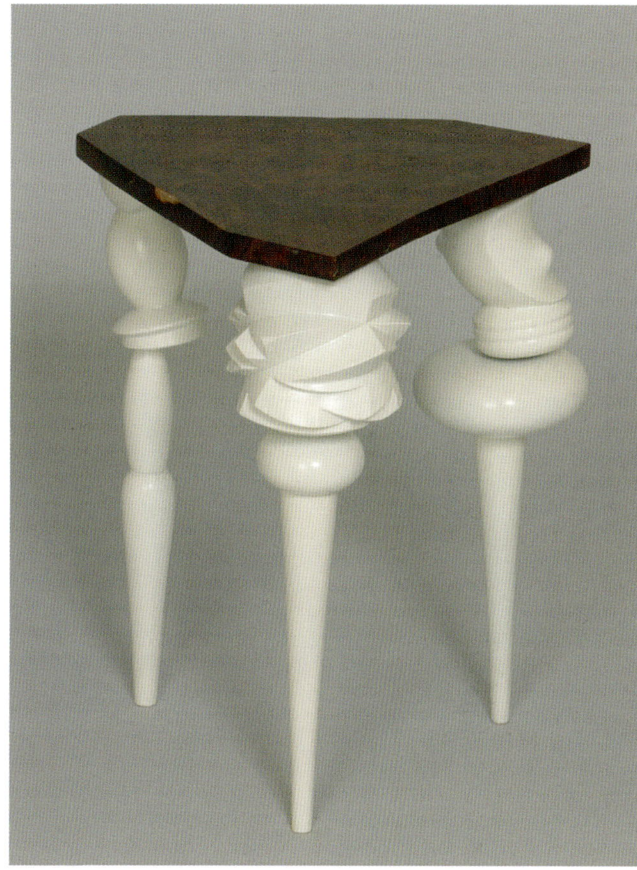

Another table made from Mark's parts, 2008

Wood turned by Mark Sfirri, Claro walnut burl, shellac19" x 15" x 15"
Photo by A. J. McLennan

Jerome Blanc

SWITZERLAND

Wood's Candy, 2012
Core (maple), red dye | 2 ⅛" x Dia. 2 ⅛"

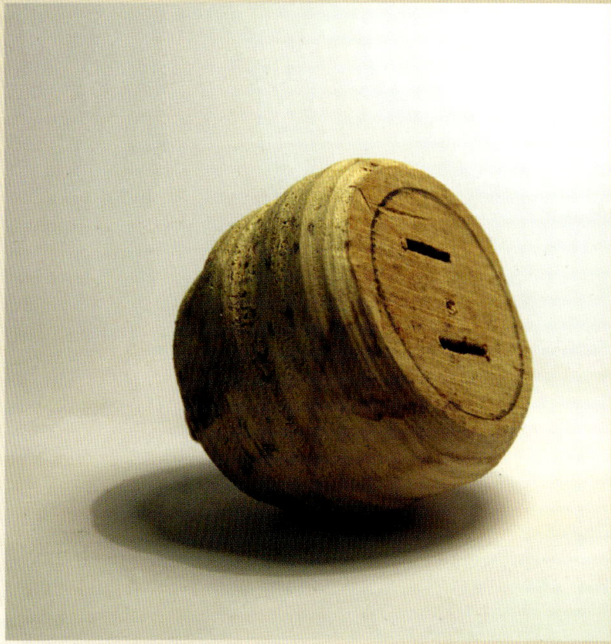

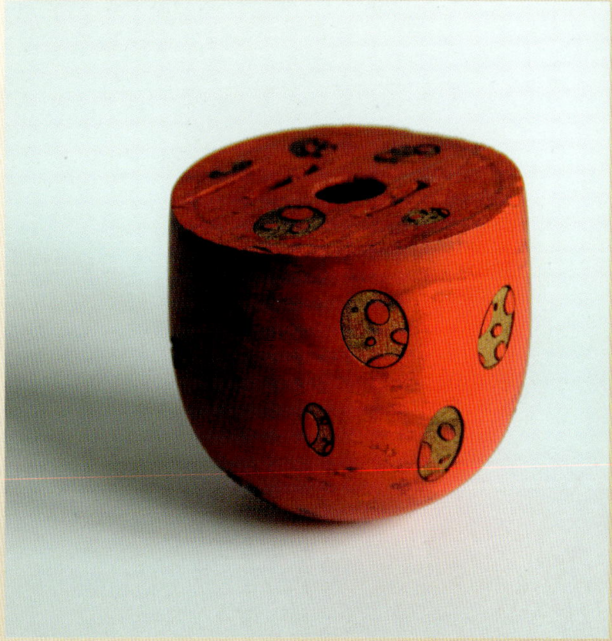

The synthesis of the world around me serves as my inspiration. Nature, unusual lifestyle, urban structure vibrate my imagination over my personal sensibility and translate into wood creations. I like clean lines, color contrasts, textures, and blends of materials. The play of light in the acrylic or gloss of the metal pieces vibrate my unique way.

The current work also follows the instinct of the moment and nuances of wood. A true dialogue with the material marks the stages of my work.

I like to go beyond my limits. I like taking risks, pushing it as an invisible border. Control of the tool must be total, because in a split second everything can change and the piece explodes into a crack suddenly. While relying on know-how, we must forget. The adventure begins: to explore and improvise in total freedom!

Combining aesthetics with technical difficulty, my creations are part of the movement of a sober and elegant design.

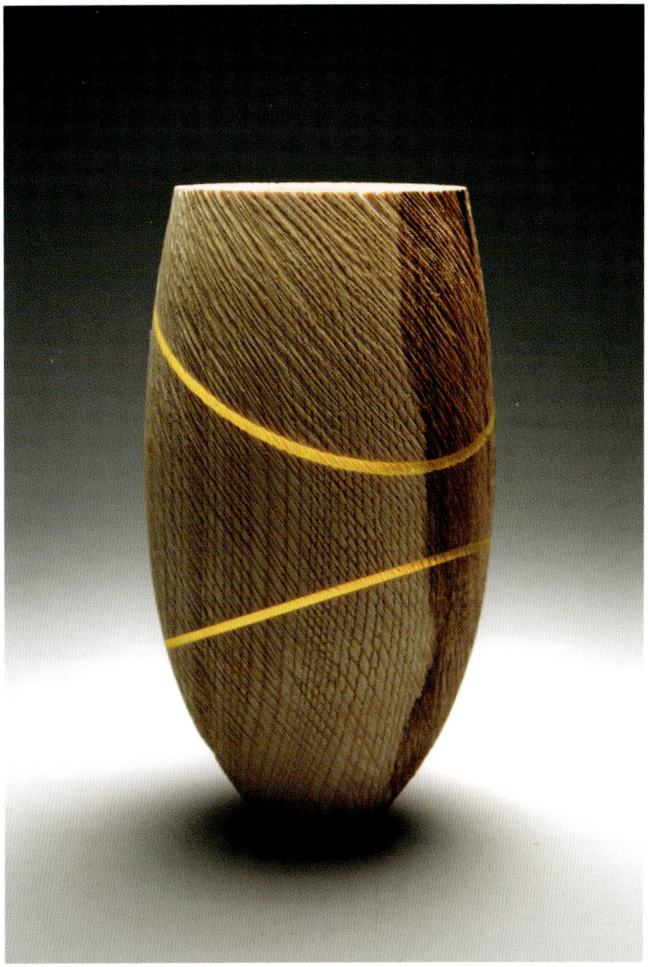

Lumi-naissance, 2011

Ash, inlay acrylic | 14" x Dia. 8"

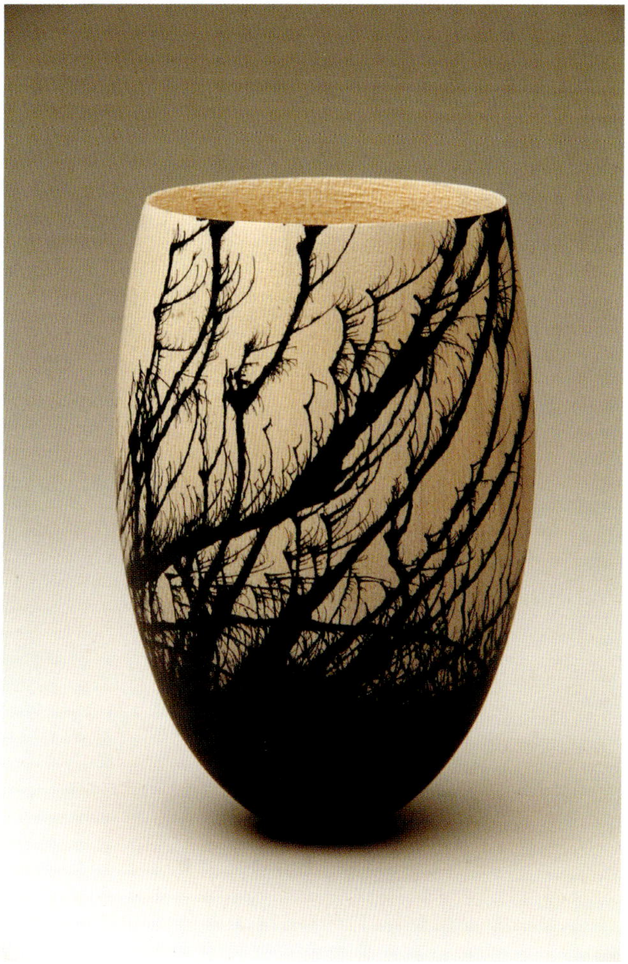

Vent et Bambou IV, 2012

Ash, ink | 18" x Dia. 6"

Jon Brooks

UNITED STATES

Norman, 2012
Core, maple, acrylic | 13" x 22" x 10"

Locally harvested tree sections from the forests surrounding my studio are configured in sculptural form as a collaboration with nature. I select maple, birch, beech saplings, and branches for their strength, durability, light weight, and color. The naturally formed shapes are carefully chosen and joined to create a dance of control and chaos.

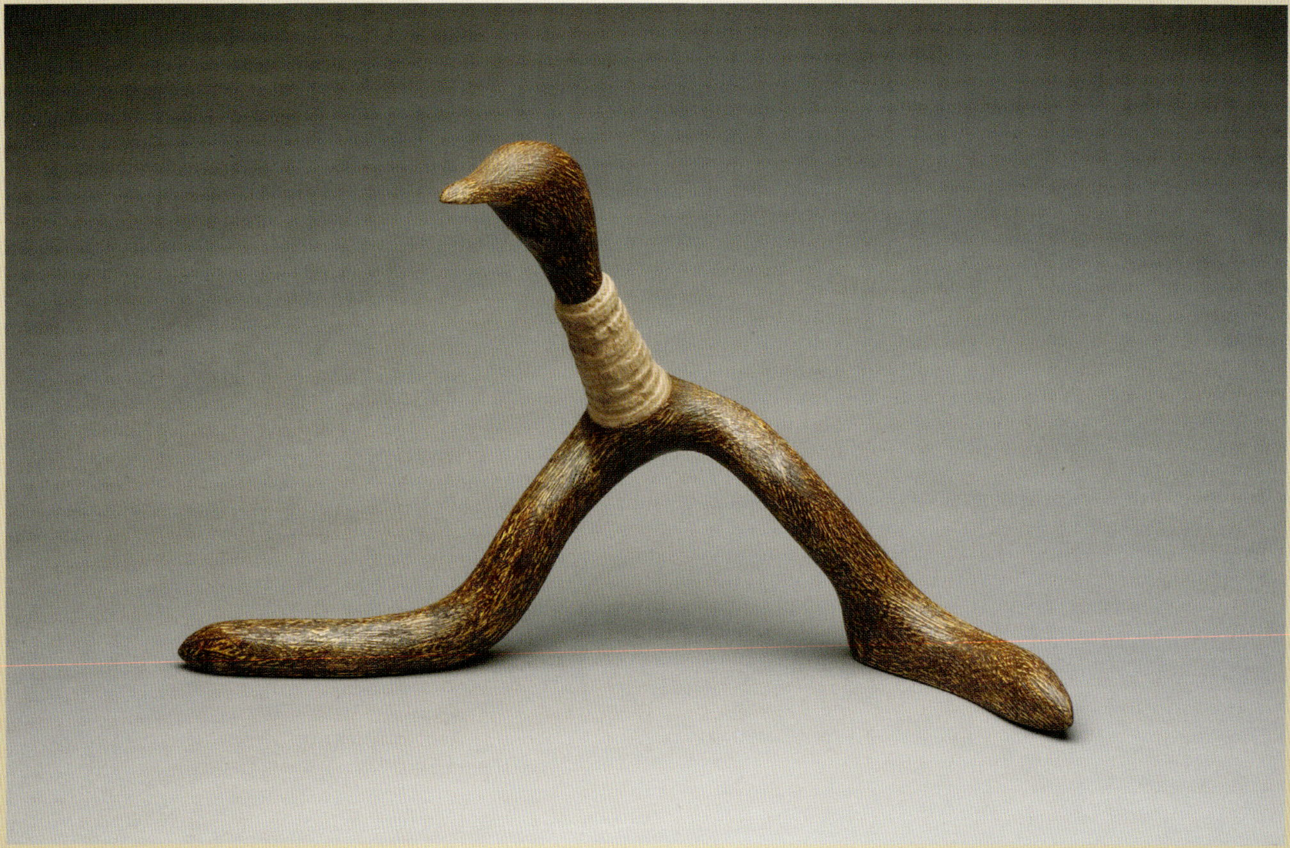

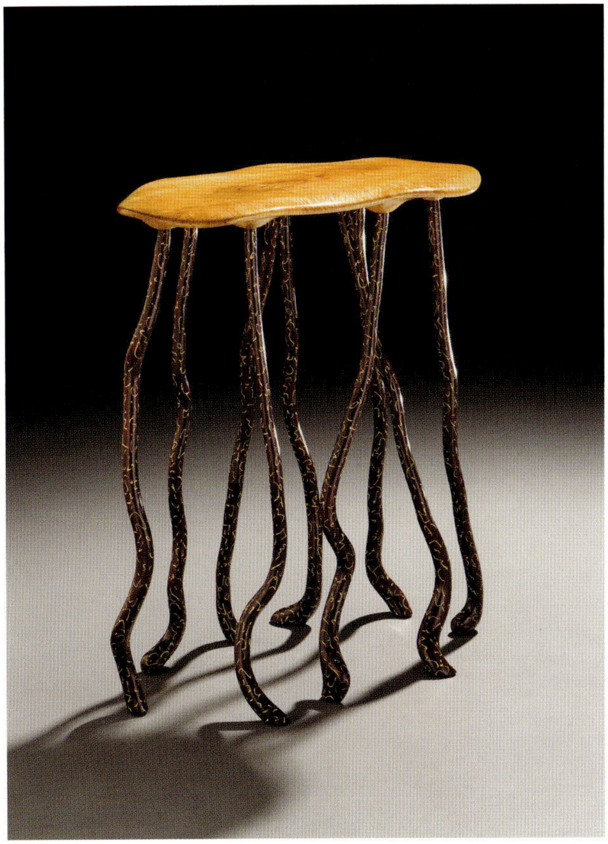

Citron Altar, 2009

Sugar maple, acrylic, color pencil, stain, varnish, lacquer | 35" x 30" x 18"

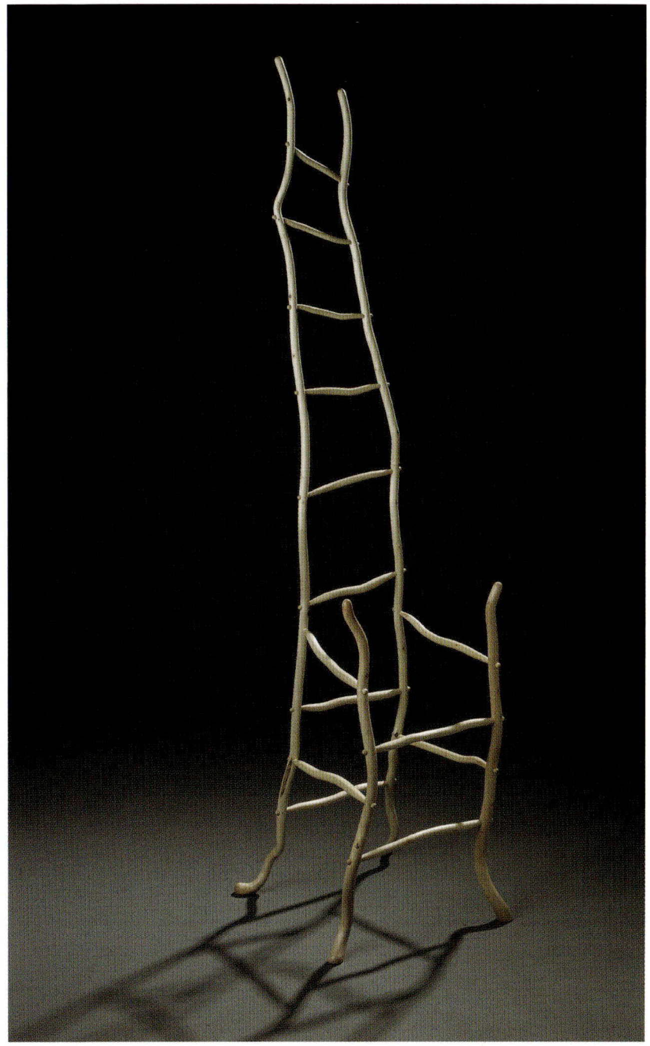

Apparition, 2012

Maple, varnish | 98" x 27" x 24"

Phil Brown

UNITED STATES

Mini Vortex, 2012
Core (beech), epoxy, oil | 1 ¼" x 2 ⅝" x 2 ⅝"

A piece so small is a challenge because it is a size I don't usually work with. The core's beet form and spalt lines suggested a flare or vortex, a form of vessel I have enjoyed creating for many years. It was a bit intimidating to undertake, for fear of messing up this one available piece, until I started turning it. I like the result.

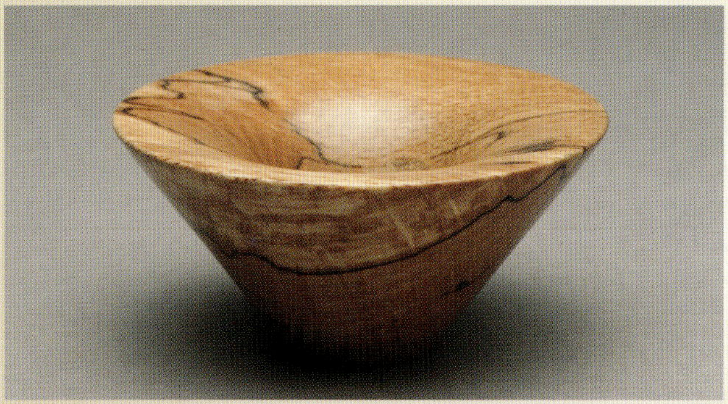

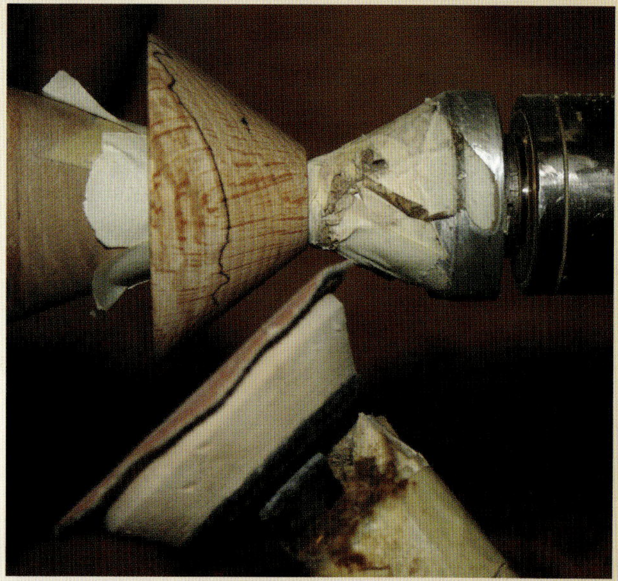

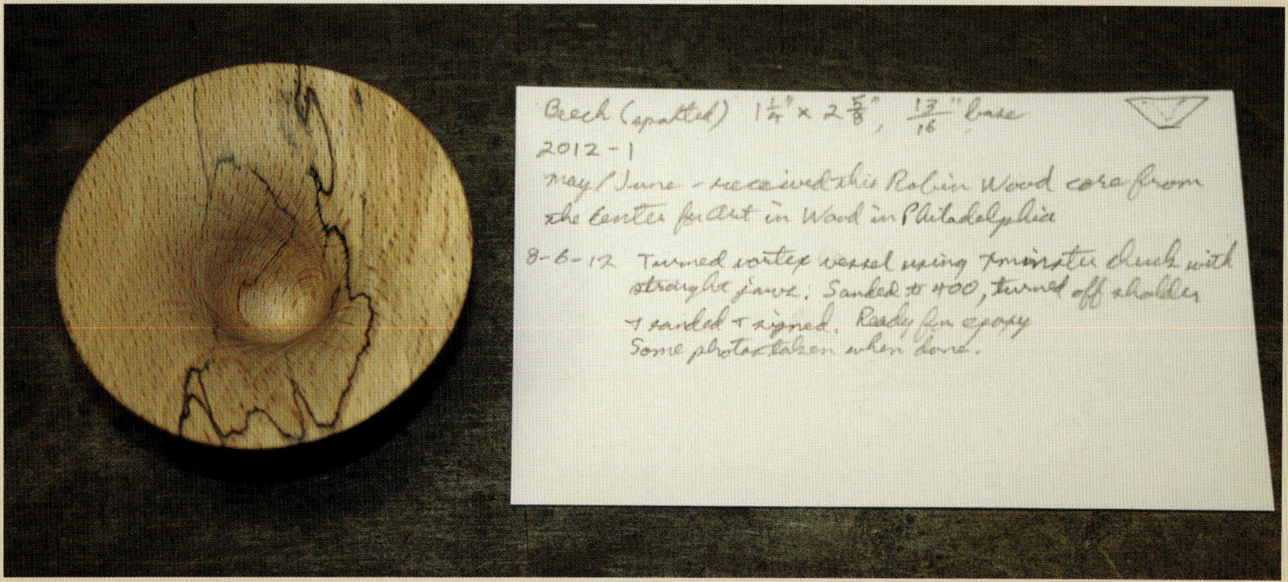

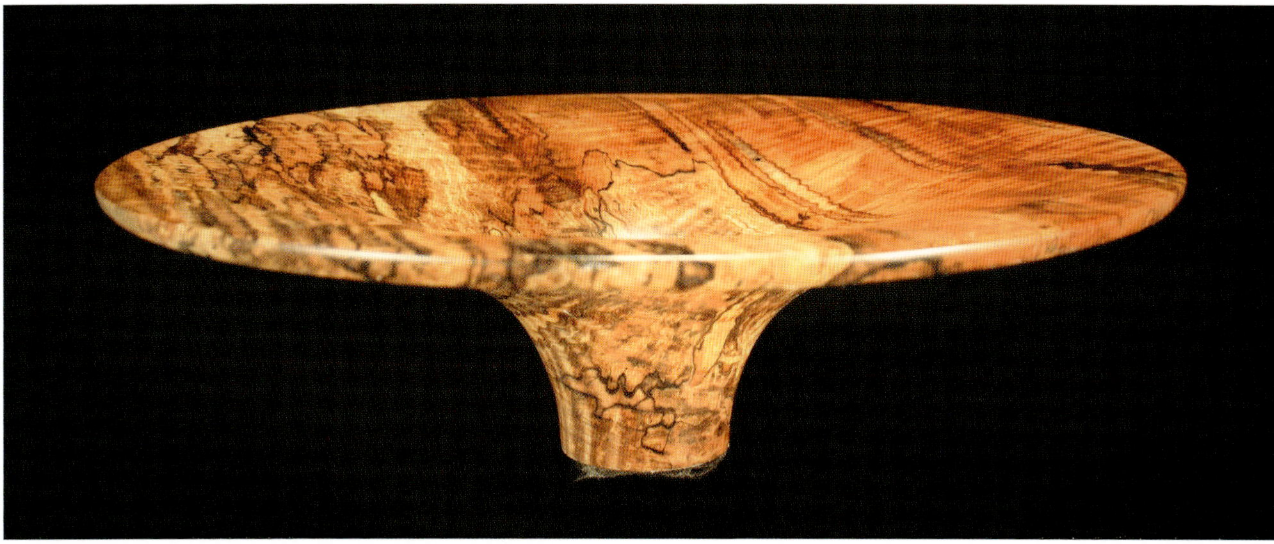

Flare, 2009 | Spalted and curly red maple | 4 ¼" x 15", base 2 ⅜"

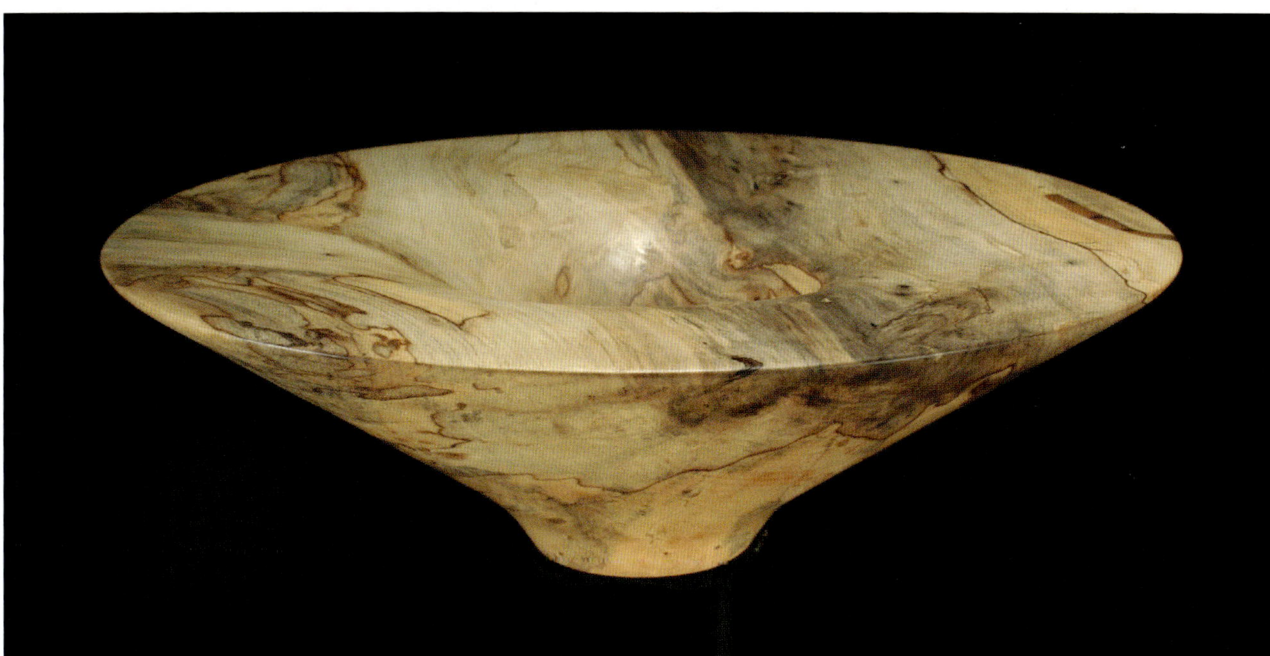

Combined flare and straight side, 2010 | Spalted maple | 5 ¼" x 15 ⅜", base 3 ½"

Zina and Sorin Burloiu

ROMANIA

Interferences 2012 | Core, paint | 1 ½" x 4 ¼"
Spinning Top: 1 ½" x 1 ⅜"

WOODEN CORES! Wood ... a living material ... CORE suggests life. These thoughts made us think of something dynamic. A bowl as a support for a spinning top that was made from the CORE of the bowl. In my traditional carving the rosette is a symbol of the sun, which means life ...

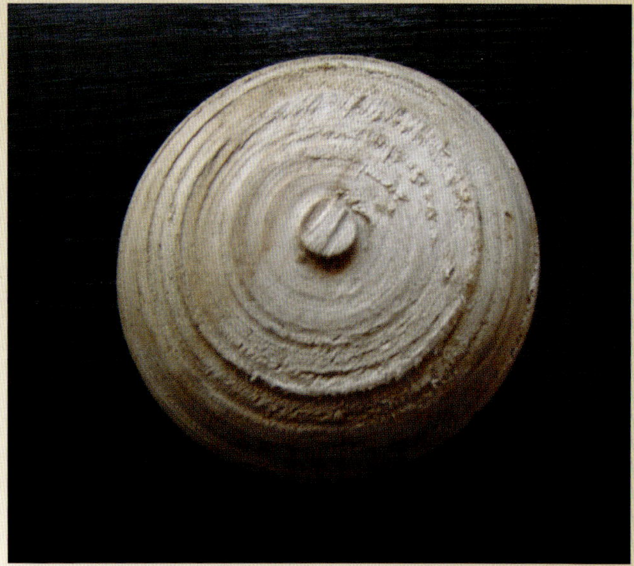

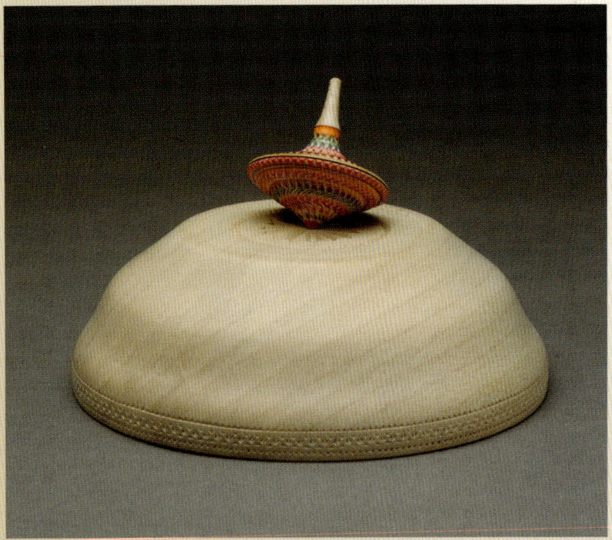

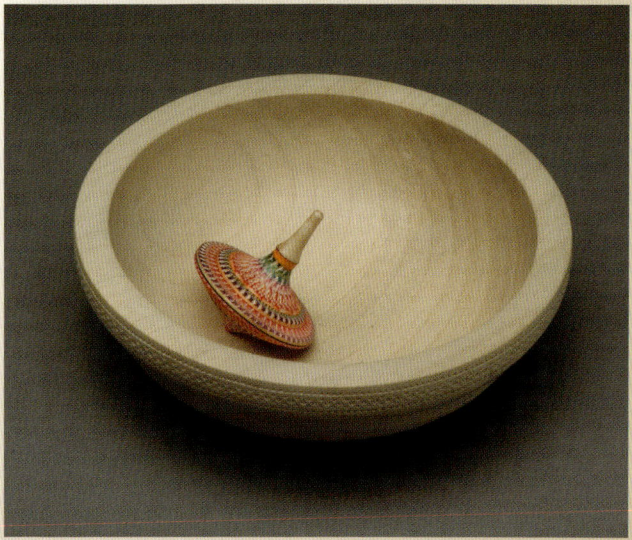

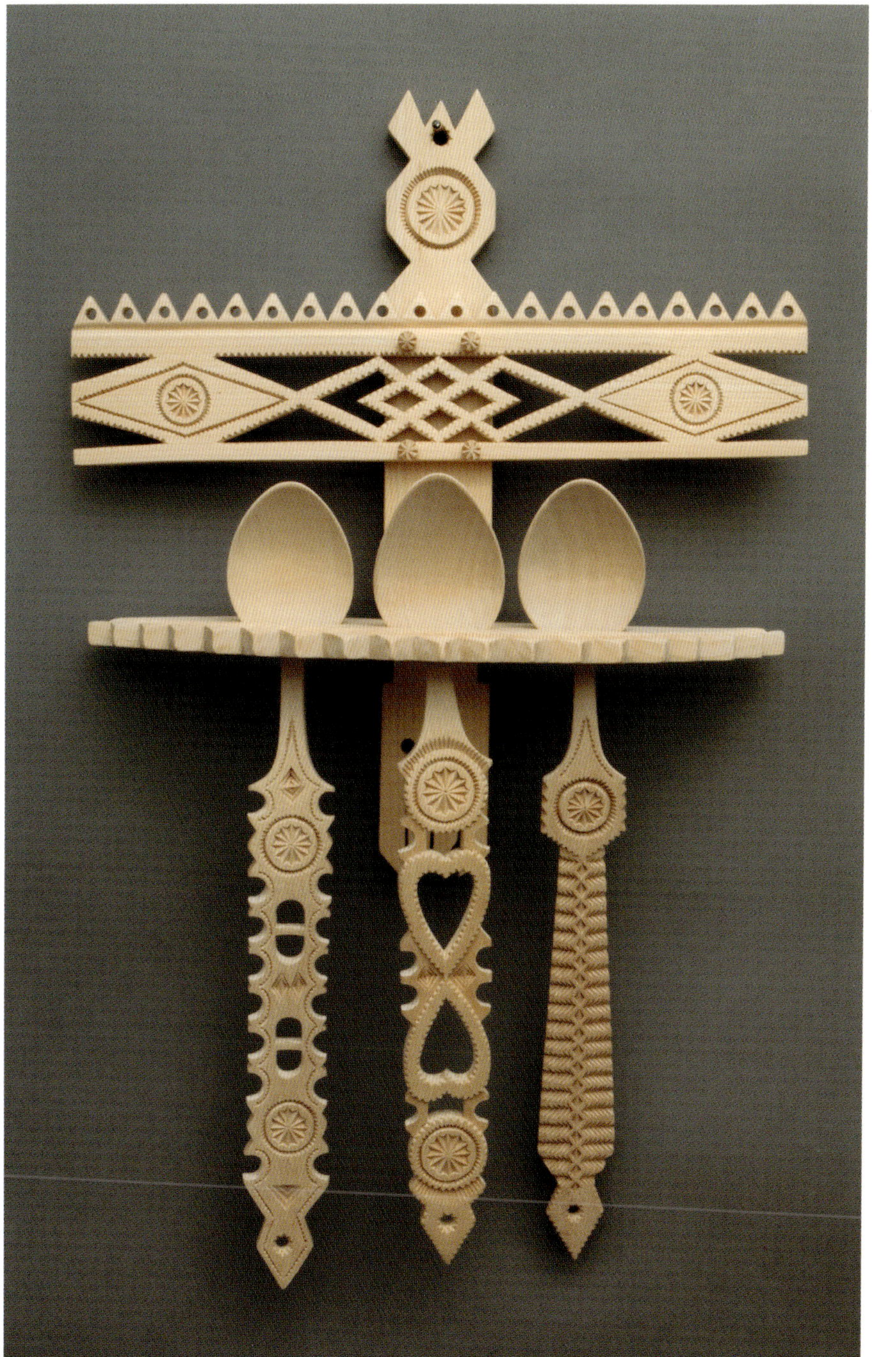

Spoon Rack, 1997

Maple | 11" × 10 " × 2 ¾"
The Center for Art in Wood
Museum Collection

Michael de Forest

UNITED STATES

Round and Round, 2012
Core, milk paint | 3 ¼" x Dia. 4 ½"

I am interested in the asymmetry of form, and within this asymmetry, the character of compound curves. I use color and texture to support line and form. Process is equal to concept.

I look at much of my work as portraiture. I am interested in the imperfections and lopsidedness of physicality, as well as psyche, and I include these aspects in the forms and surfaces of my work.

I use various methods of subtracting and adding, bending, and joining wood to create asymmetrical forms with compound curved surfaces. I have turned, cut into segments, steam bent, bent laminated, carved, veneered, painted, and stitched together. I use vacuum bags, steam, spray guns, dental tools, sewing tools, woodworking hand tools, and machines. My training is furniture making; my inclination is sculpture.

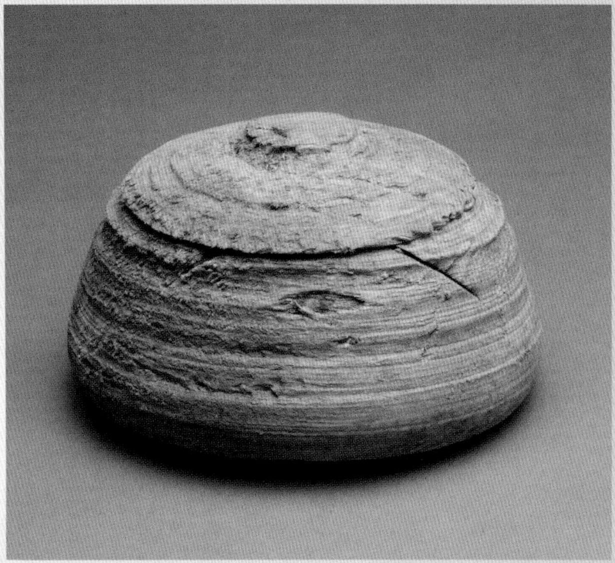

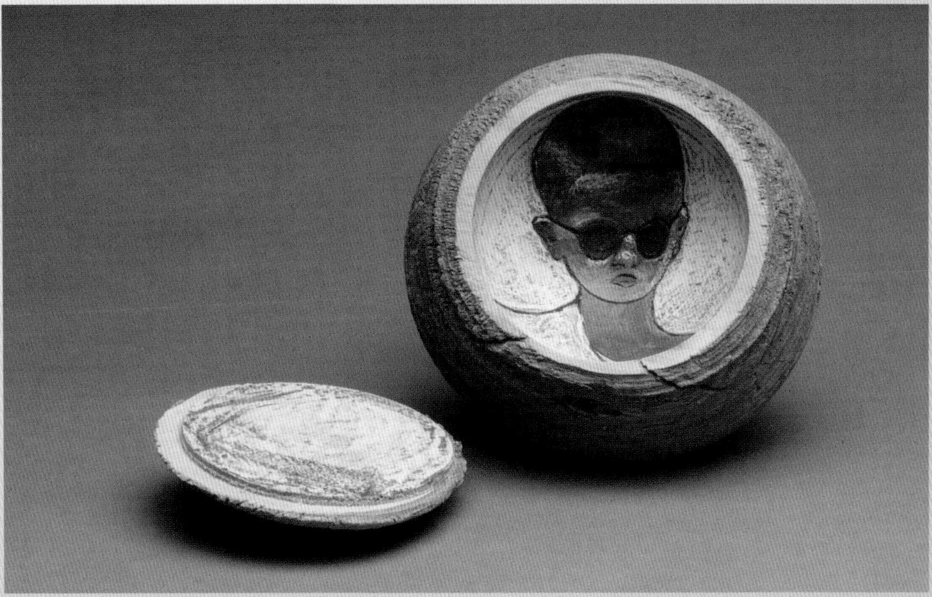

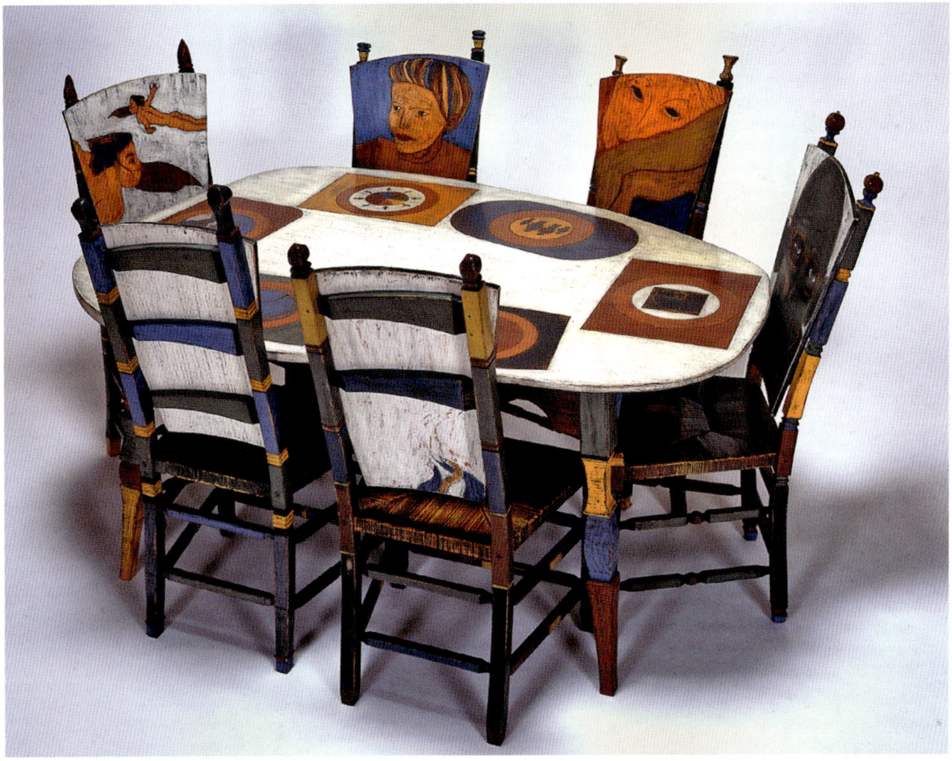

The Family, 1997

Various Woods,
incised line carving,
milk paint
Table: 26" x 63" x 45";
Each Chair: 43" x 20" x 22"

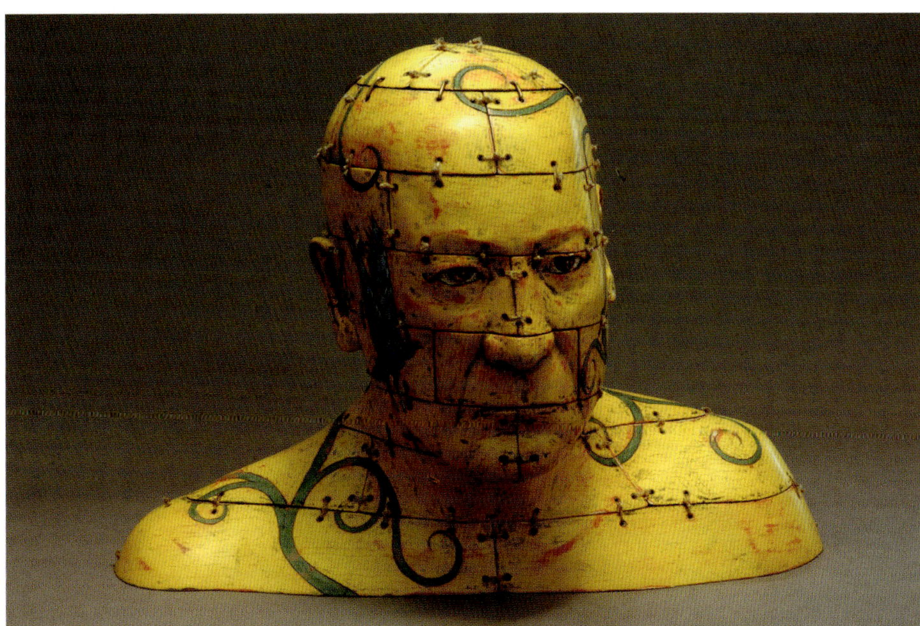

The Crow, 2003

Basswood, incised line
carving, milk paint,
waxed nylon sinew
13 ½" x 19 ½" x 12"

Luc Deroo

BELGIUM

Butterfly, 2012
Core, black gesso | 3 ⅓" x 3 ⅓" x 3 ¾"

Born in Brussels in 1967 and trained as a furniture maker, I've been involved in fine woodworking since the mid-'80s. After exploring furniture making for several years, I now focus on lathe-turned sculpture.

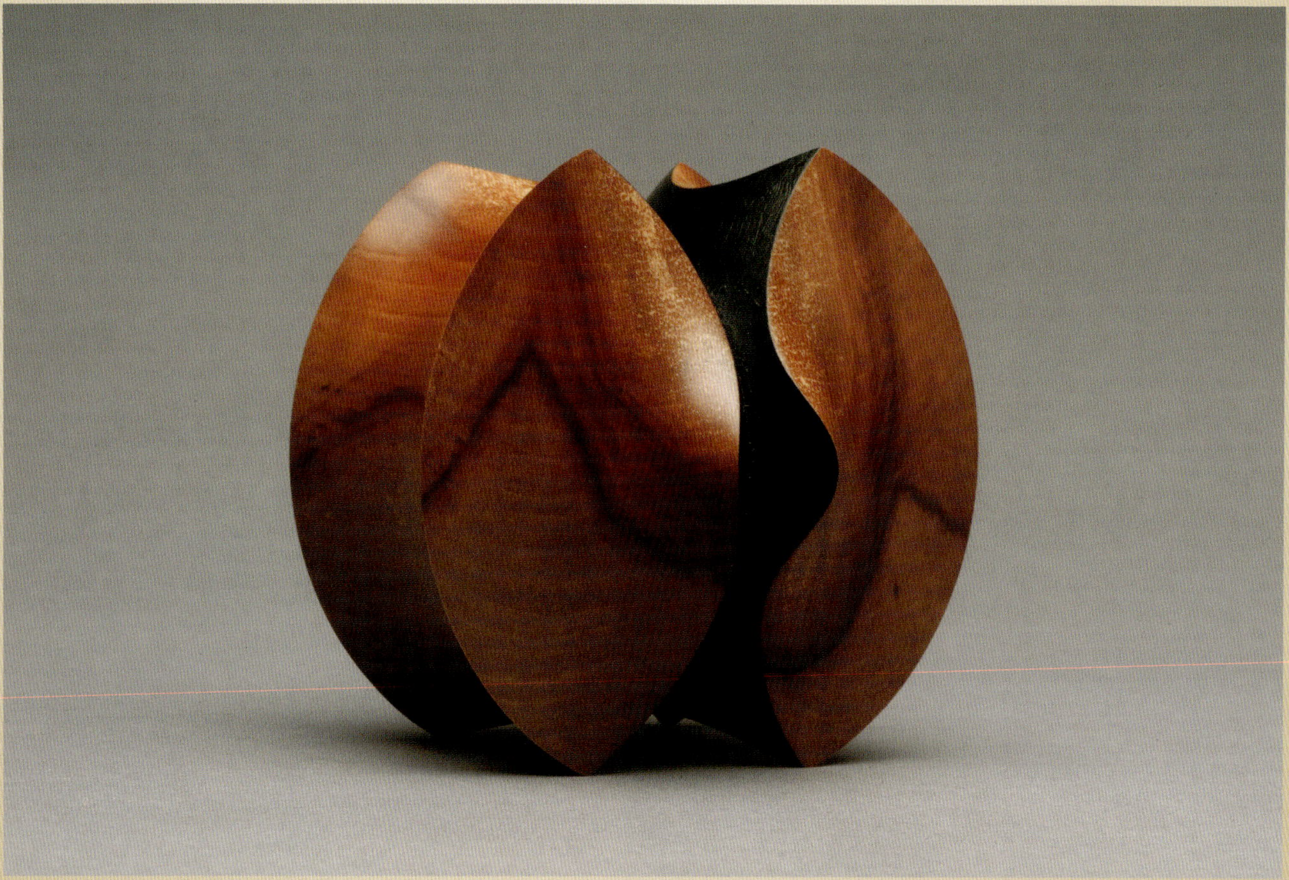

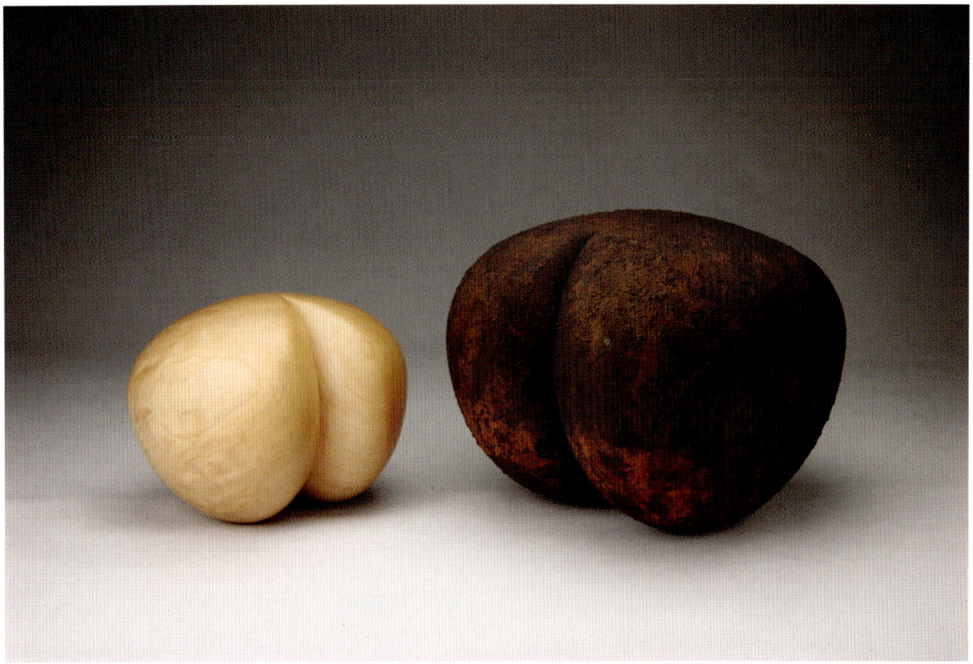

Lunar landscape # 13-1, 2013

Maple and rusted steel
Left: 5" x 5",
Right: 7" x 5"

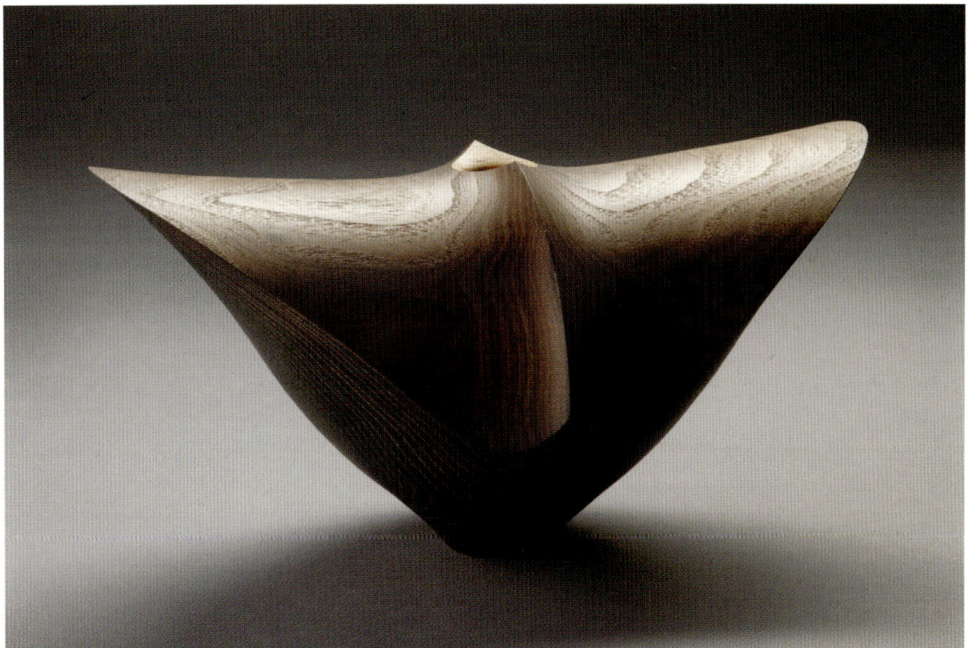

Tenue de soirée #4, 2010

Ebonized locust
7" x 7" x 13"

Neil Donovan

UNITED STATES

Timping Gauge, 2012
Core, pipe, cherry, brass | 10" x 15" x 2"
Before photo by Mark Fainstein;
after photo by John Carlano

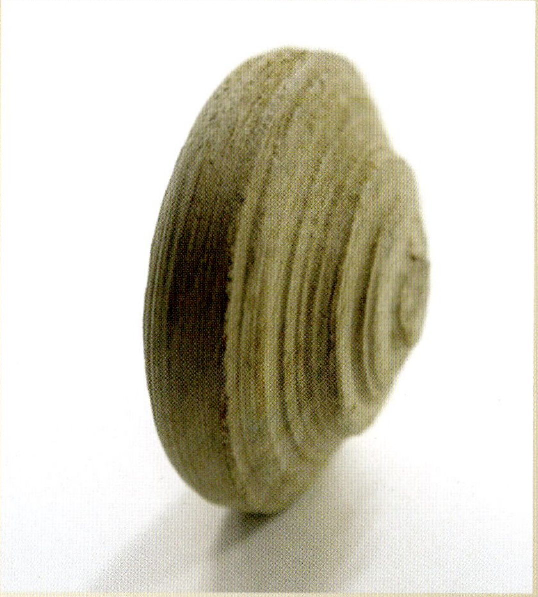

I envision my imaginary tools and machines in an exhibition with visitors moving from object to object. I hope passersby will stop and ask, "What is this? It is familiar but I can't name it. What does this thing do, what is it?" If the works are successful, the viewer will engage, at least momentarily, beyond casual visual inspection. Ideally, the viewer will want to handle the piece, study it, and perhaps feel some level of frustration at not being able to fulfill that human need to name and categorize the object.

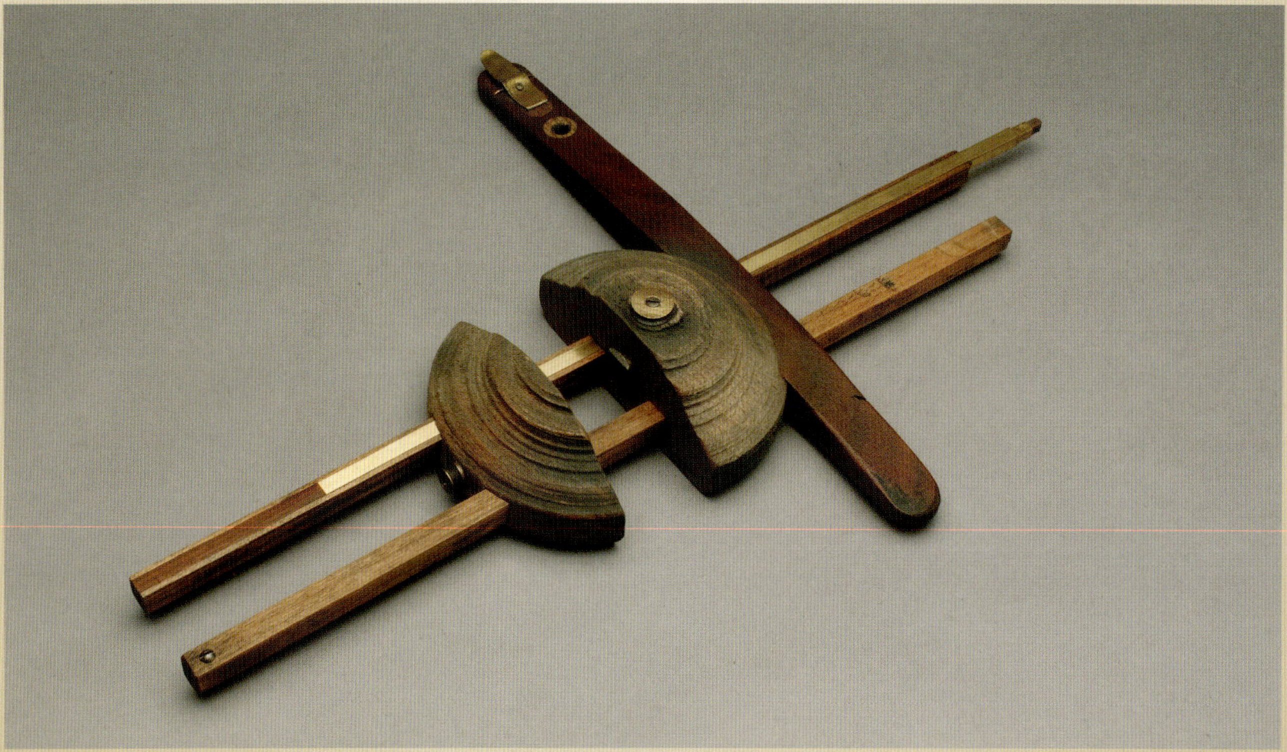

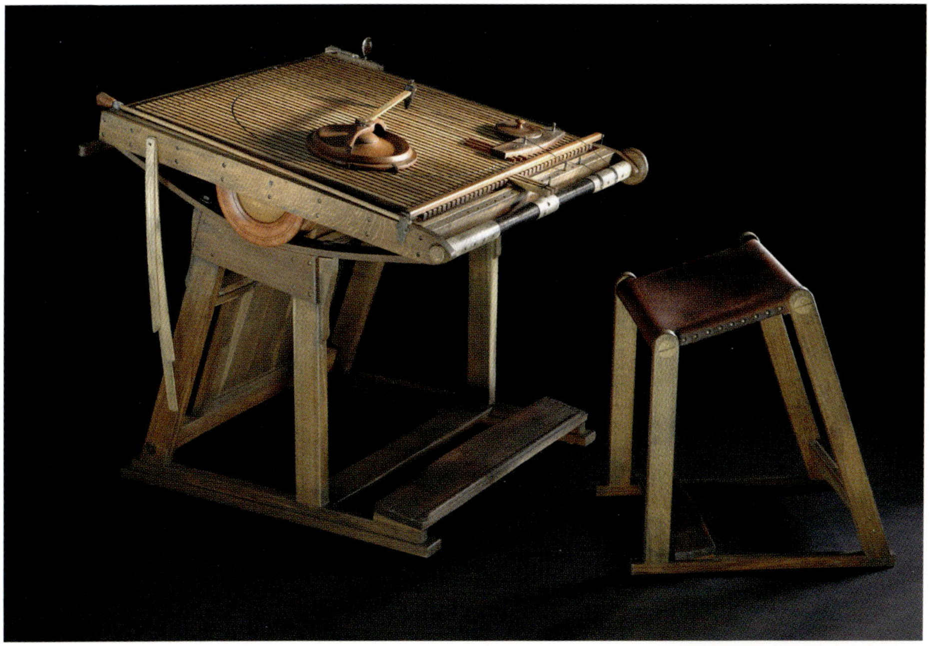

Arc and Cord Engineer's Field Bench, 2010

White oak, maple, mahogany, leather
42" x 34" x 34"
Photo by Mark Fainstein

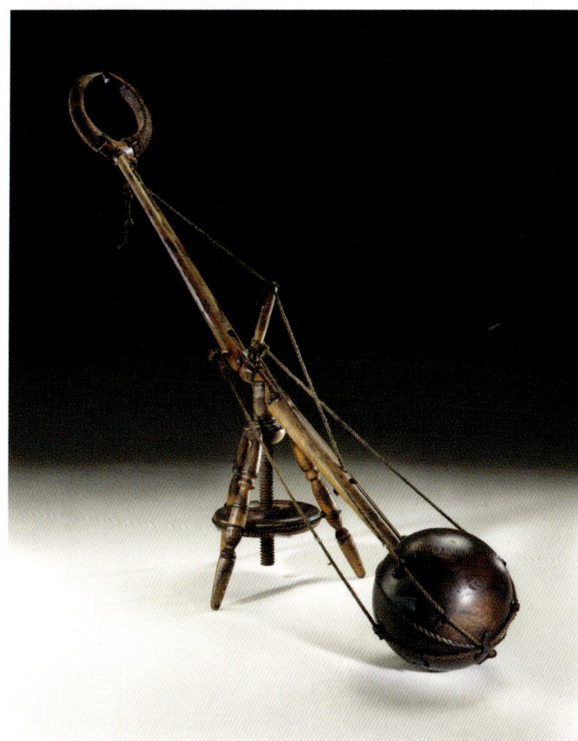

Mono-Totter II, 1994

Walnut, maple, Douglas fir | 60" x 20" x 84"
Photo by Mark Fainstein

Peter Exton

UNITED STATES

Rough-Cut Diamonds, 2012
Core, cocobolo | 3 ½" x 2 ¼"

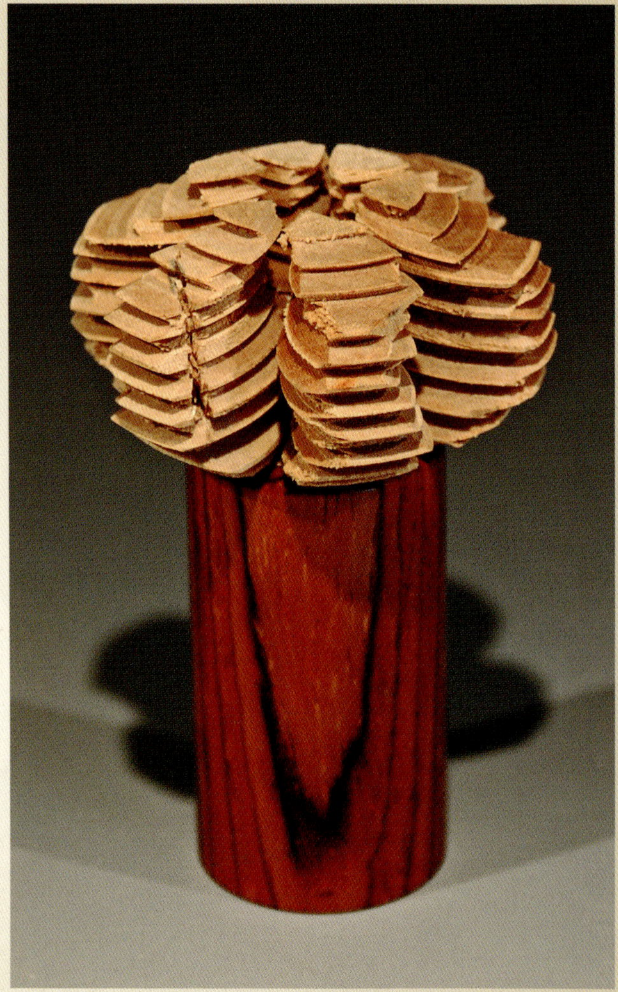

I thought it would be fun to make a diamond turning out of my core. In *Rough-Cut Diamonds,* I've attempted to contrast an ordered arrangement with some loose, freehand tool work, allowing for rips and tears and breaks. The idea was inspired by a desire to break with previous refined work, and by ancient ruins, which even as they crumble can be very evocative.

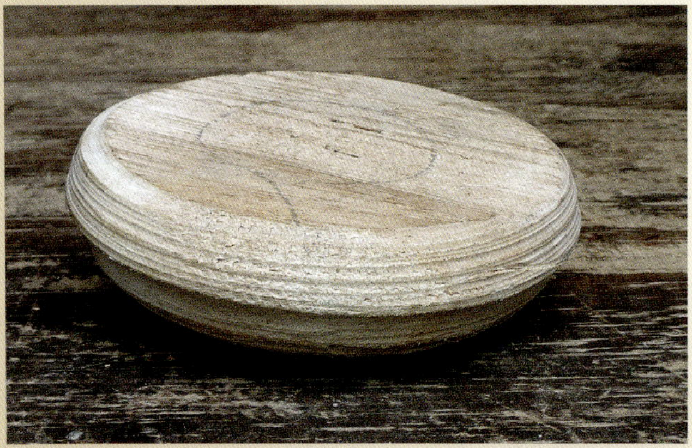

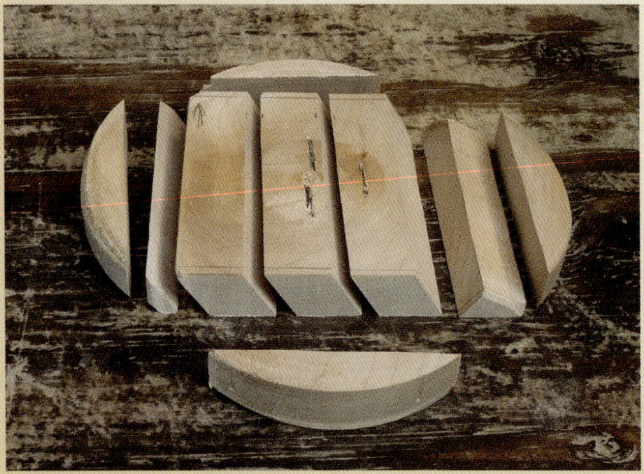

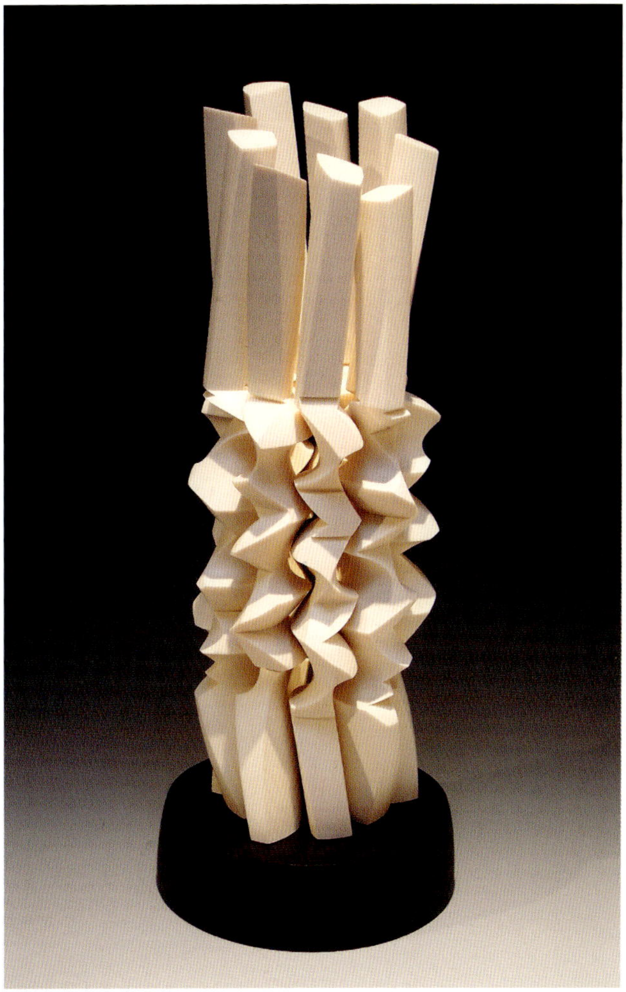

Complex Forms Activated by an Axis, 2006

Bleached maple | 18" x 7" x 7"

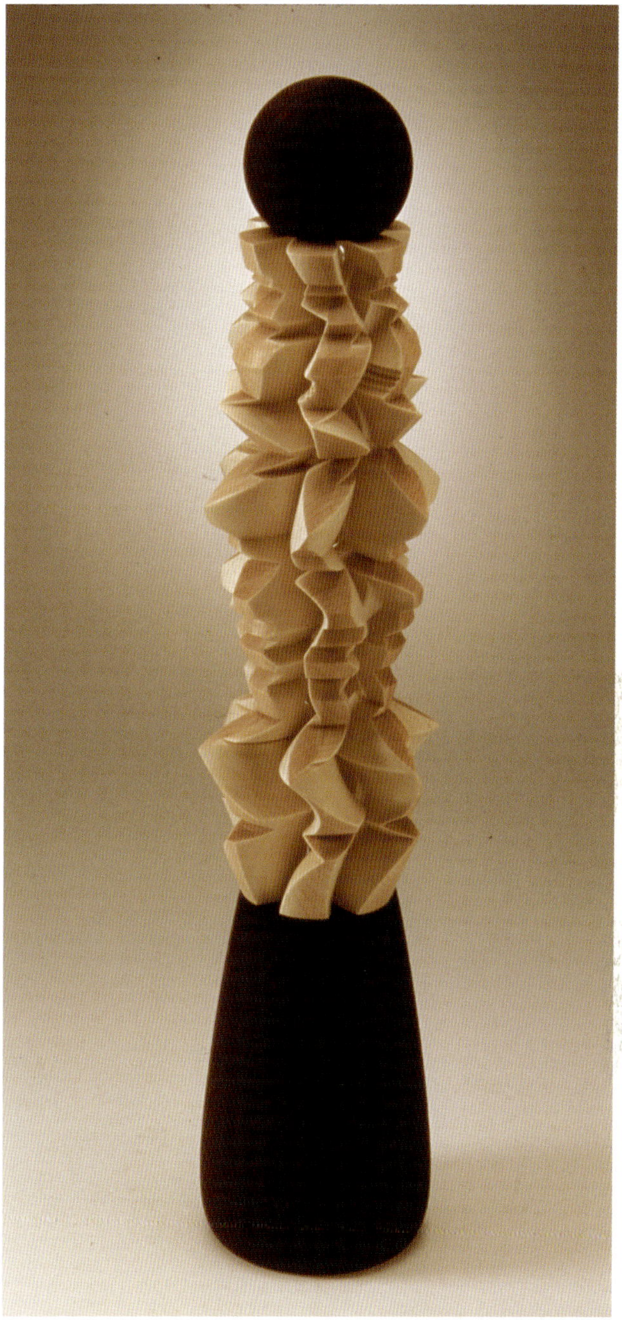

Form Study, Six Diamonds, 2001

Bleached maple, dyed elm | 20" x 4" x 4"

Doug Finkel

UNITED STATES

The Modern Stone Age Family Rover, 2012
Core, boxwood, walnut, red oak | 7 ½" x 7 ½" x 13"

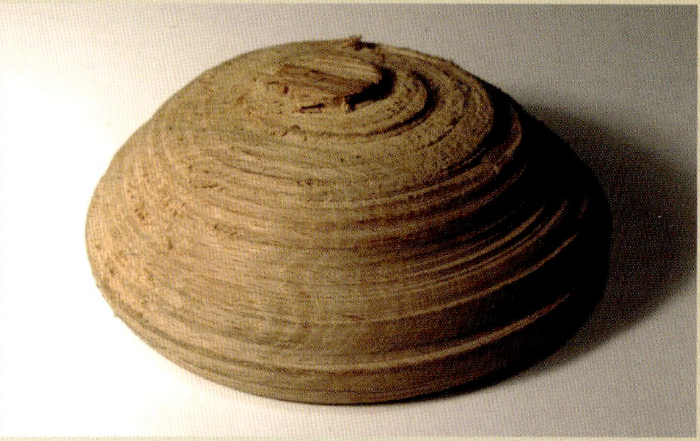

From right out of the box, my core put into my mind this drawing by H.R. Giger, which became the inspiration for my piece. (The drawing was done as an idea sketch for the making of the movie *Dune.)*

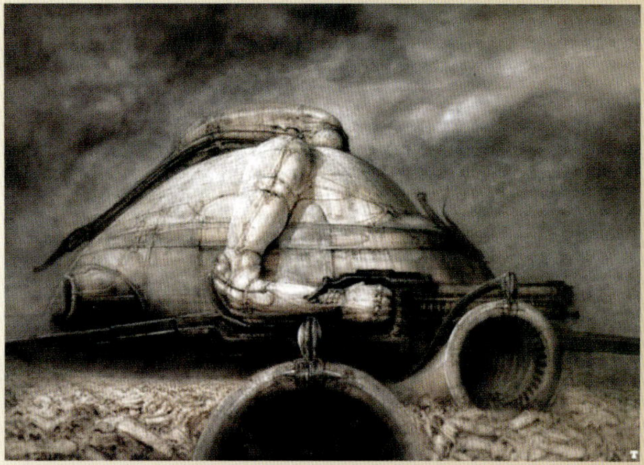

The form of the drawing's subject has an obvious relation to the form of the core, but I was also cognizant of the conceptual elements that they shared in common. The core was created here and now in the twenty-first century on a lathe that harkens back to an ancient technology; Giger's drawing speaks to a sci-fi future, à la *Bladerunner,* that has experienced a long and tumultuous past. Each embodies a blending of technology, time, and human-ness. This idea, in fact, left me feeling reluctant to change my core too dramatically for fear it would lose this aura.

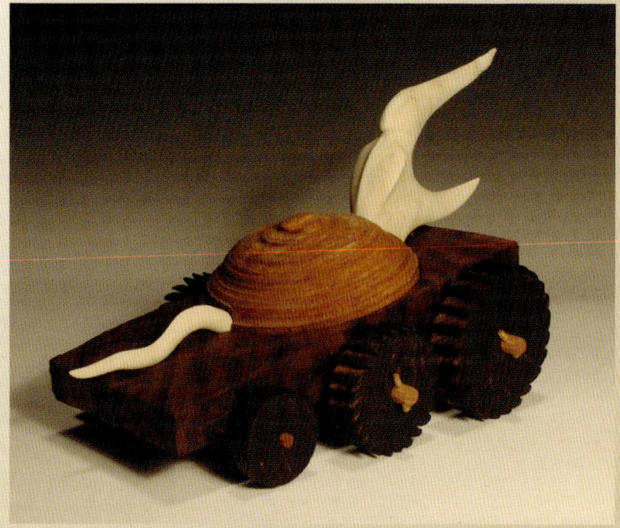

I've also been teaching woodworking to middle school students for the past two years and simple cars are a common project in my classes. This exhibition seemed like a perfect opportunity to try my hand at one myself. I enjoy making fun pieces that are inspired by cartoons. My hope is that Fred Flintstone would enjoy a day-trip in this modern stone-age family rover.

In the past ten years or so, the wood that I use has come primarily from locally found sources. The process of working from the downed tree to finished object harkens back to traditional techniques that require a thorough understanding of the biology of wood and connects the maker intimately to her tools and materials. The objects that I've made from trees that I "knew" are particularly special to me. In my teaching, this attention to wood as a resource has led me to develop a green woodworking curriculum that, in addition to the standard woodworking curriculum, is designed to embrace history, science, and the responsibility that comes with using the resources that nature provides.

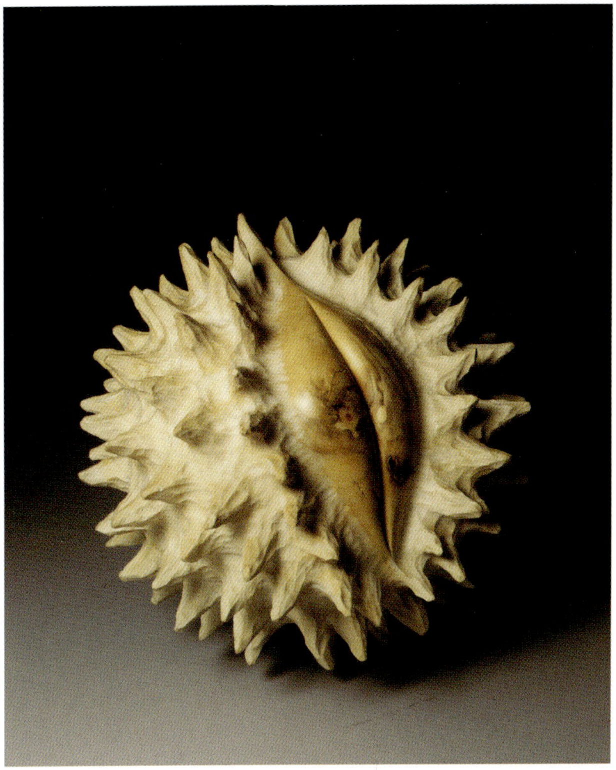

The Face of Boe, 2008

Bleached boxwood | 6" x 6" x 6"

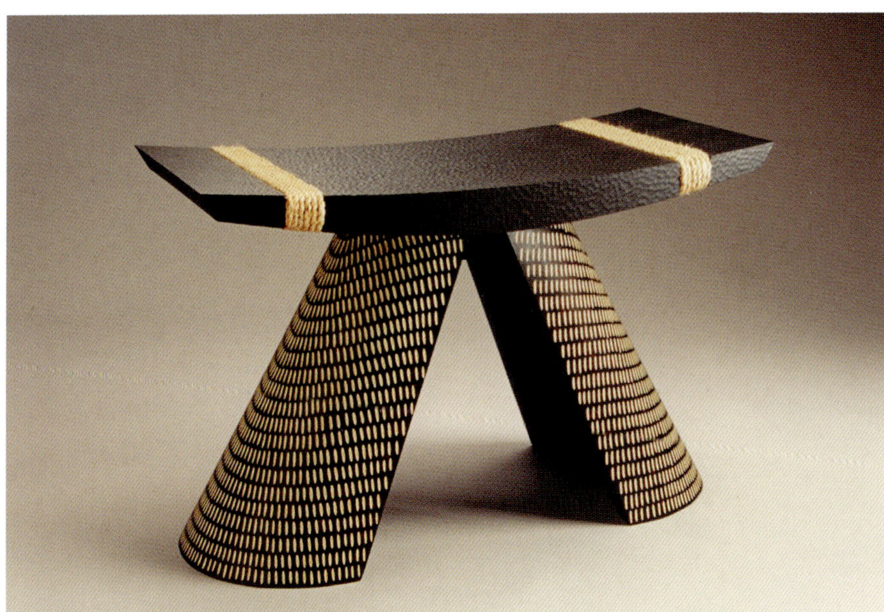

Source Bench, 1999

Poplar, paint, rope
27" x 12" x 17"

Ron Fleming

UNITED STATES

Fern Platter, 2012
Core, dye, acrylic | 1" x Dia. 4 ¼"

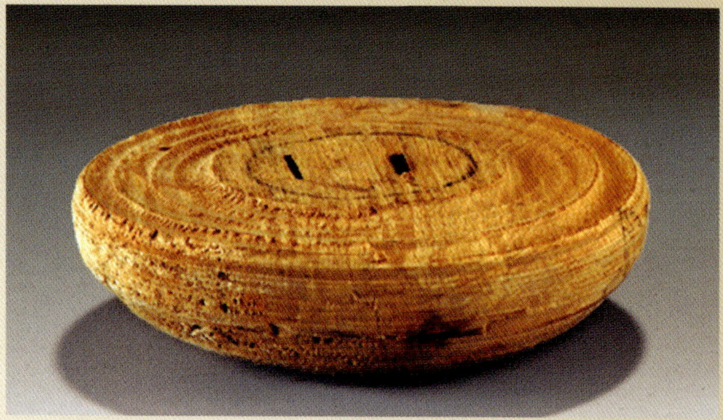

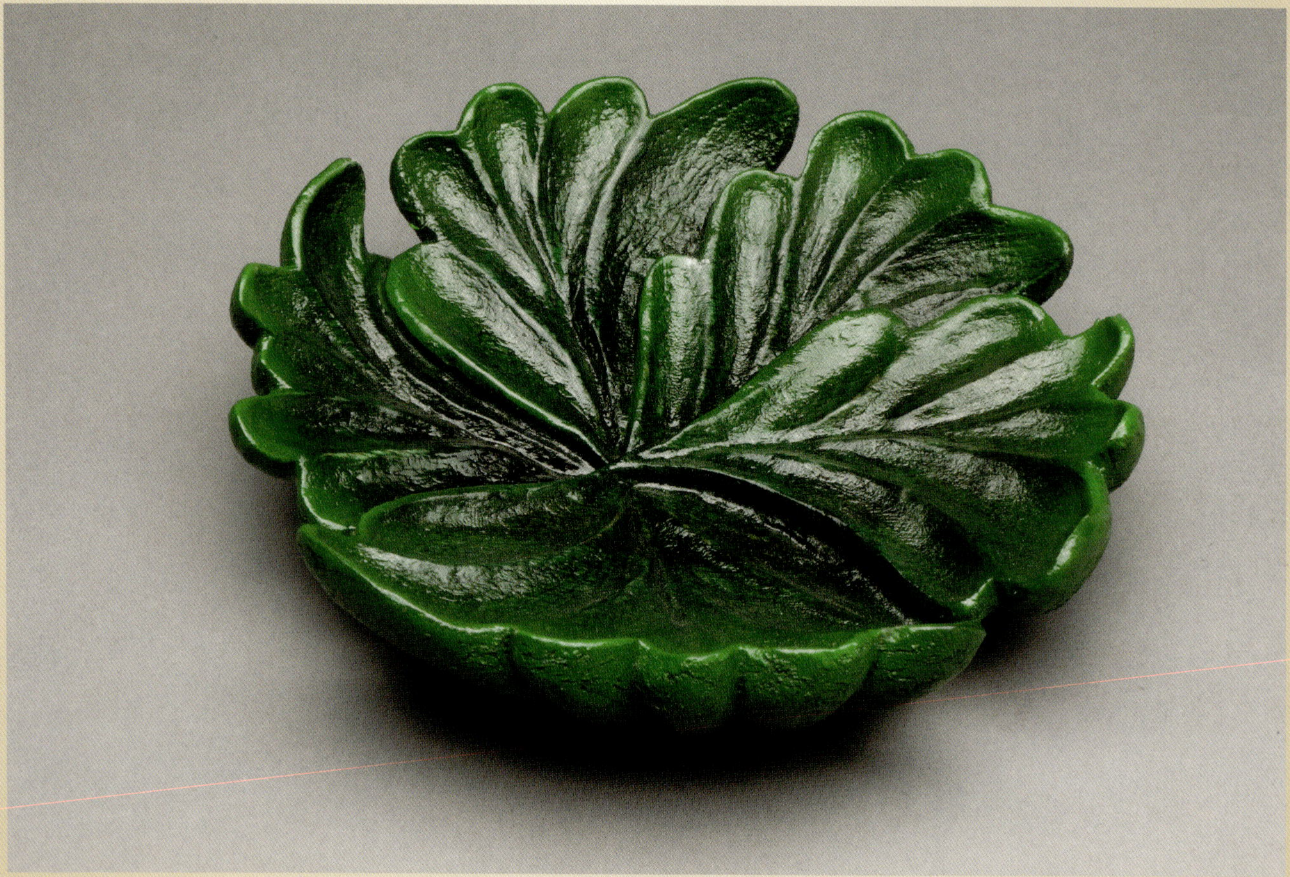

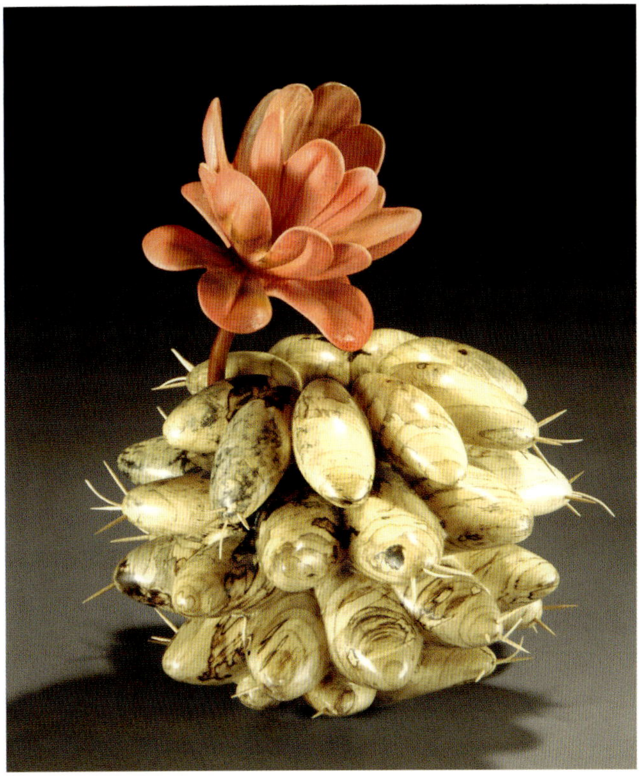

Bickle, 1998

Hackberry, mahogany, acrylics, maple | 15" x 10"

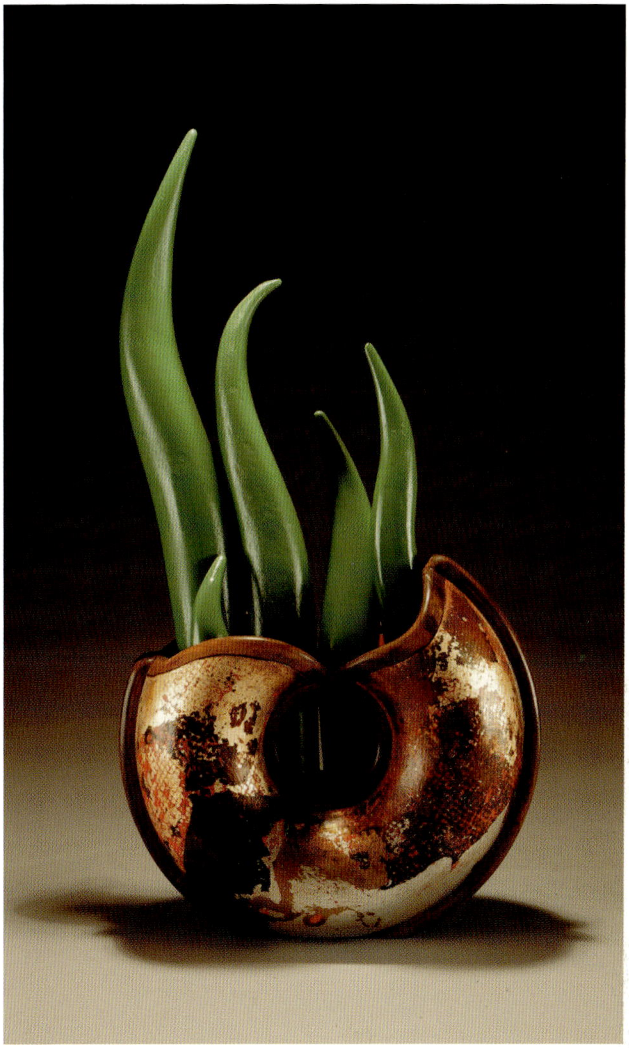

Isopod, 2013

Mahogany, acrylics | 22" x 5 ½" x 11"

Satoshi Fujinuma

JAPAN

Dear Robin, Thanks tasty cake. Sincerely yours, Japanese wood worm, 2012
Core | 1 ⅜" x 2 ¾" x 4"

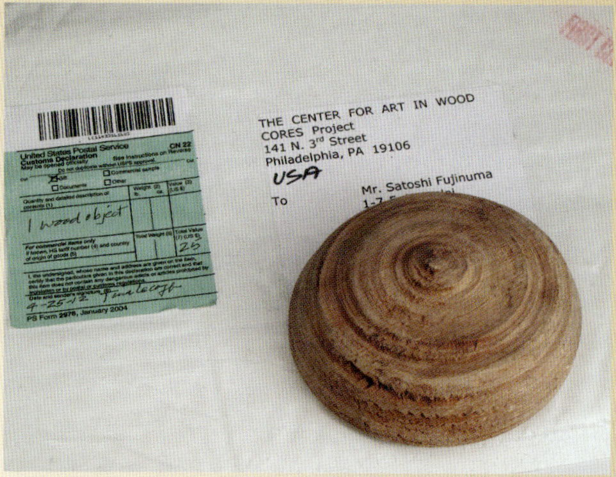

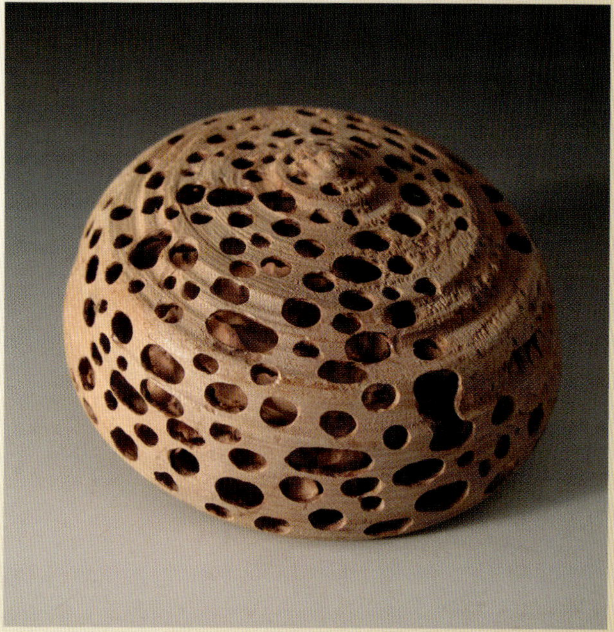

I have a strong interest in "nature."

When I am in nature, I pay detailed attention to nature by using all my senses, including vision, hearing, and smell. Then I come across "something unique" and I am surprised: "What is that?" and "Why?"

I am overjoyed by finding something I had never seen before or by stimulation of intellectual desire.

I like to create art by using "What is this?" and "Why?" in nature as my inspiration.

Nature has pattern and regularity. However, there are some inconsistencies and irregularities. That's where I find beauty.

I am especially interested in plants and animals of nature. And I study them in depth. That's when I find interesting shapes and patterns.

I rebuild these images in my memory together to create my sculpture. You will not find the exact same thing in nature as I create.

My art is abstract, but it is realism abstract art. What that means is: I make something that doesn't exist.

But you will think of my art as if it could exist or as if you had seen it somewhere before.

I think that sense can stimulate the synapse of people's memory. I explain this as "biomimetic expression."

I want people to pick up my art in their hands and look at it from every direction—the same way I observe nature.

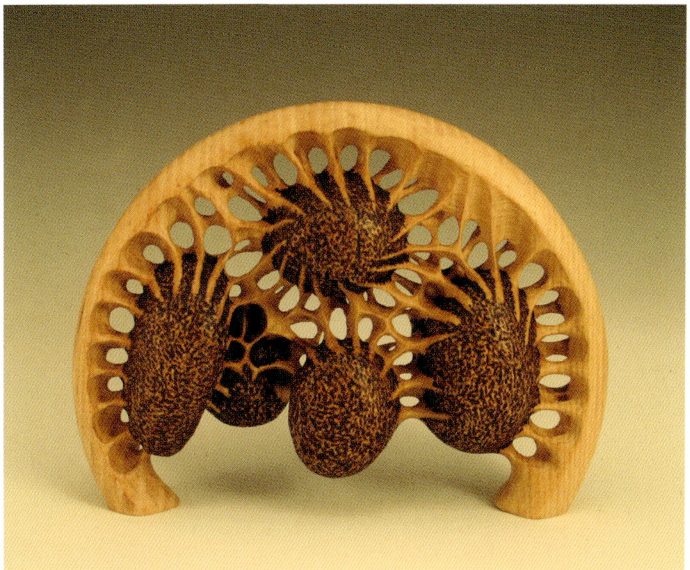

Untitled, 2011

Hickory | 4 ¼" x 1 ½" x 4 ¾"

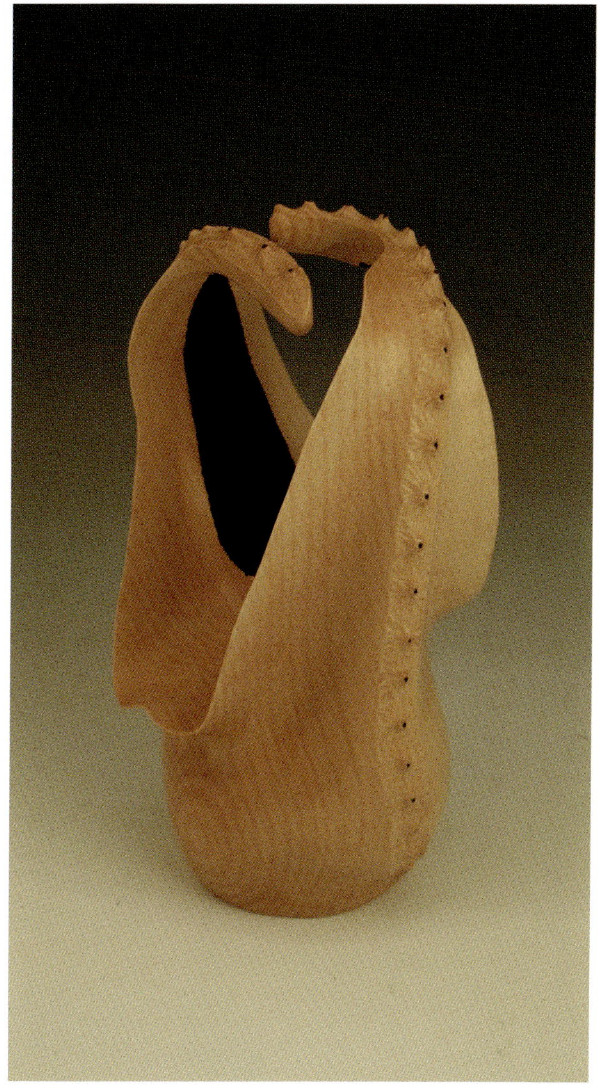

Untitled, 2011

Japanese Clethra | 5 ¼" x 2 ¼" x 2 ¼"

Laurent Guillot

FRANCE
Core than precious, 2012
Core | 2" x Dia. 5"

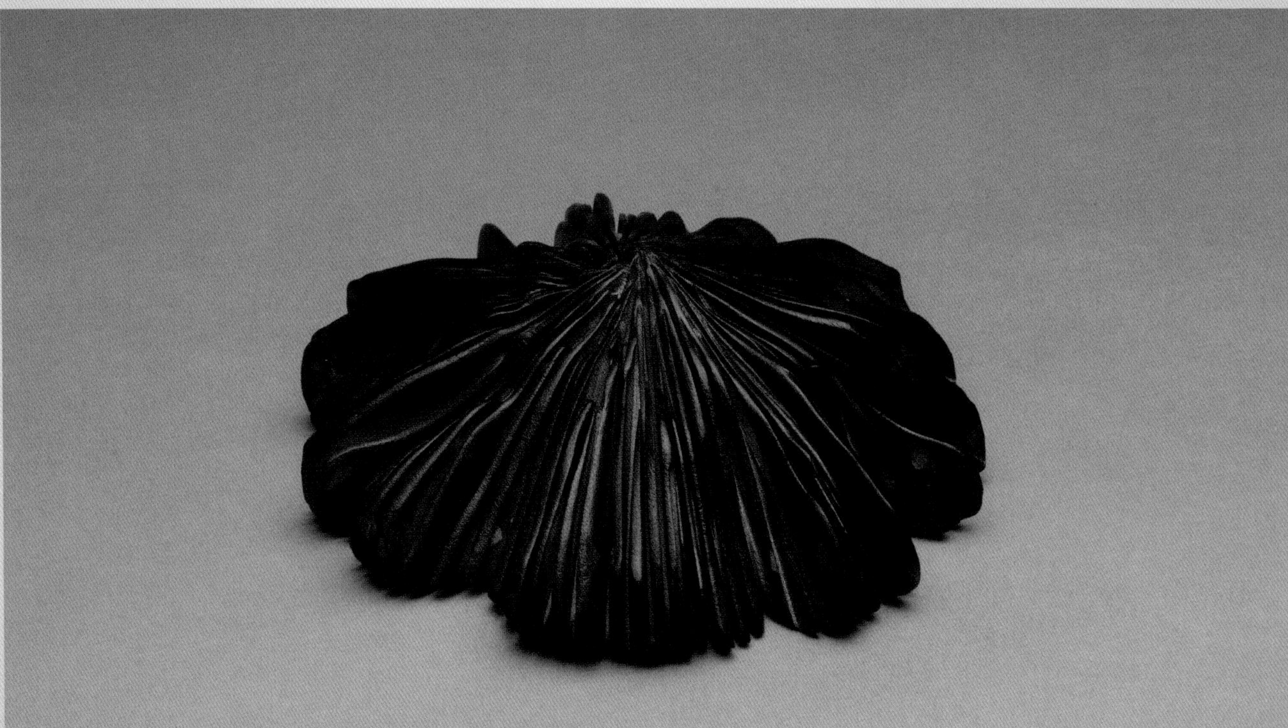

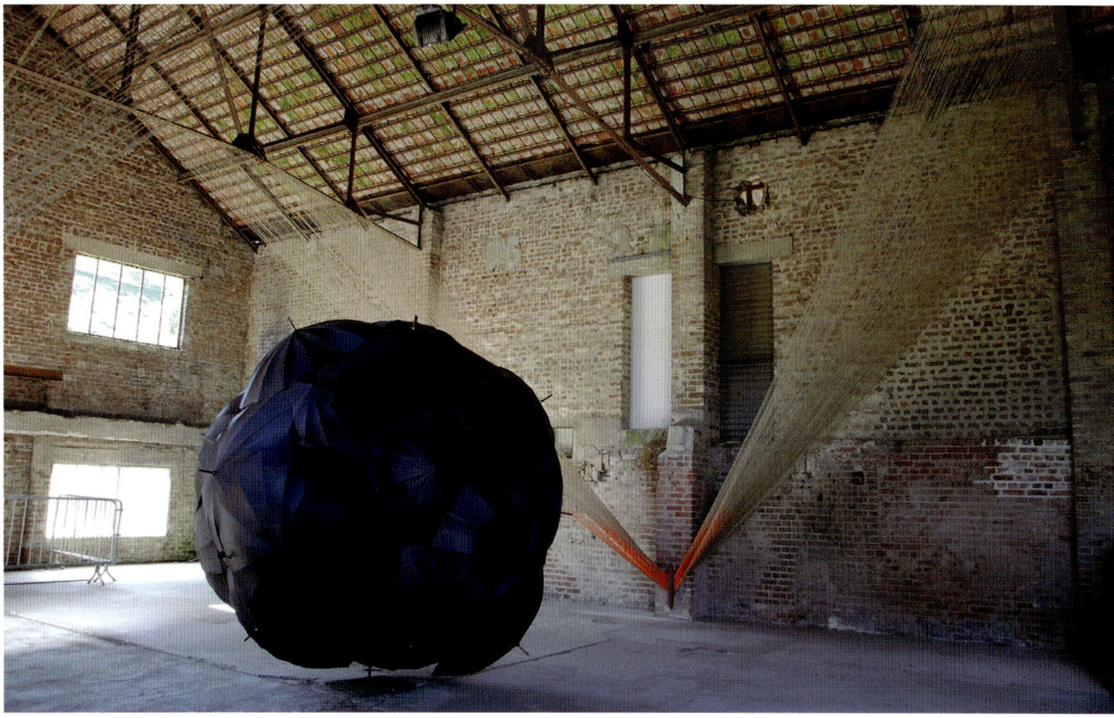

Femmes et Leak et Sysiphe, 2012

8,749 yards of flax string braced the iron carpentry, with an umbrella's sphere 78 ¾"

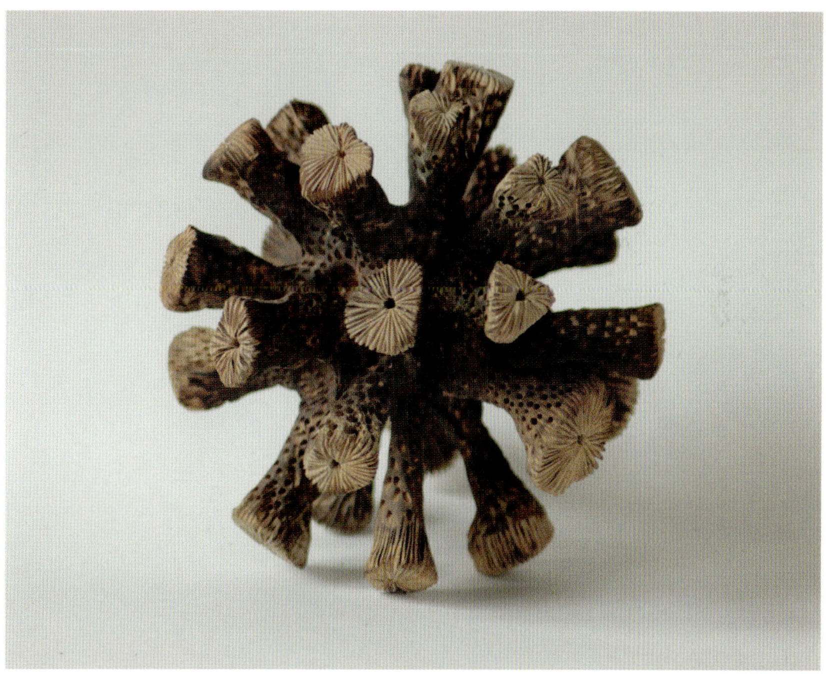

Touchons des Yeux, 2007

Apple tree, turned, carved and sandblasted Dia. 7"

Peter Harrison

UNITED STATES

Rotary, 2012
Core, sapele, stainless steel | 7" x Dia. 10 ½"

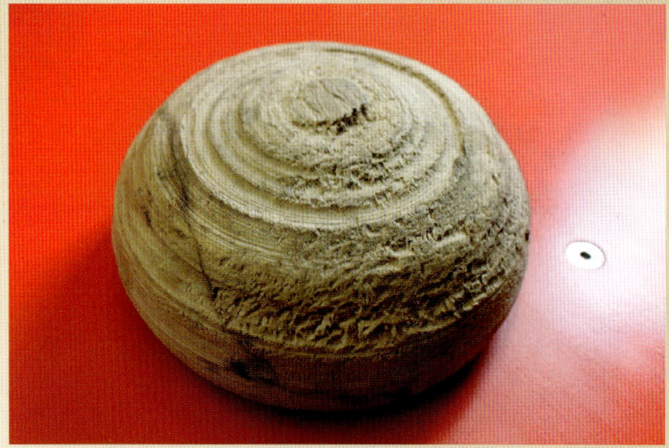

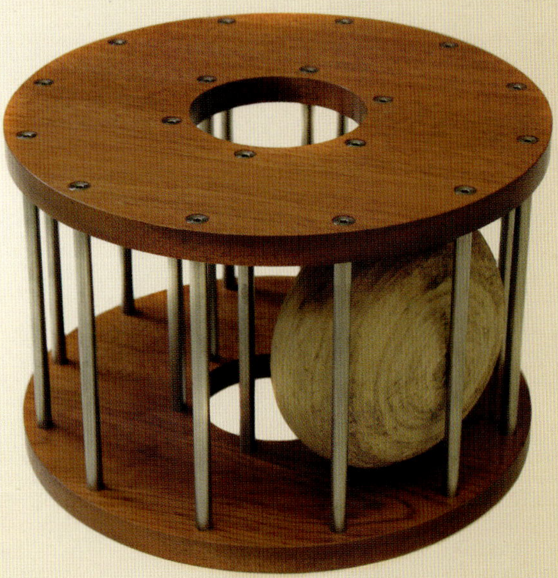

It was important to me to keep the core unaltered. I saw it as an object to build around, rather than a piece of wood to be used. I decided to surround it with a cage using stainless-steel rods and sapele. As the design evolved, it became interactive, where the core could roll about within the cage.

The style of my furniture grew out of a desire to build without traditional woodworking joinery. This began as a method of making furniture, but quickly became integral to the composition and design of my work. I use three materials: wood, metal, and concrete. Each has characteristics that are specifically suited for different elements. The aesthetic nature of the elements long ago became more important than their convenience.

It is important to me to create complete pieces. I strive for my furniture to entice the viewer from across the room and captivate him or her upon closer inspection. Designs must be bold and details crisp. This is a combination of design and craftsmanship. My furniture is openly constructed with exposed fasteners. The heads of stainless-steel screws get polished and used as details. They are a view of exposed structure, yet not a complete vision. It is intended as a glimpse of what is inside, a celebration of the beauty of structure rather than a moment of too much information.

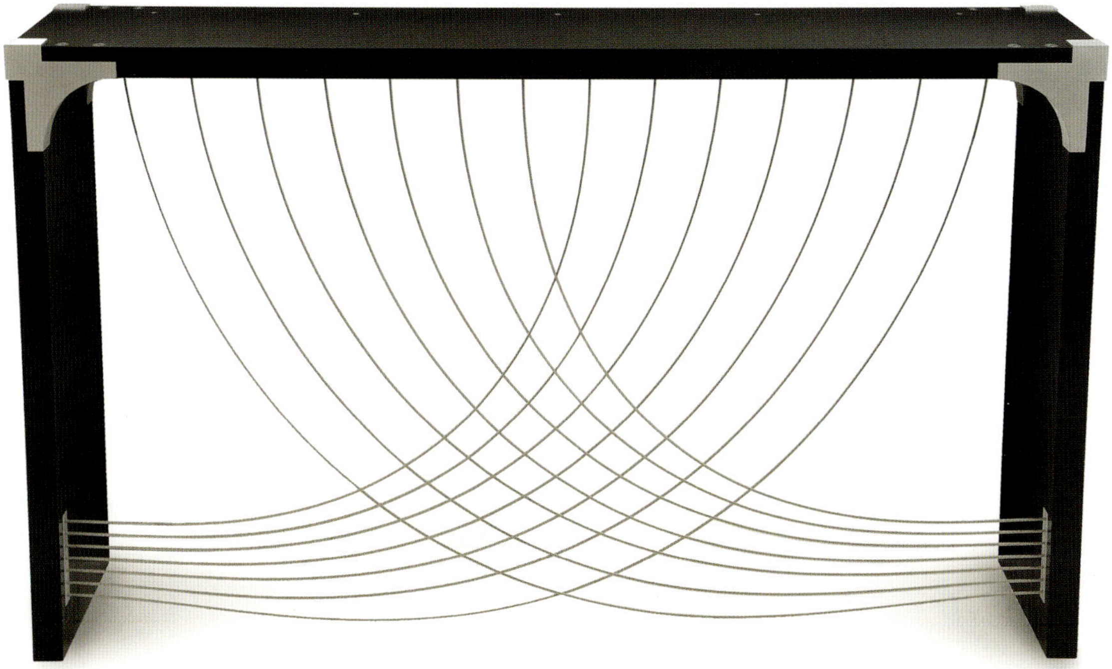

Divergence, 2011

Sapele dyed black, stainless-steel cable, aluminum | 36" x 60" x 12"

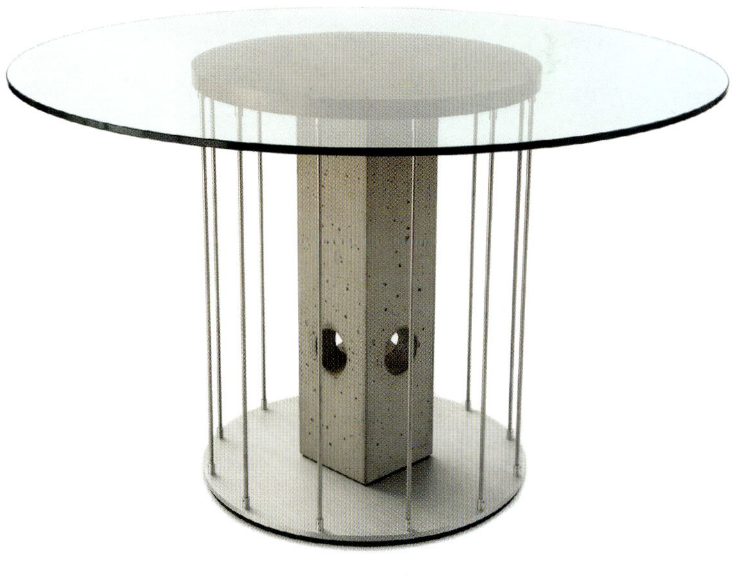

Lithium, 2011

Sapele, concrete, stainless steel, aluminum, glass | 29" x Dia. 48"

Doug Haslam

CANADA

***Adamski Call Home!*,** 2012
Core, pernambuco, mixed media | 6" x 4 ½" x 5 ½"

When I was growing up, George Adamski's *Inside the Spaceships* was part of the family library. His descriptions of meetings with "space brothers" and voyages to Venus piqued my curiosity, but it was the line drawings of flying saucers and motherships that really fascinated me.

Although I can't actually remember if I believed any of it or not, memories of times looking at the book have become an important part of my personal nostalgia, reminding me of an innocence not entirely left behind.

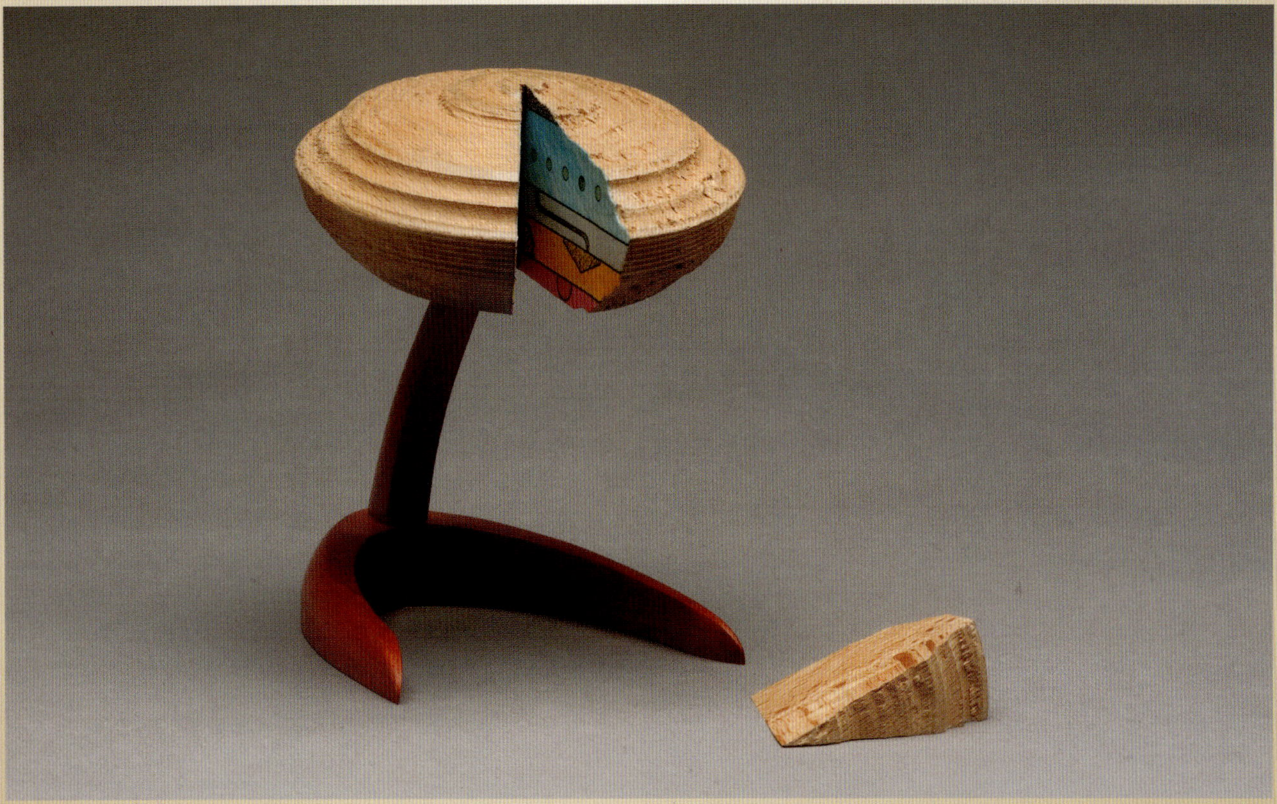

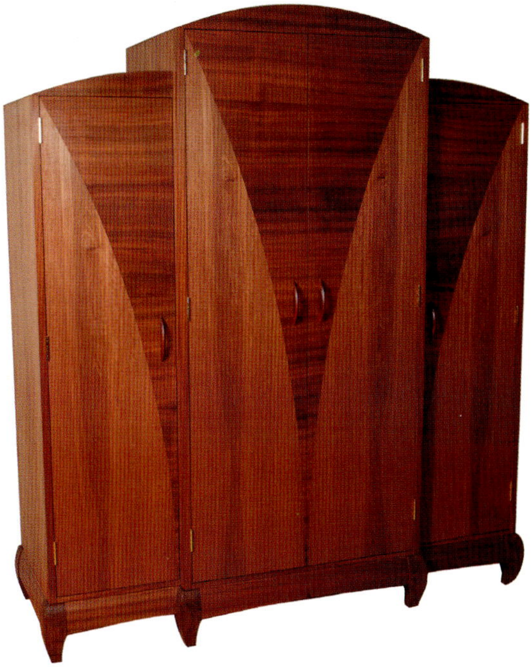

Bernstein Armoire, 2007

Jatoba, bloodwood | 86" x 75" x 25"
Private Collection

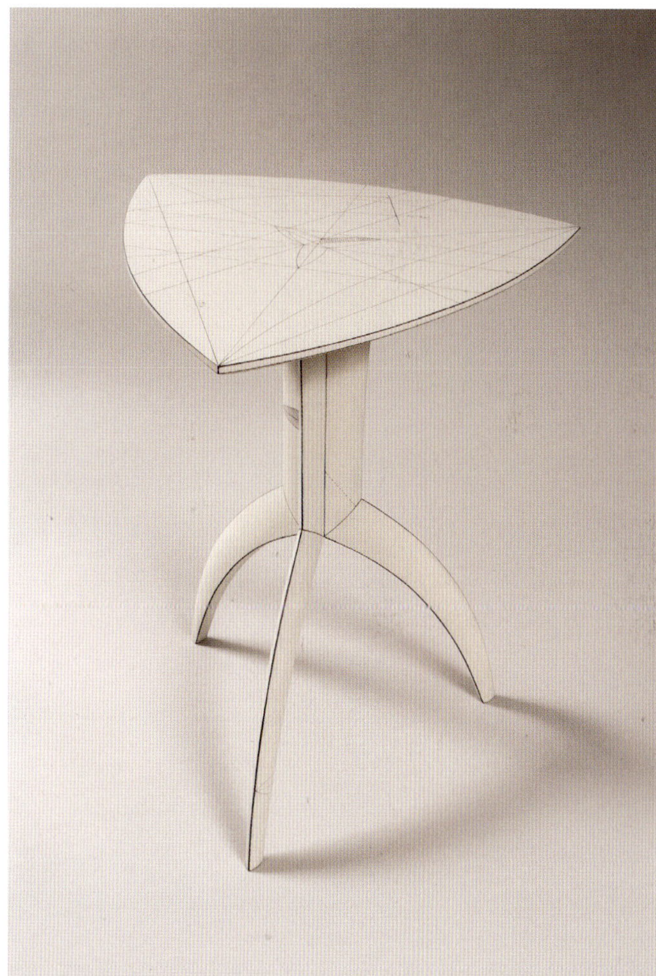

Triagram, 2007

Alder, milk paint, ink |
23 ½" x 19 ¼" x 18 ½ ", Collection of
the Alberta Foundation of the Arts

Michelle Holzapfel

UNITED STATES

Cores Collage Arranged According to the Laws of Chance, 2012
Core, mixed woods, found objects | 32" x 18" x 6"
Photo by David Holzapfel

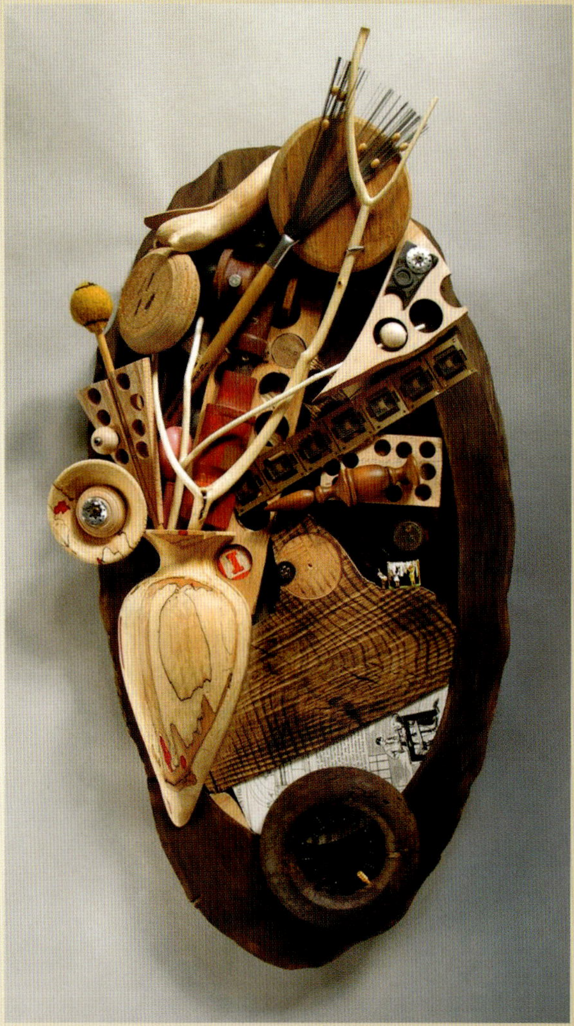

I adapted the title from a 1917 work by Hans Arp called *Collage with Squares Made According to the Laws of Chance*.

I chanced to see this title as a clue to a crossword puzzle I was engaged in while working on this piece. I was also inspired by the work of Sophie Taeuber Arp, who made a wide variety of Dadaist works, some in wood.

I visited the Center and chose a core. Then I got another one in the mail. That's how I chanced to end up with two cores. I imagined them as two "blooms" in the arrangement that went through a couple of iterations before the final piece.

What follows here are the lineages of the elements that I incorporated, which illustrate their randomness.

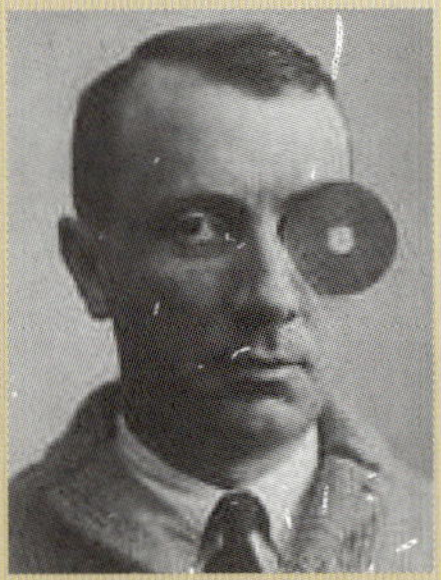

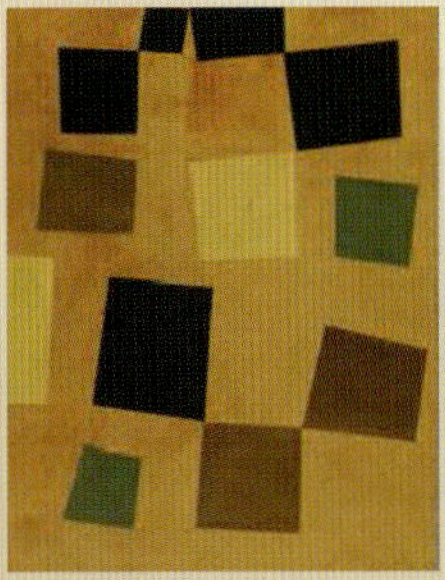

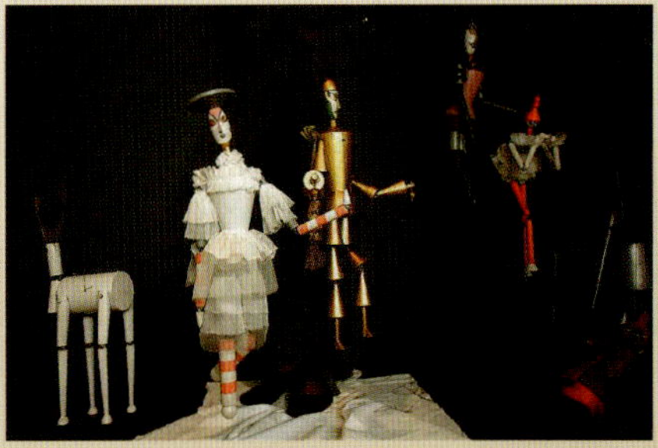

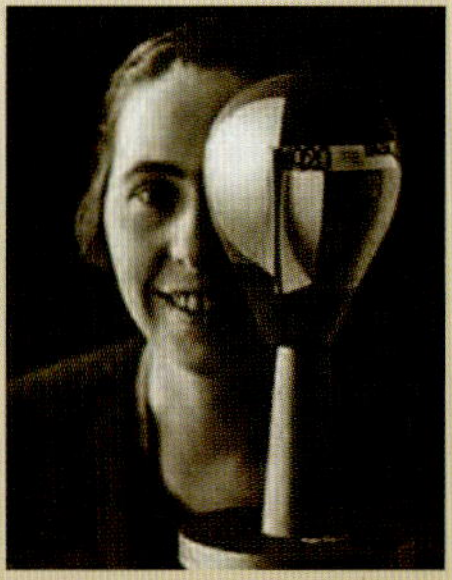

Materials—Found wood, turned and otherwise:

Frame: A few decades ago, my husband, David, cut out and sanded a piece of butternut to frame a mirror, but he never finished it. I found it and scorched it before using it as a foundation/frame in both the early iteration and the final work.

Amphora: s=Spalted maple. I turned a dozen of this same amphora shape for the solo show *Inner Circle* in 2000 at del Mano Gallery. This is half of one extra. I don't often turn multiples; but it coincidentally echoes the multiple nature of the cores.

Yellow birch ring, scorched: Similar to the cores in that it was "waste," parted off while turning another form. I've got lots of these; can't seem to discard them. Found cribbage peg "teeth."

Spalted maple funnel: Made for another piece but never used, until now.

Banana: Carved yellow birch, made c. 1989, then sat in a box, waiting.

Plug-cutting scraps: Cherry, maple, oak. My first arrangement —ultimately a discarded attempt—was mostly made of these. I like their random/regularity. I eventually eliminated most of them.

Other: Scorched oak chunk/ebony scrap/ebony button/ two maple sticks/two walnut plugs/peppermill kit top piece/turned balls: Woodcraft Supply/Pink darning "egg"/ Alphabet block: all stuff found by chance in various places.

1 soft mallet/1 wire brush (from percussionist David Moss).

2 patternmaker's samples (from Albert LeCoff).

Hepplewhite bed finial: In the late 1980s I was commissioned to make replacement finials for a client's Hepplewhite four-poster bed. She wanted finials of the same wood and proportions, but carved to resemble spruce "cones." She gave me this one as a model, and never asked me to return it. Several decades later it serves here as an homage to earlier American woodturning.

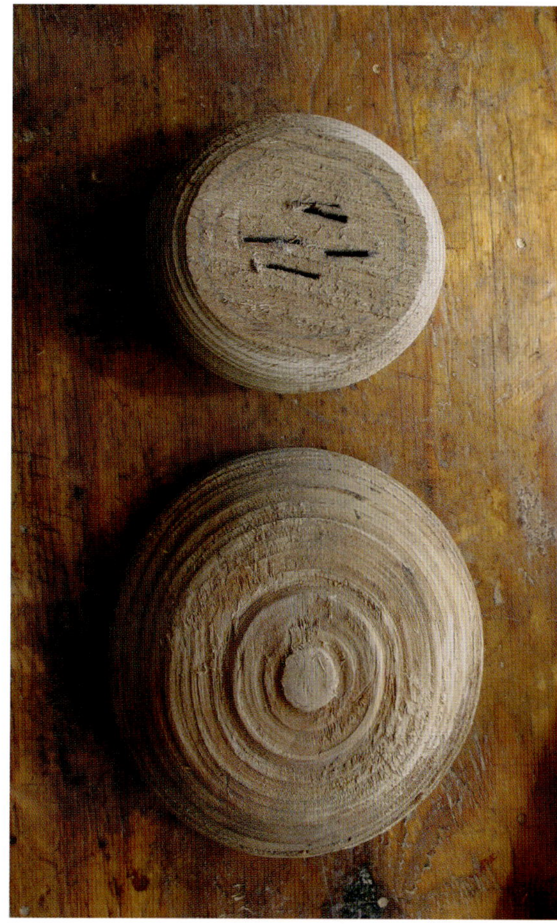

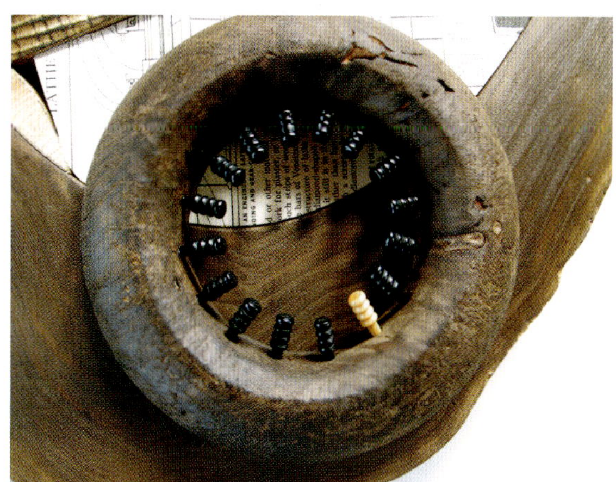

Michelle Holzapfel

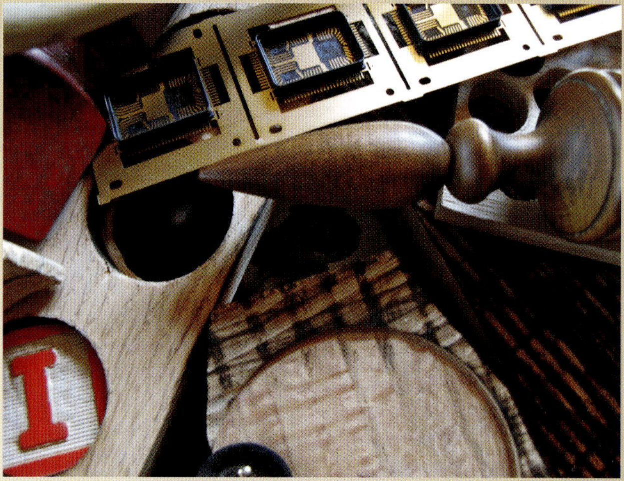

Materials—Found metal objects and hardware:

Brass locker key tag #55 / "Lion" key / "19" Tack

A trial run of a molded lead frame housing for an ASIC (customized integrated circuit) and MEMS (miniaturized mechanical and electro-mechanical) device. Basically, a box with a built-in wiring harness for a sensor. (From my brother, David Chasse, precision tool & die-maker.)

Sheetrock discs/electrical wire staple/screws.

Other objects:

Preiser German HO-gauge model railroad figures (1:87 ratio). I bought these long ago and used them in *Birthday Cake*, *Piazza Pie*, and *Because it's There* in the mid-1980s. Still have many and love their realism, especially the Laundry group.

Page entry for "Lathe," 1942 Encyclopedia Britannica.

Background: White birch bark/ Luan plywood.

Finish: I used a red Sharpie to fill in some "spalted" areas of maple amphora. Light application of Krylon clear.

Many small surprises will reward the careful viewer.

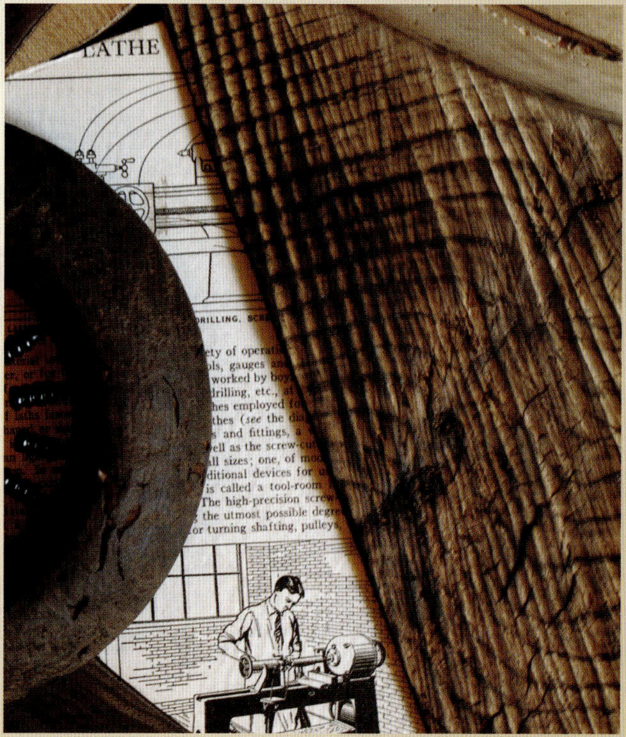

Thanks to Robin Wood

I first encountered the work of Robin Wood when curating the Wood Turning Center's Challenge VI exhibit in 2000. His clear and moving statement for Star Bowls is an exemplar of a maker speaking his mind. I remembered it when I saw all those cores. I've edited it a bit:

"The inspiration for the work is a single bowl found during excavations of a mid-fifteenth century deposit in Braunschweig, Germany. From 600–1600 AD, thirty generations of Europeans ate from turned wooden bowls. Whilst this fact is little known at a conscious level there is a lasting legacy: the humble wooden bowl is as much a part of our cultural identity as fine ceramics are for the Chinese.

"I have handled thousands of these medieval wooden bowls and have developed a deep respect for the turners who made them. This work is a homage to those turners. I could easily have changed and developed the form in order to make it "my own," but felt no need. I could make this bowl a thousand times and still no two would be the same. None would be the same as the original, and still I would be developing, refining.

"Look closely: pick them up, feel the marks of the tools, feel where the weight lies. Put them down and hear the difference in resonance as they touch the table: subtle differences in balance and form make one bowl sing whilst another doesn't.

"I use no measuring tools to make them; I turn and carve them by eye.

"I use only these historical tools: the pole lathe, the axe, the knife—not out of some nostalgic vision but because they work efficiently and give the variation in texture and form which I desire.

"Each is an approximation of the perfect Star Bowl that lives in my mind—as it lived in the mind of the turner of the original, 500 years ago."

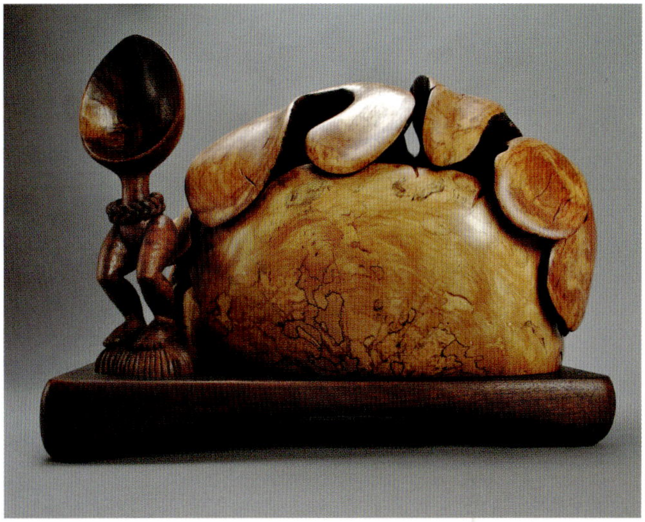

Grandfather, 2003

Red maple burl, walnut spoon and base13"x16" x 10"

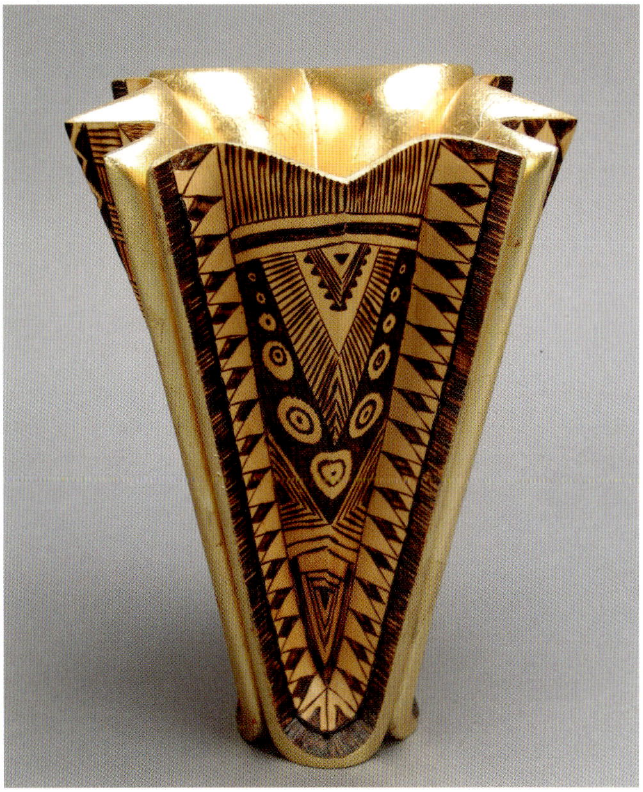

Tattooed Vessel, 2007

Burned/gilded basswood bound with waxed linen | 9" x 7" x 7"

Richard Hooper

UNITED KINGDOM

Reactor Core, 2012
Core, glass, metal | 4 ½" x 23" x 5"

The piece I submitted was an attempt to contrast (and even, by bleaching the core, to exaggerate) the difference between the surface of a traditional turned wooden pole-lathed form and more contemporary non-organic materials. I wanted to keep the form of the core intact as far as possible by not working into it and even to open it up by splitting it with a chisel to expose the fibrous nature of the wood.

The pierced linear elements provided a means to create a dynamic composition in contrast to the static mass of the core.

The title alludes to the translucent green color of atomic cores (well at least as depicted by that reliable source of facts about the atomic industry: *The Simpsons*!)

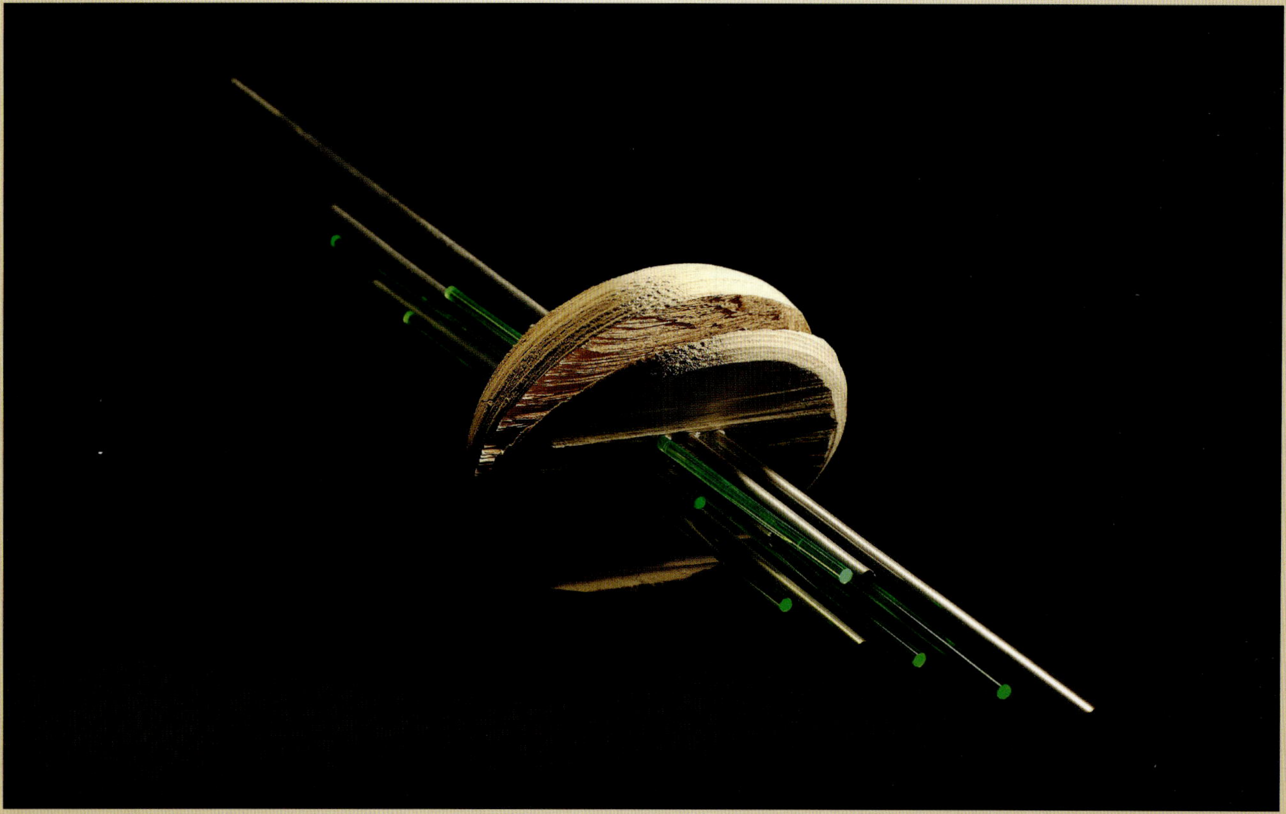

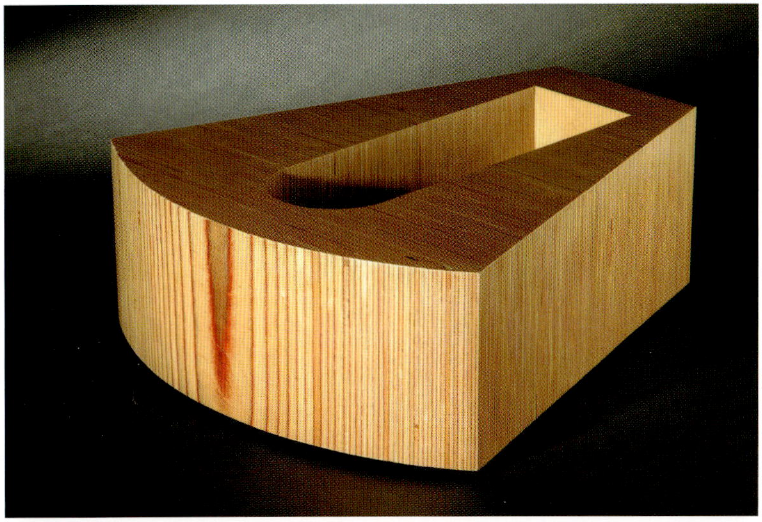

Sector Bowl, 1999

Birch plywood
16" x 15" x 6"

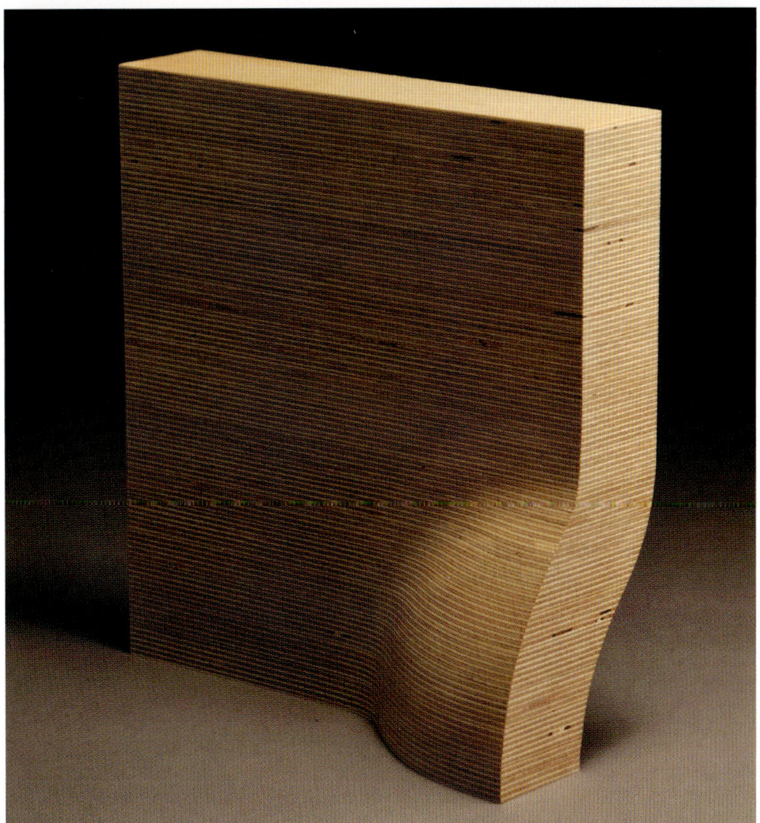

Wave Wall, 2005

Birch plywood
12" x 12" x 5"

Beth Ireland

UNITED STATES

Metamorph, 2012
Core, milk paint | 2" x 11" x ¾"

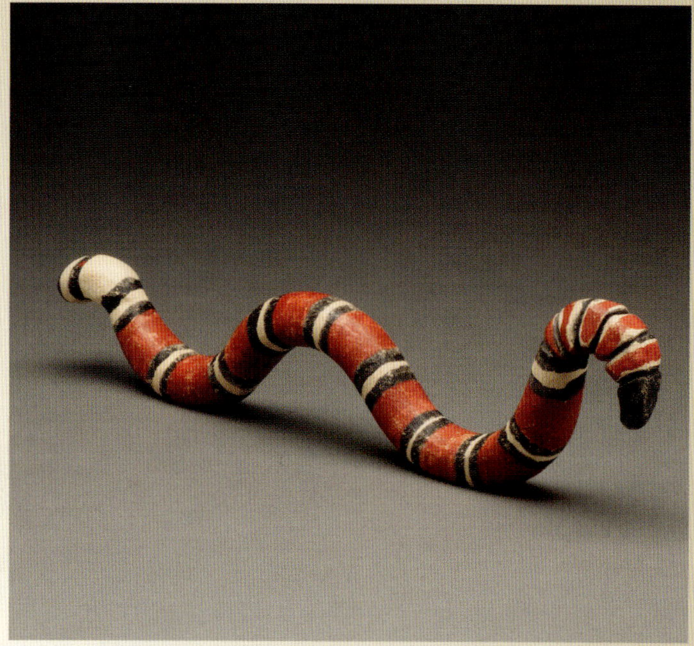

My work reflects my life as a professional craftsman and artist. I have always loved the meditative act of turning a pile of balusters, newel posts, columns, or bowls. I am enthralled with the meaning we place on objects, whether it is a trinket given by a loved one that becomes magic through time and memory, a tool that performs a function, or an archeological object that reflects the life and skill of a maker from another time. These investigations inspire me to create. I am committed to promoting the act of making in our culture and see empowering people through teaching as another aspect of creating.

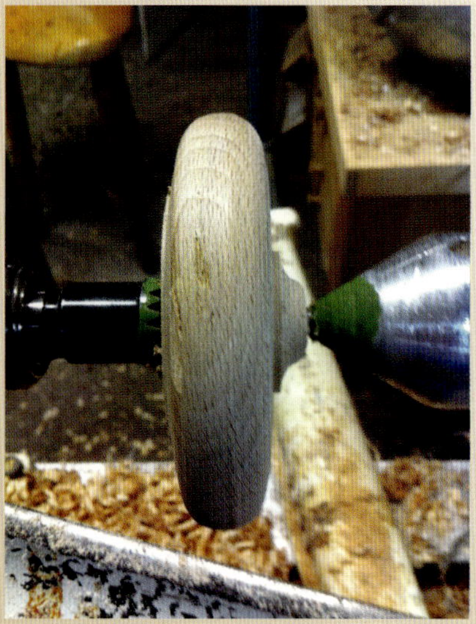

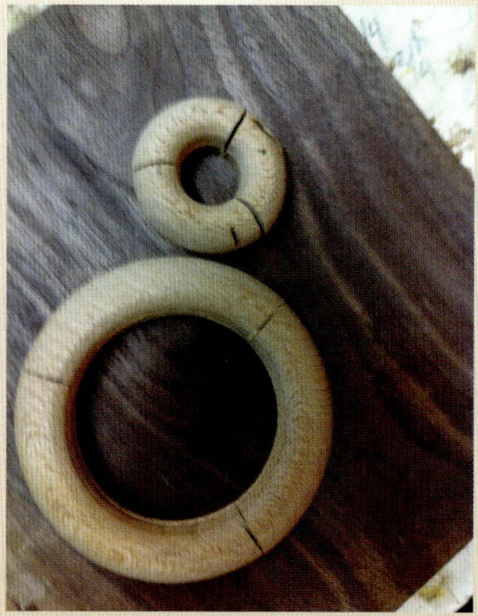

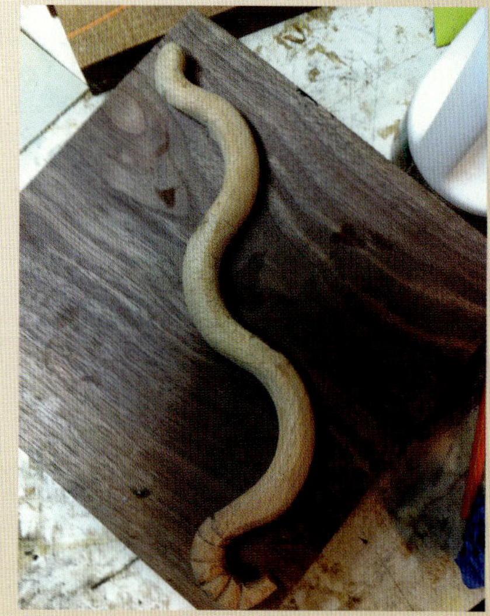

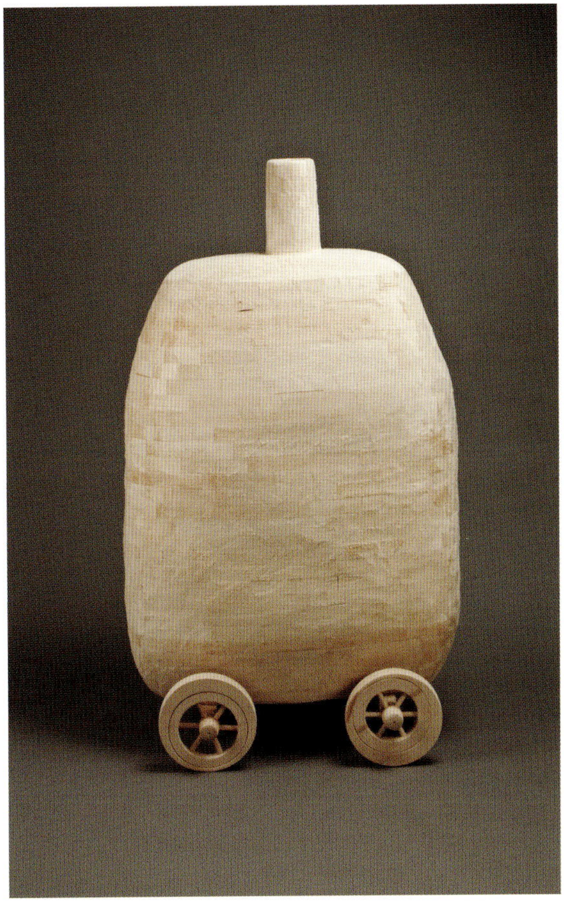

Tribute; 2011

Basswood | 62" x 32" x 15"

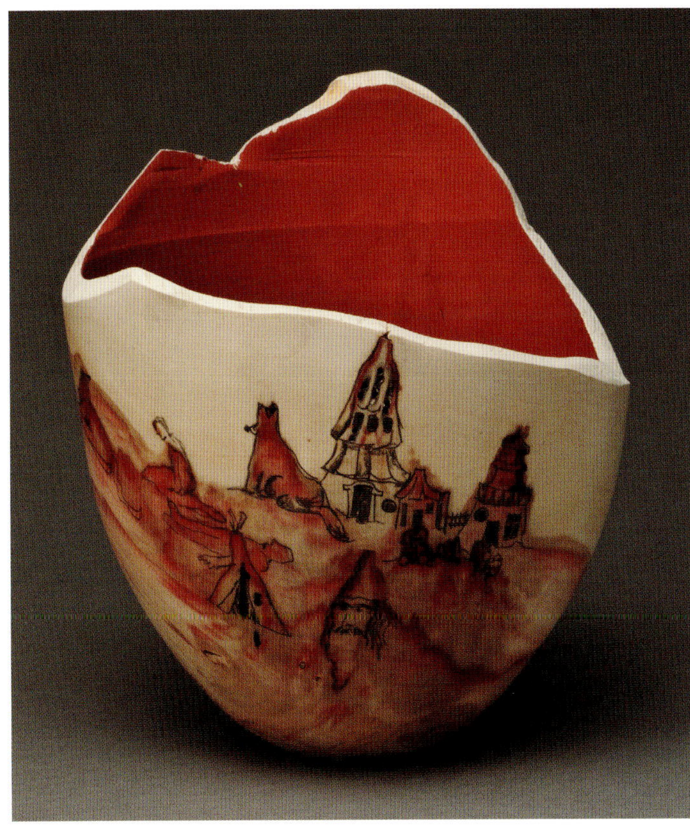

Cow Contemplating Liberty; 2011

Box elder and graphite | 9" x Dia. 6"

Michael Kehs

UNITED STATES

Hint of Flight, 2012
Core (maple) | 3" x Dia. 4 ½"

In order for this to be a more collaborative effort between Robin and myself, I decided only to minimally alter the shape. I've been experimenting with textures lately and continued this experiment on this project. As I am a caver (some might say spelunker), I wanted to add a touch of this world in my work. So the bats were carved and the texture applied, then sandblasted. This gives the piece a feeling of being fossilized into a cavern wall.

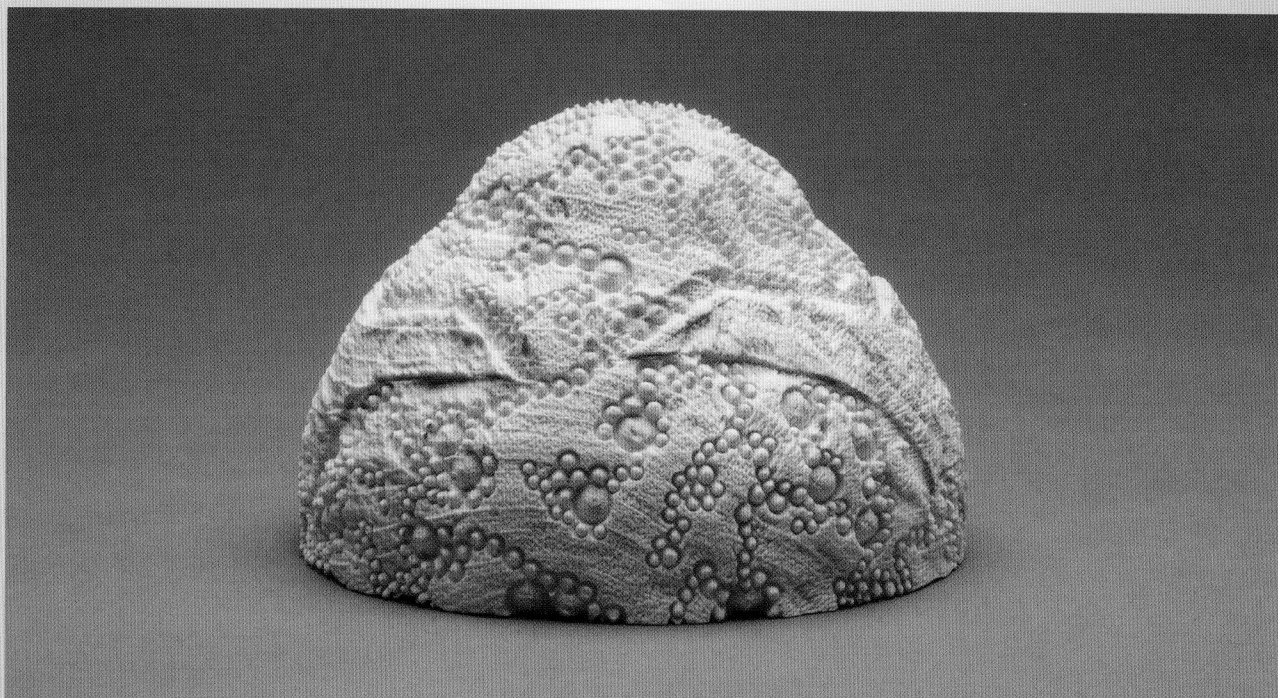

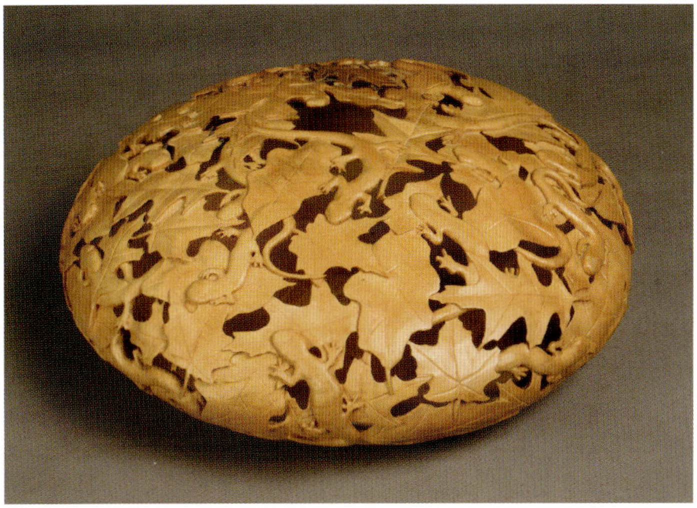

Among the leaves, 2008

Norway maple | 6" x Dia. 14"

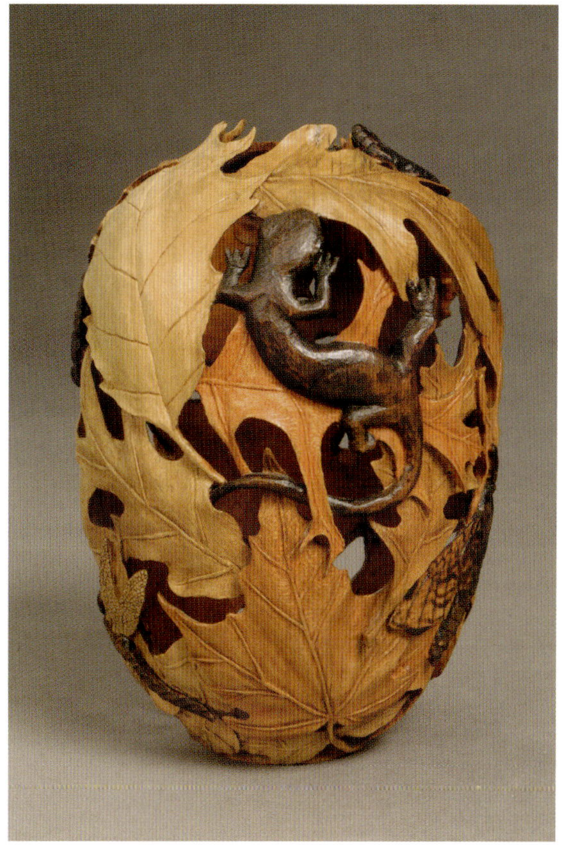

Forest Critters, 2010

Cherry | 7" x Dia. 4"

Max Krimmel

UNITED STATES

CORE Dreams, 2012
Core, color photography | 9" x 5" x 5"
Photo by Max Krimmel

What? That's my core? This isn't useable for anything but firewood. Sheesh. Well that's what I've got. I signed up for this. OK—I'm thinkin'. But I could stare at this thing all day and not come up with anything. Think, think, think. I've got about as many ideas as Rodin's *Thinker* probably does—ZIP—NADA. This thing isn't big enough for a butter dish, let alone something useful, like a salad bowl. It's not even as big as Escher's globe. Actually it's probably about the size of a boob on the *Venus de Milo*. If I had two of them I could make a coconut bra for her. If only it were bigger. Hah—how about if it were really big, big enough to be the cupola on the Dome of Florence. Dang, I'd rather be marooned on a desert island than turn this into something artistic. I'd rather be in outer space than turn this chunk of firewood. I've had more luck finding Waldo than finding an idea for this project. Hey, maybe I'm on to something after all. Art—it's all about ideas. Craft, it's all about objects, even useful ones occasionally. Eureka! Added bonus, you have to handle it to appreciate it, just like any good piece of craft. Perfect, something you have to touch in a typical "no touching" exhibit.

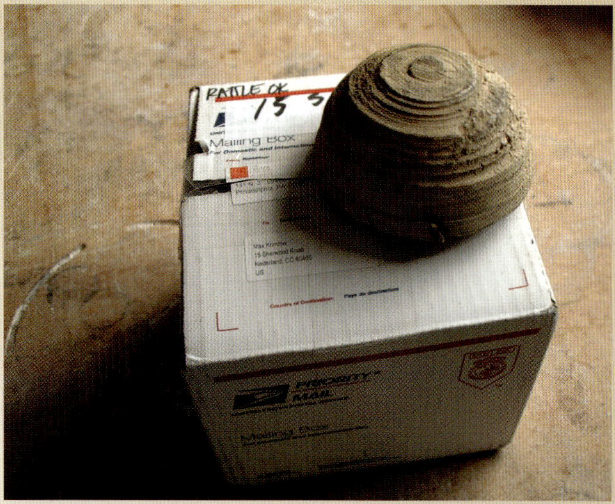

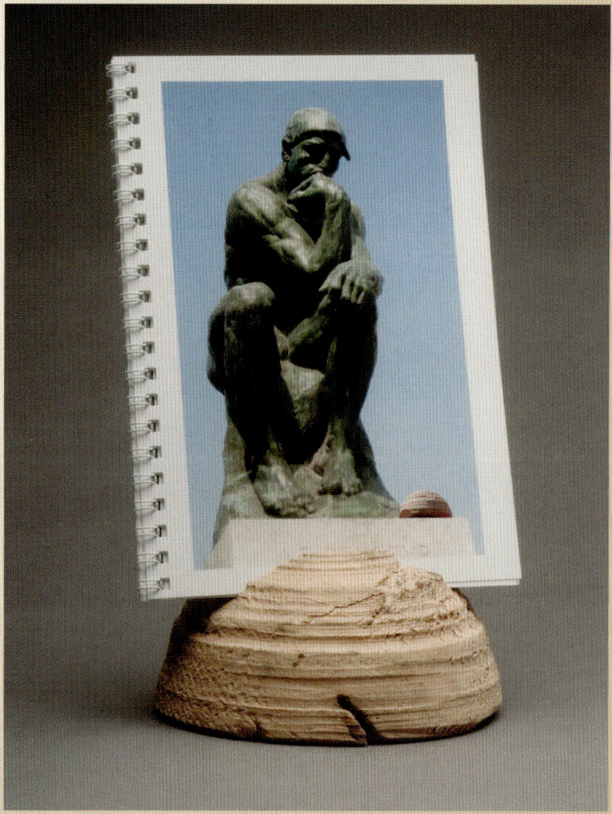

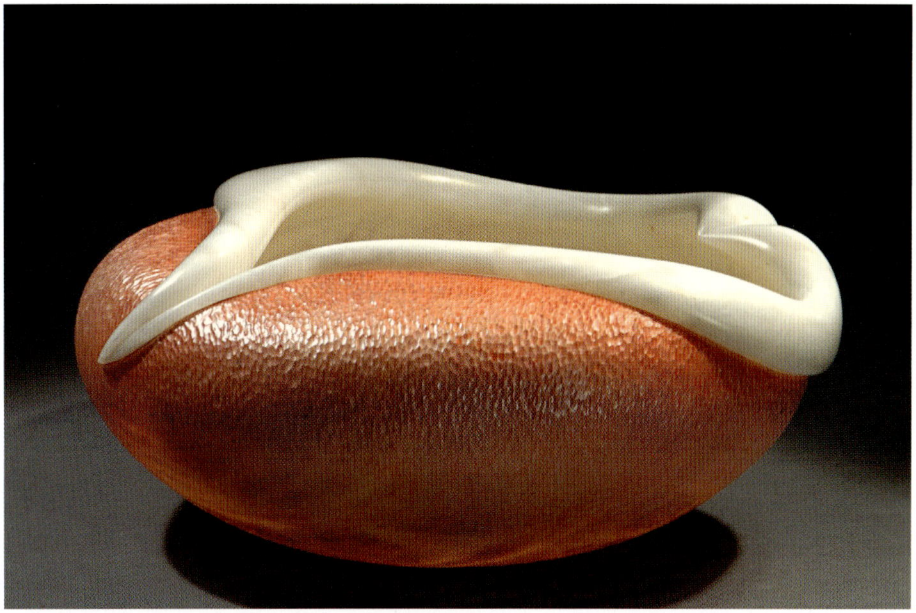

Vessel #686, 2006

Alabaster
4 ½" x Dia. 10"

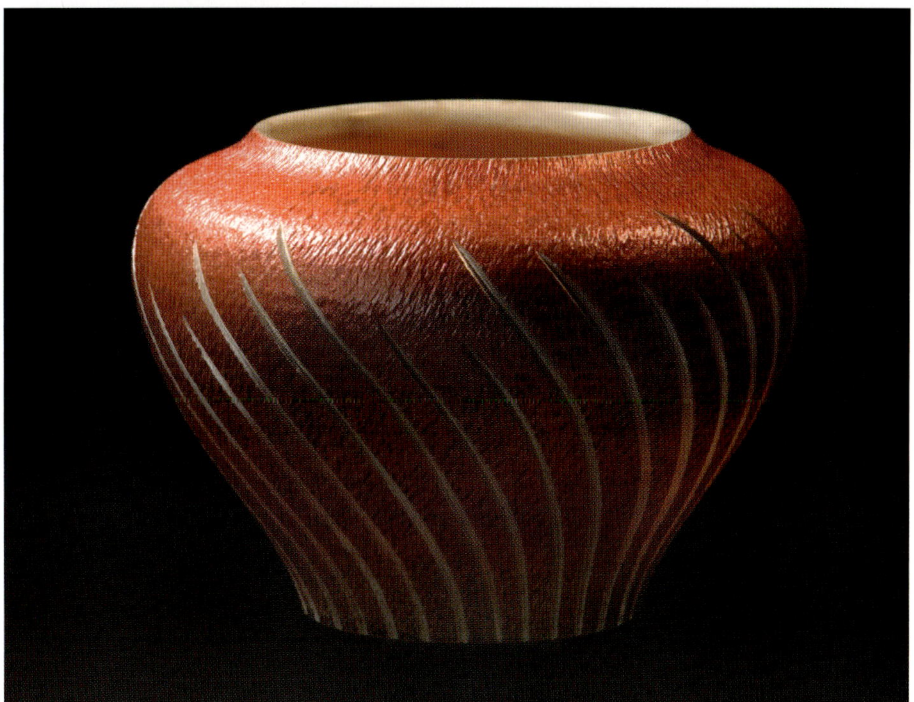

Vessel #726, 2011

Alabaster
4" x Dia. 5 ½"

Simon Levy

UNITED STATES

Night Owl, 2012
Core, metal | 2 ¼" x 2 ½"
Photo by Simon Levy

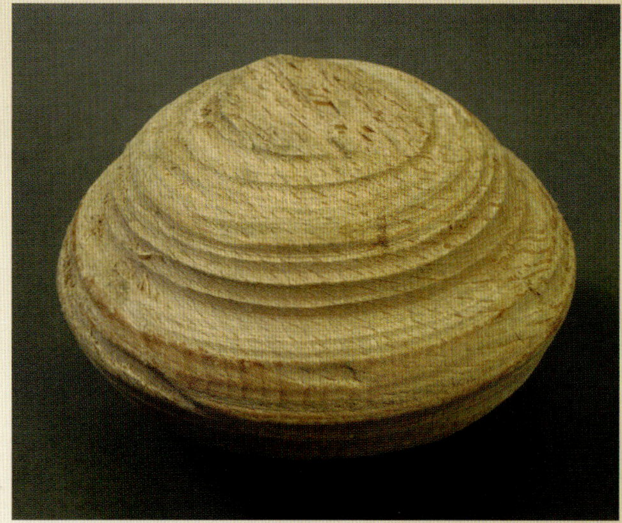

Wood is an ideal medium for sculpting; each piece is naturally unique, containing attractive and supple qualities.

By design, the lathe-turned vessels here (some with lids and additional support elements) are purely intended to bring everlasting enjoyment. Distinctive abstract surface applications give further individual identity to these one-of-a-kind objects.

Born in 1946, in Los Angeles, California, I attended the Art Center College of Design, Los Angeles, California (1966–69). My studies included drawing, painting, graphic design, and photography. Then I served as an art director in the recording industry for more than twenty years, involved with album package design, print advertising, and marketing.

With a lifelong and deeply personal interest in the visual arts, making the transition in 1996 from two-dimensional graphic design to three-dimensional form was a natural progression. The process is basically two-fold. First, the vessels are lathe-turned; then complementary elements are created, surface designs are developed and applied utilizing: freehand drawing, pyrography (woodburning), carving, and low-relief engraving; some are enhanced with pigment.

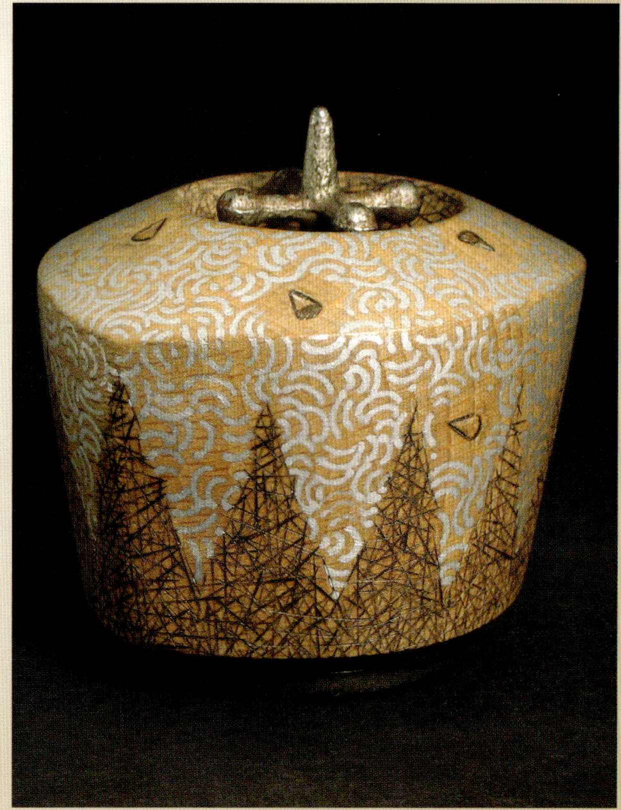

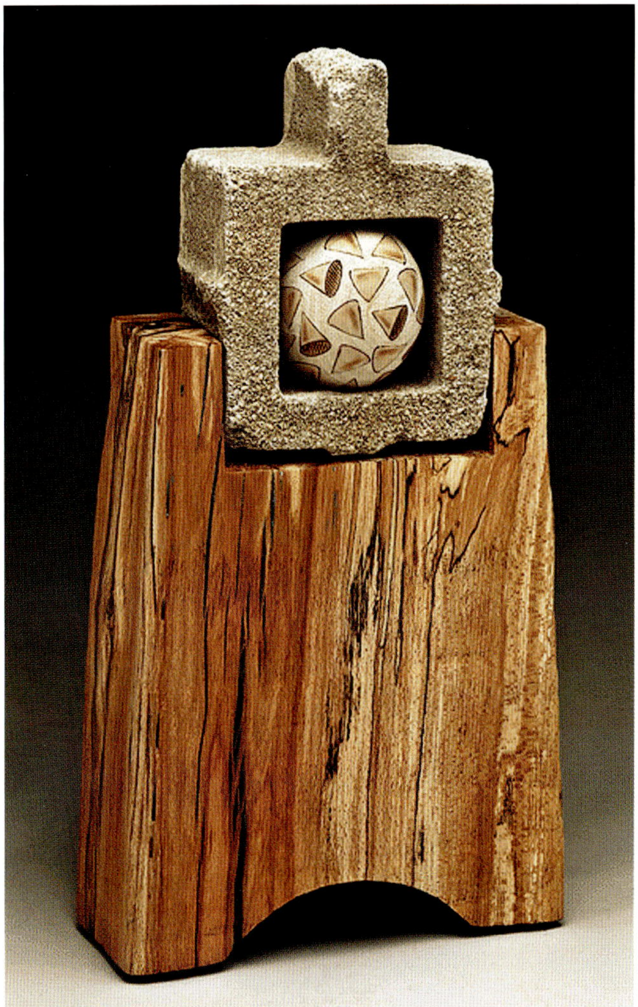

Inside Out, 2012

Poplar, beech, cinder block fragment, engraving, pyrography | 18 ⅜" x 10" x 3 ½"

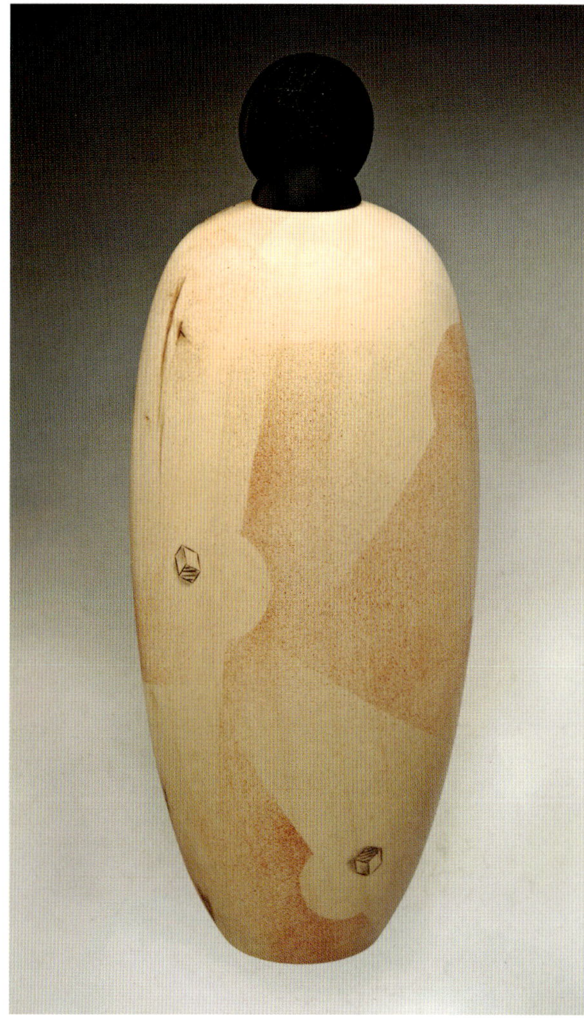

Ultralight, 2013

Boxelder, pyrography | 11" x 4 ¼" x 4 ¼"

Yoav Liberman

UNITED STATES

Artifact, 2012
Core, mahogany, canvas, steel, cardboard
6 ½" x 5" x 3"
Photo by Yoav Liberman

My piece is a take on the reverence with which we choose to handle and display important artifacts from prehistory or antiquity. It includes an archeologist's scale (in centimeters) and delicate painted steel arms to ensconce the precious object. I treated the core with bleach to lighten it, giving it the appearance of a bone or clay artifact, hence the piece's name: *Artifact.*

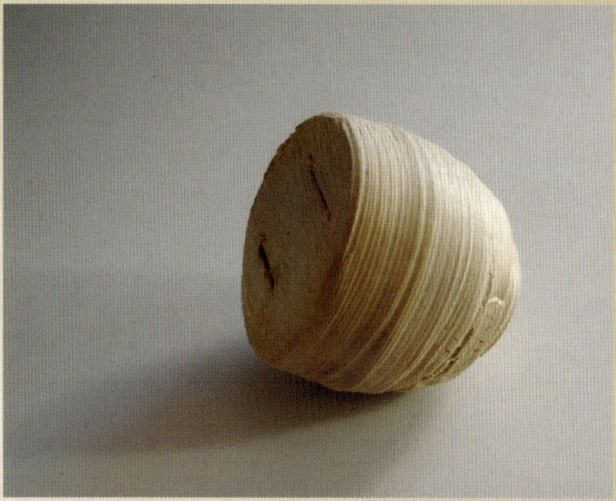

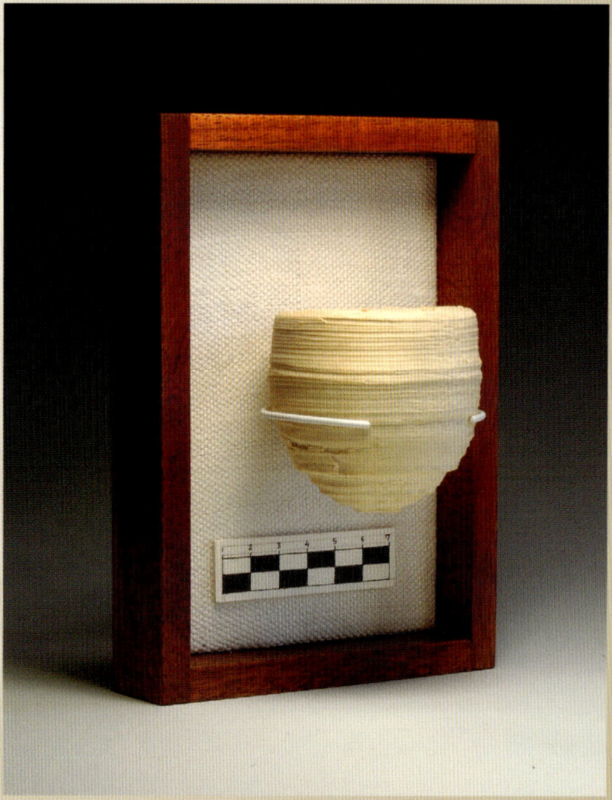

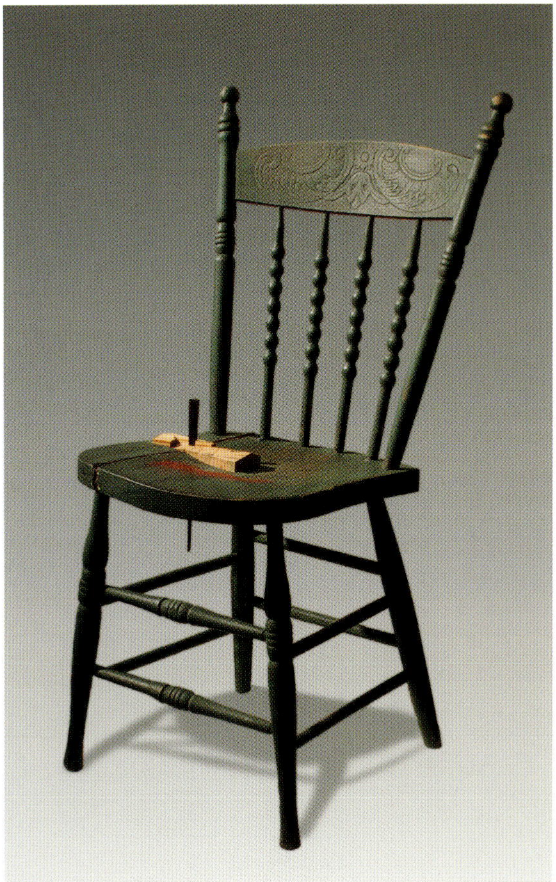

A House Divided, 2007

Found Windsor chair, spalted maple, southern yellow pine, West African wenge, pigment | 36" x 17" x 17"

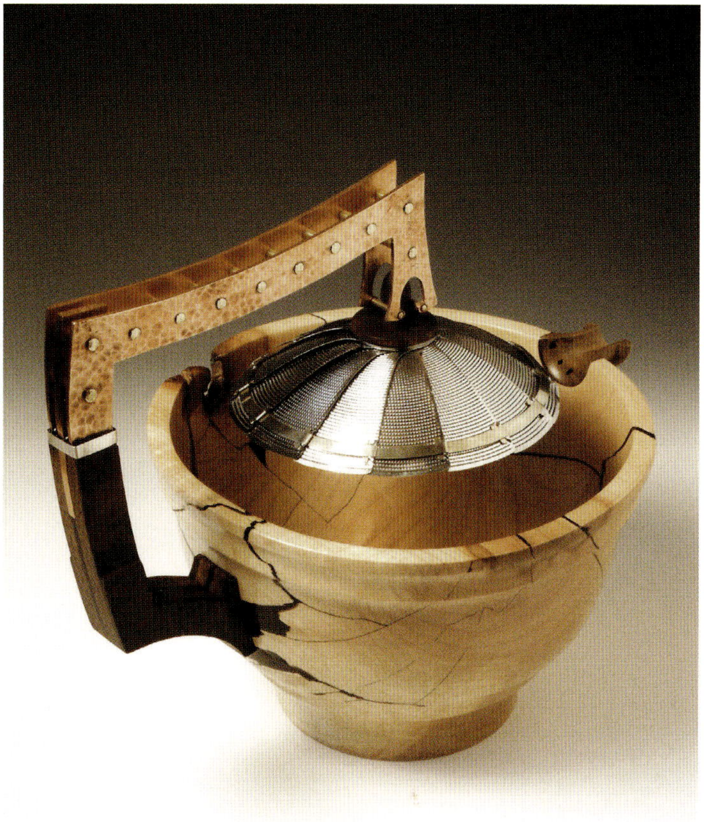

Flash Teapot, 2005

Found maple, found collapsible flash reflector (fan), walnut, copper, brass, epoxy | 9" x 7" x 9"

Robert Lyon

UNITED STATES

The Doodler's Dream 2012
Core, pencils, erasers | 8" x Dia. 4 ¾"

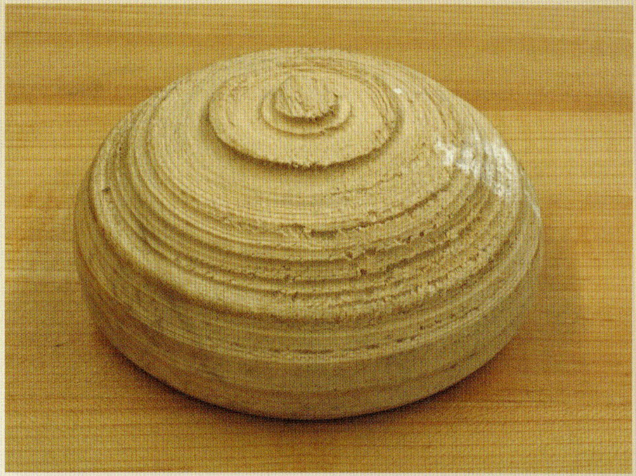

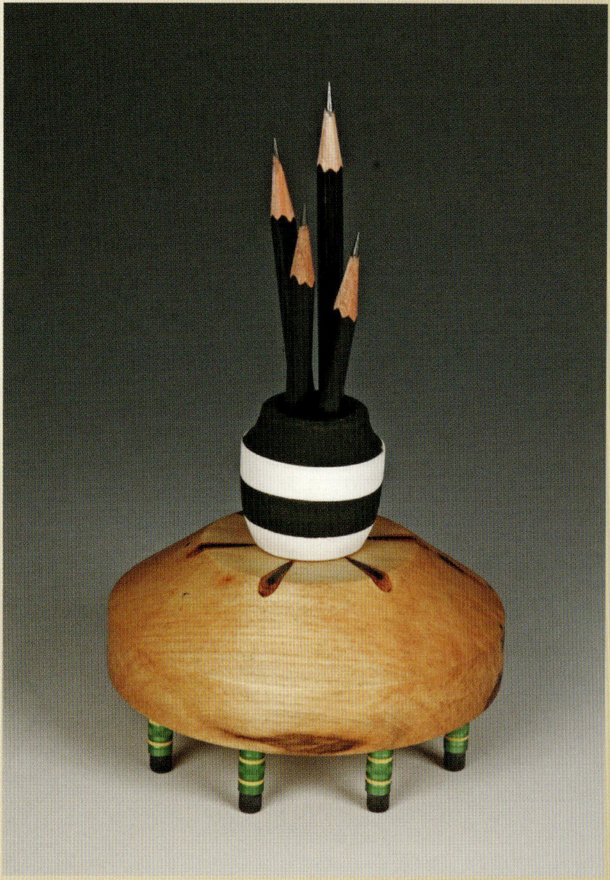

Robert Lyon's interest in architecture, especially the cylindrical forms of Italian architect Aldo Rossi, including small granaries from the Ivory Coast, and the ancient towers of Iraq, led him to making circular forms. Looking for a practical method of working with these forms brought him to working with the lathe.

Rather than simply relying on the beauty of the wood and traditional forms, Lyon is concerned with form and color and their ability to express his ideas. Beauty, fragility, memory, and our connection to the earth have been continuing themes in his work. Using wood, along with other materials, Lyon tries to make the effects of his hands evident.

His continuing lathe work with pencils originates from an interest in memory. Prior to her death, Lyon's mother had suffered significant memory loss during her illness. Her memory loss made him question the source of our thoughts and where they go. Through the artwork, he realized that graphite and erasers were good visual metaphors for the way our brain works. The smear of graphite is like memory, always fleeting, never permanent.

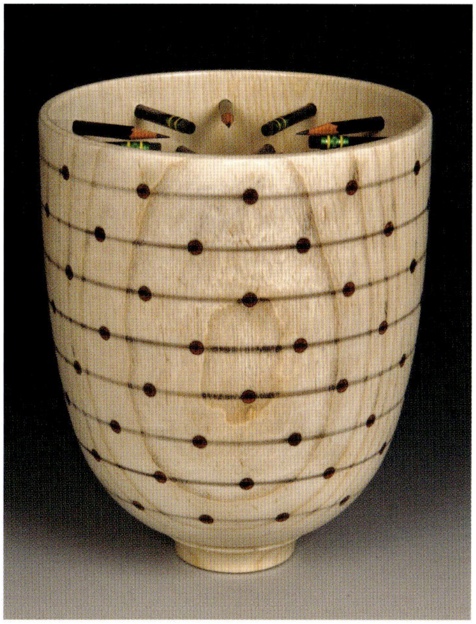

Chasing Memory, 2012

Ash, pencils, erasers | 9 ¾" x Dia. 8"

Eraser Dreams, 2012

Maple, pencils, erasers | 7" x 13" x 4"

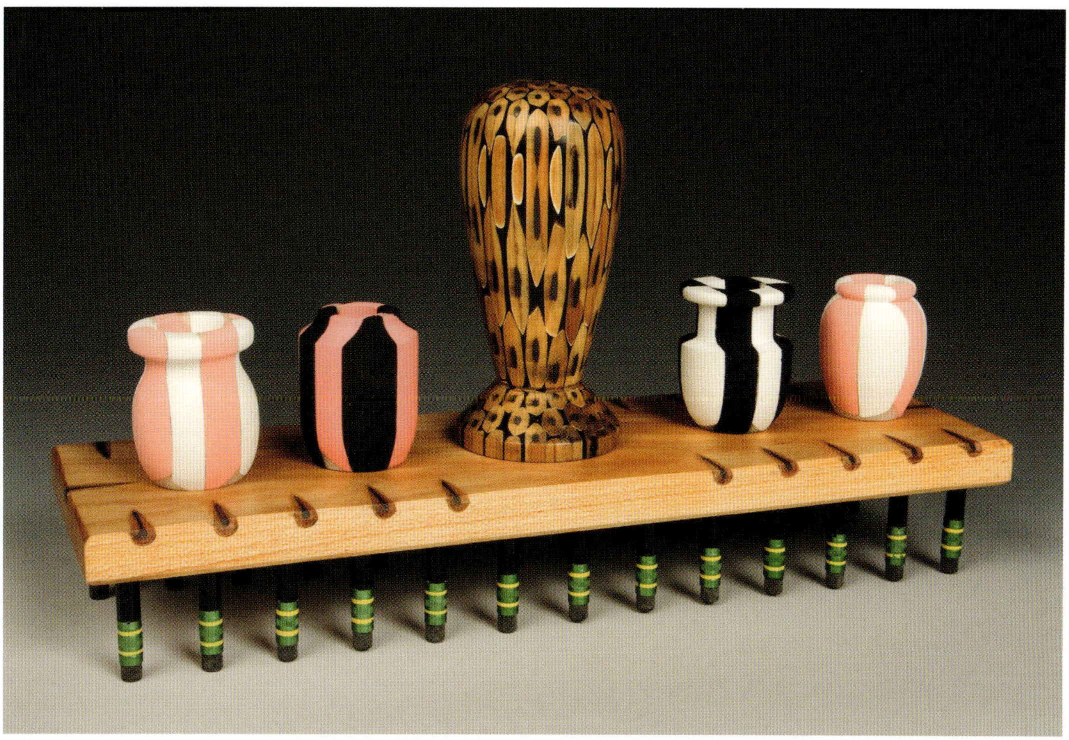

Gord Peteran

CANADA

"Before" and "After", 2012
Two color photographs | 18" x 21" each

Wood Floats.

I can imagine Robin Wood standing at his lathe in a sea of cores, intently focused upon producing yet another very lovely ... Core—the collateral fallout, the aftermath, the wake, the tsunami, the evidence, the side effect, the symptom.

"Life is what happens while we're busy doing something else" (author?)

Because the subconscious never sleeps, it always gets its way, but it's the rational intention of a focused physical task that seems to tempt and coax buried conceptual meanderings out into the visible.

I'm not sure I have anything specific to say with the core given to me, but I was fascinated by this exhibition's proposition. The making of something from an "off cut." Extending this equation in perpetuity—make something from the leftover, then make something and keep the garbage, now make something out of that garbage but hang onto the remaining pieces, now make an artwork out of those and keep the leftover to create an artwork. There could potentially be no finite conclusion ... like ripples.

Last summer I threw the wooden core that Albert sent me into the lake, snapped a photograph, and sat most of a lovely August afternoon watching as it gently drifted out across the lake.

I watched until I could not see it any more.

Perhaps my photographs are simply evidence, collateral fallout, the remains from that event, ... but also a beginning, ... like any artwork.

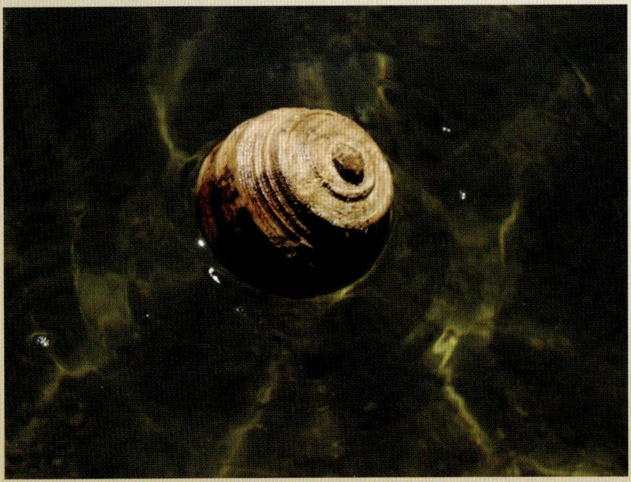

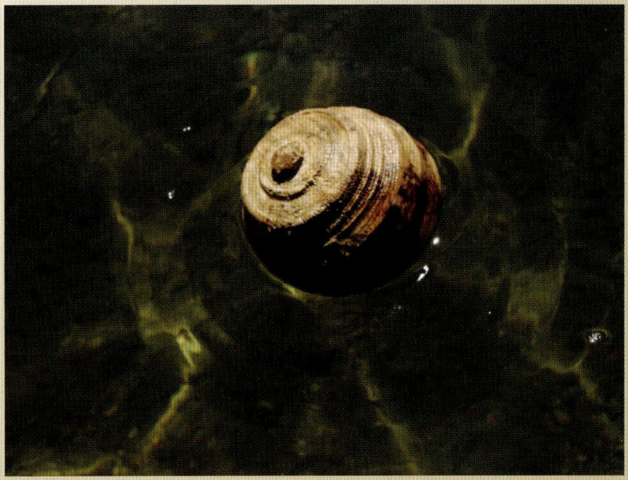

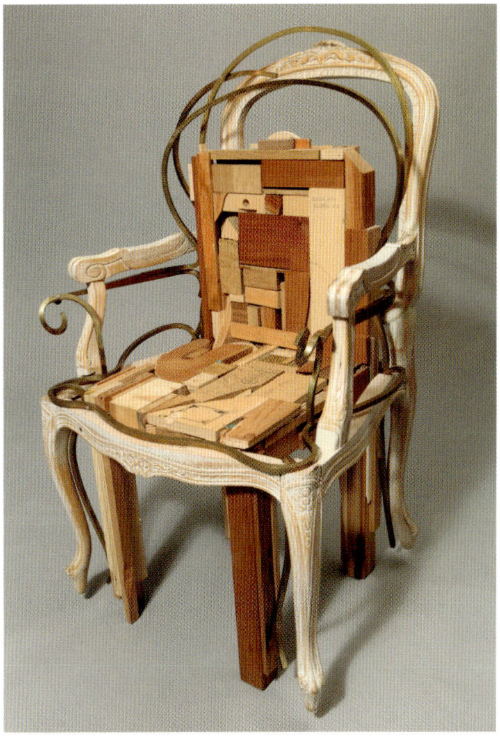

Elaborinth, 2013

Gord Peteran and Donald Fortescue

Made of scrp wood, wound in brass, and inserted with a Louis XV frame

38" x 24" x 24"

Photo by Jill Kitchener

Two, 2006

Wood, brass | 22" x 64" x 16"

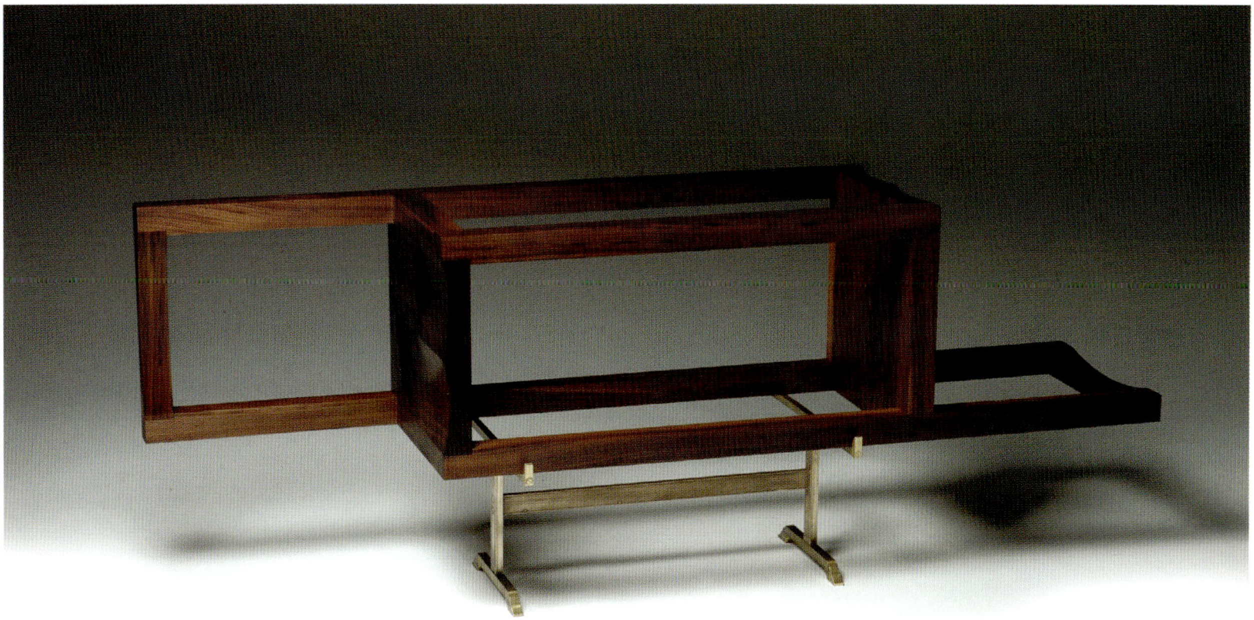

Michael Peterson

UNITED STATES

Untitled, 2012
Core (oak) | 2 ½" x 3 ½" x 3 ⅛"
Photo by Jean Peterson

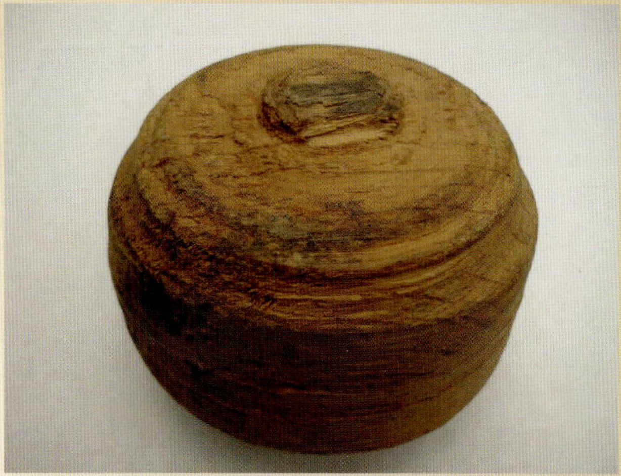

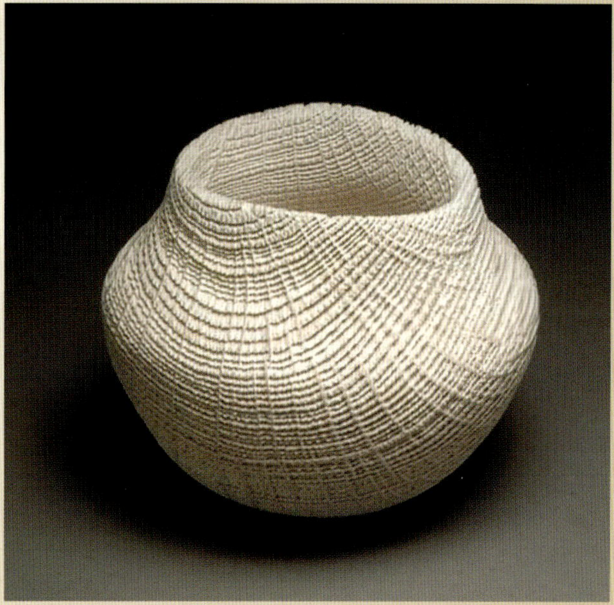

I admit that this piece was approached rather cautiously and conservatively, with a real admiration for Robin Wood's work and the process represented in the oak core I received. "Hand carved" seemed in accord with the core's origin. It was a pleasure to explore the potential of an unfamiliar material with my familiar surface treatments. I like the intersecting lines.

Untitled Landscape Series, 2013

Sandblasted/pigmented Madrone burl
18" x 23" x 5"
Photo by Jean Peterson

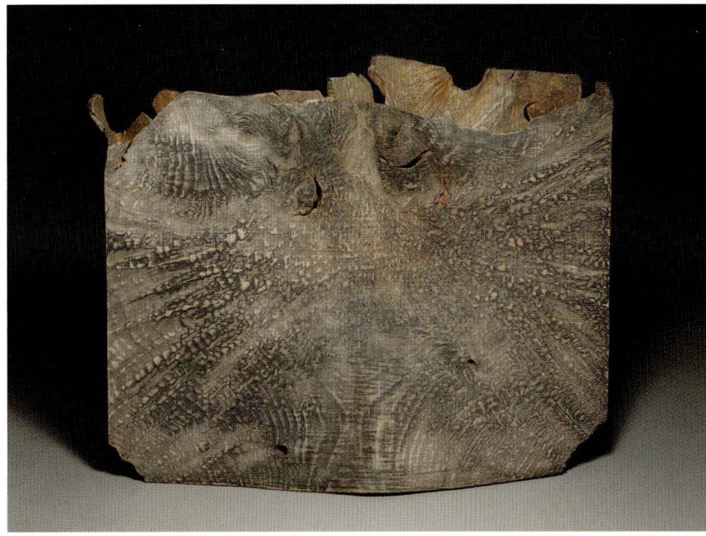

Still Life, 2012

Sandblasted/bleached/pigmented locust and Madrone Burl 9" x 24.5" x 8"
Photo by Jean Peterson

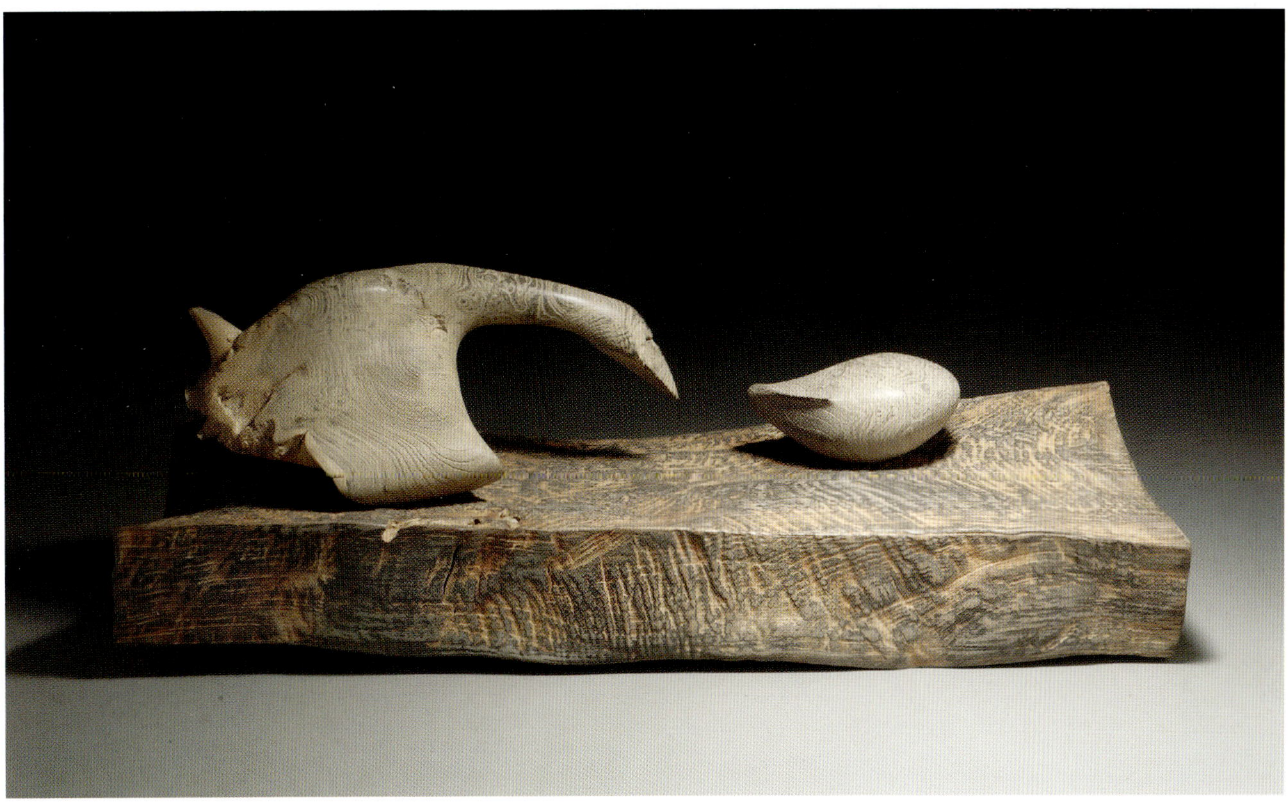

Hilary Pfeifer

UNITED STATES

Have Nothing In Your House That You Do Not Know To Be Useful And Believe To Be Beautiful (For Todd Akin) 2012
Core, mixed media | 17" x 5" x 4"
Photo by Hilary Pfeifer

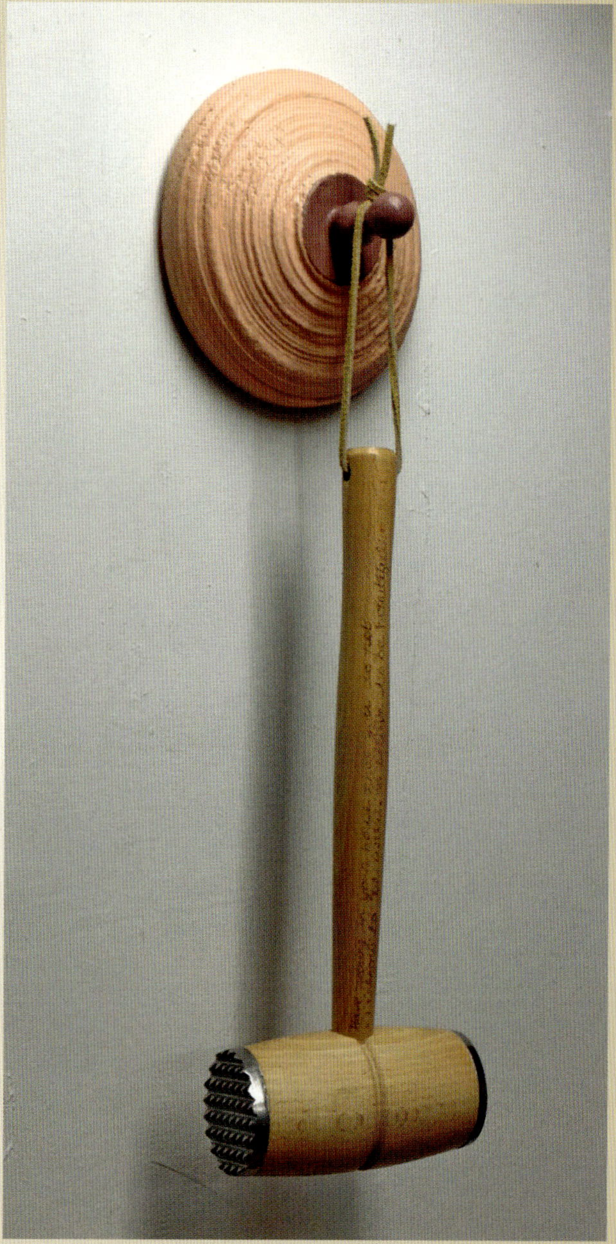

I was settling into work on this piece when news broke of Missouri State Representative Todd Akin's misinformed statements about a woman being able to biologically defy pregnancy in the case of a "legitimate rape." My work often incorporates altered found objects, and I loved the idea of combining a simple shaker peg with the core to create a suggestive tool holder: in this case a meathead cleaver.

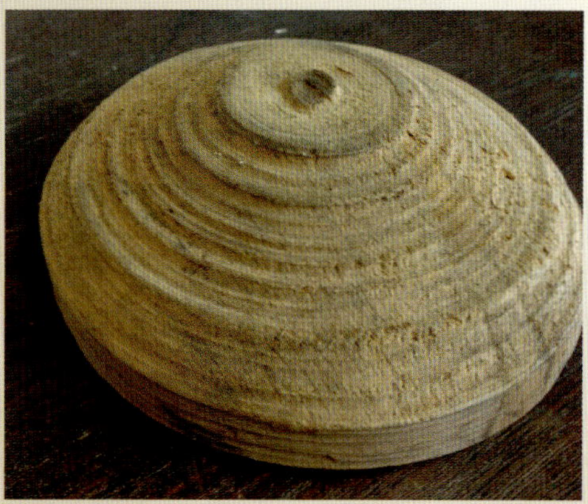

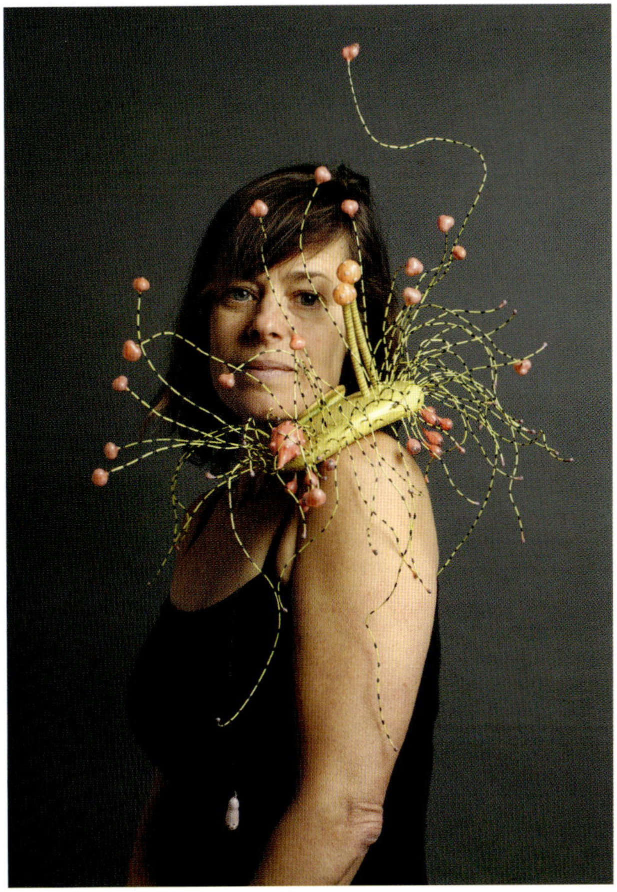

Epiphyte, 2011

From an ongoing series of wearable sculptures that interact with the human body; wood, mixed media

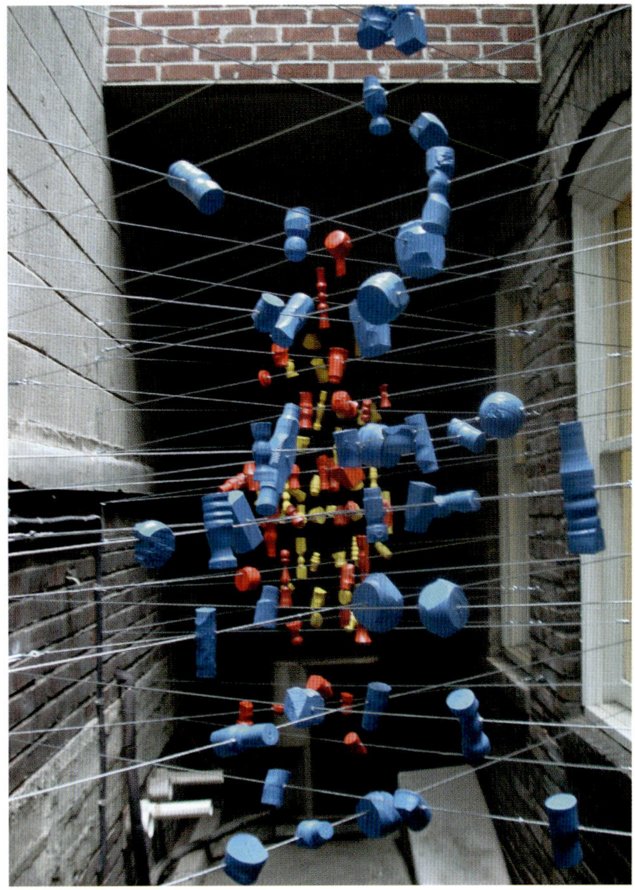

Liminal Space, 2006

An installation at the then Wood Turning Center; wood, metal, mixed media

Carl Pittman

UNITED STATES

From Earth to Oxygen, 2012
Core (pear tree), copper wire, ammonite, book pages from ***Turning to Art in Wood*** | 2" x 3 ½" x 1 ⅜"

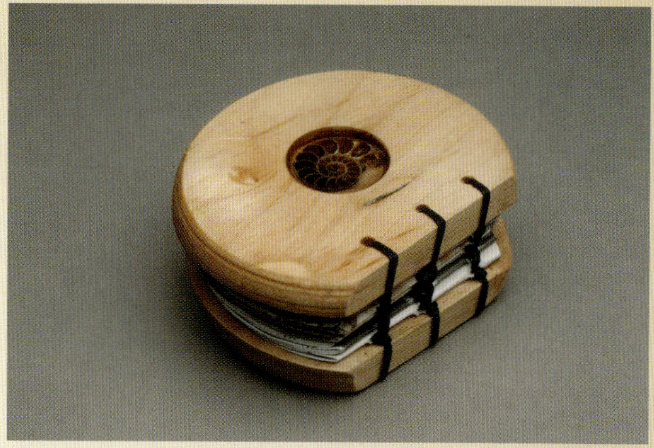

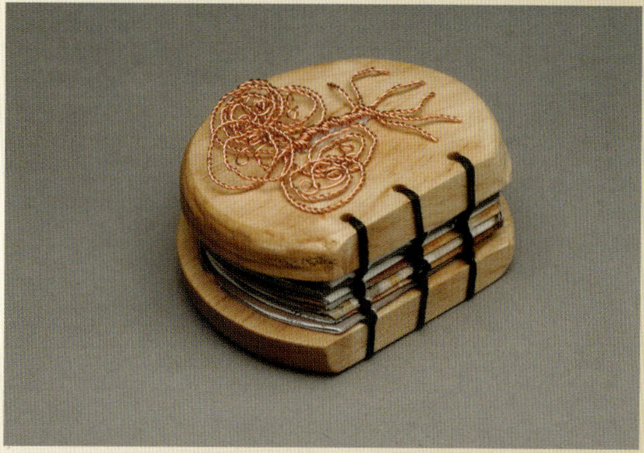

I have wanted to pursue book making for several years, but until I was ready to put my full focus on it, I let it stay a thought in my mind. Two months ago I dove in head first and began the book-making process. The process from start to finish is rather long, yet so fulfilling! After much consideration on the core, I chose to make a book, as that is where a lot of my focus is directed now. When I found that I had a little wood left over, I decided to make earrings as well. That is where the rest of my focus is directed as of late. Jewelry is sculpture on a small scale and apart from books it has captured my attention for well over a year now. The book is my first that you look at and not write in. A lot of time went into choosing pages that resonate within me. From Albert LeCoff to Mark Lindquist to Robin Wood to George Peterson (my mentor), each page has a little piece of what inspires me on my creative journey.

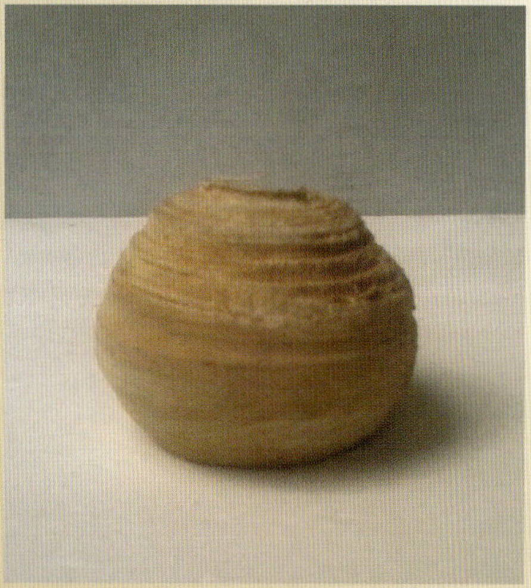

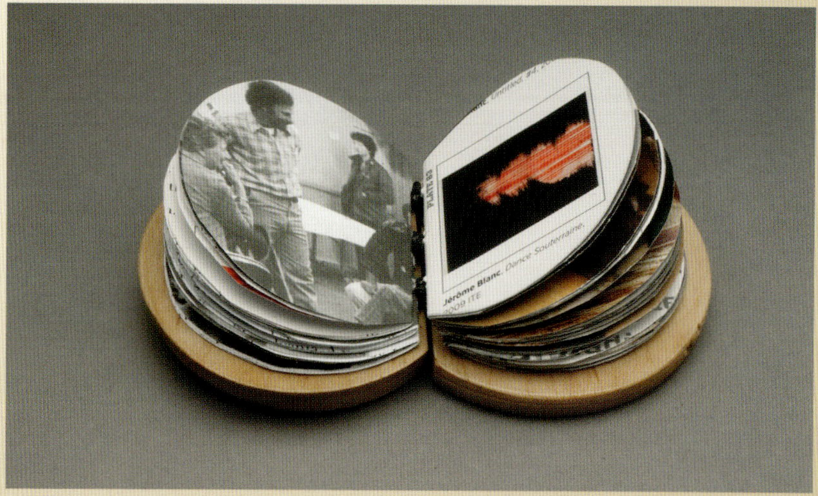

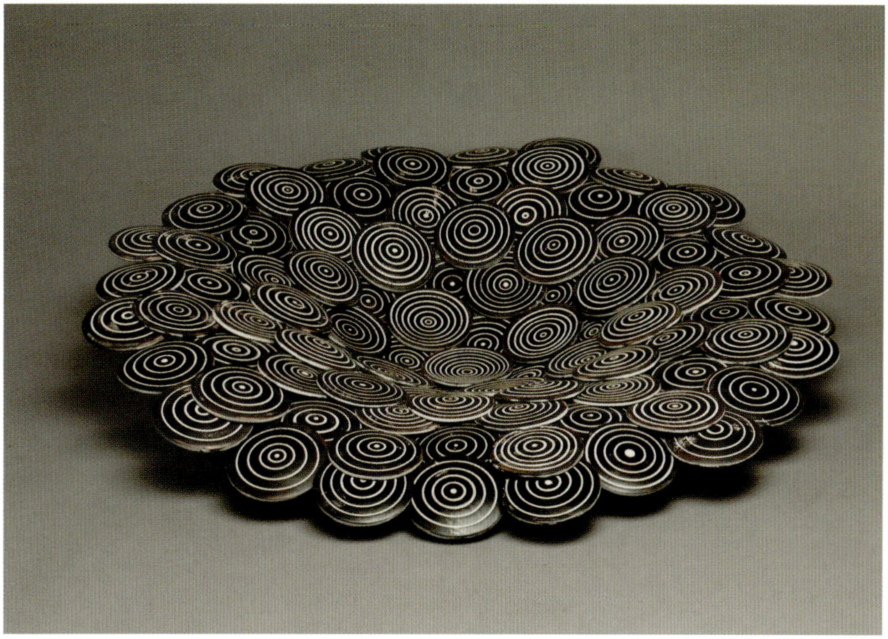

Welcome to the New Paradigm, 2011

Silver maple, milk paint, waxed linen
11" x 31" x 32"

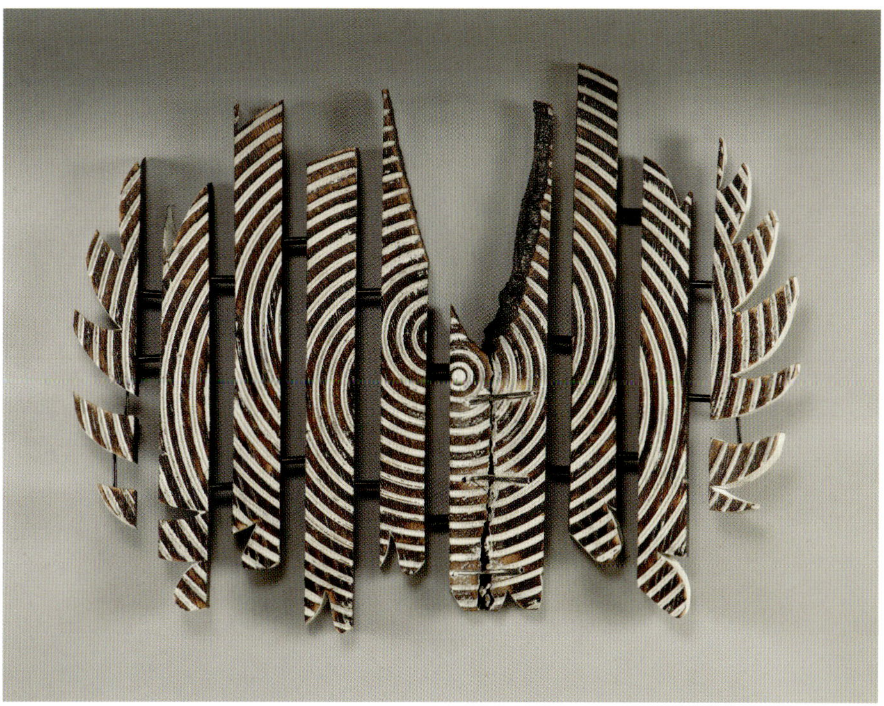

Energy Lines, 2008

White oak, iron oxide, milk paint, steel, waxed linen, epoxy
24" x 30" x 3"

Jeannette Rein

WESTERN AUSTRALIA

Sea Urchin, 2012
Core (walnut), silver, acrylic paint, carnauba wax
1 ¼" x 1 ¼" x 1 ¾"

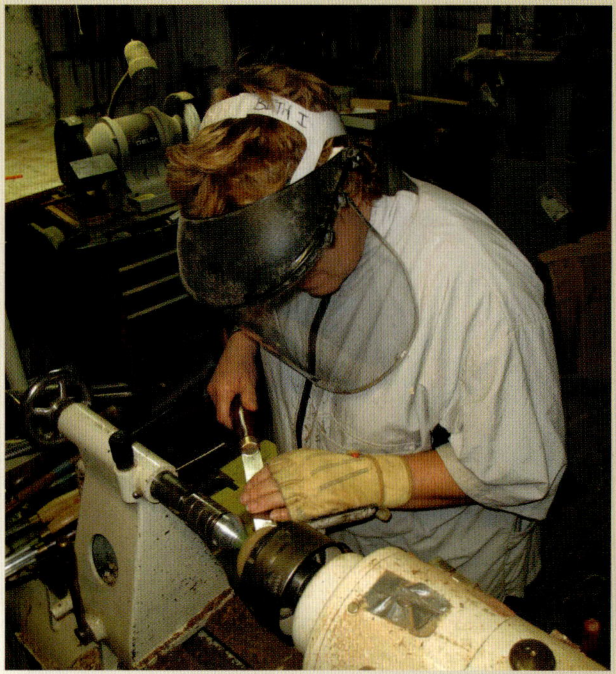

The origins of my sculptural forms evolve from the study of the dynamics and power of the natural world. My art practice is centered on the use of Western Australian timbers, challenging the boundaries of woodworking techniques and the conceptual framework surrounding fine wood sculpture. The jewelry is influenced by the art deco architecture I saw during my International Turning Exchange residency at The Center for Art in Wood in Philadelphia in 2012. The use of geometric forms such as the triangle is one of the basic elements in many art deco compositional arrangements.

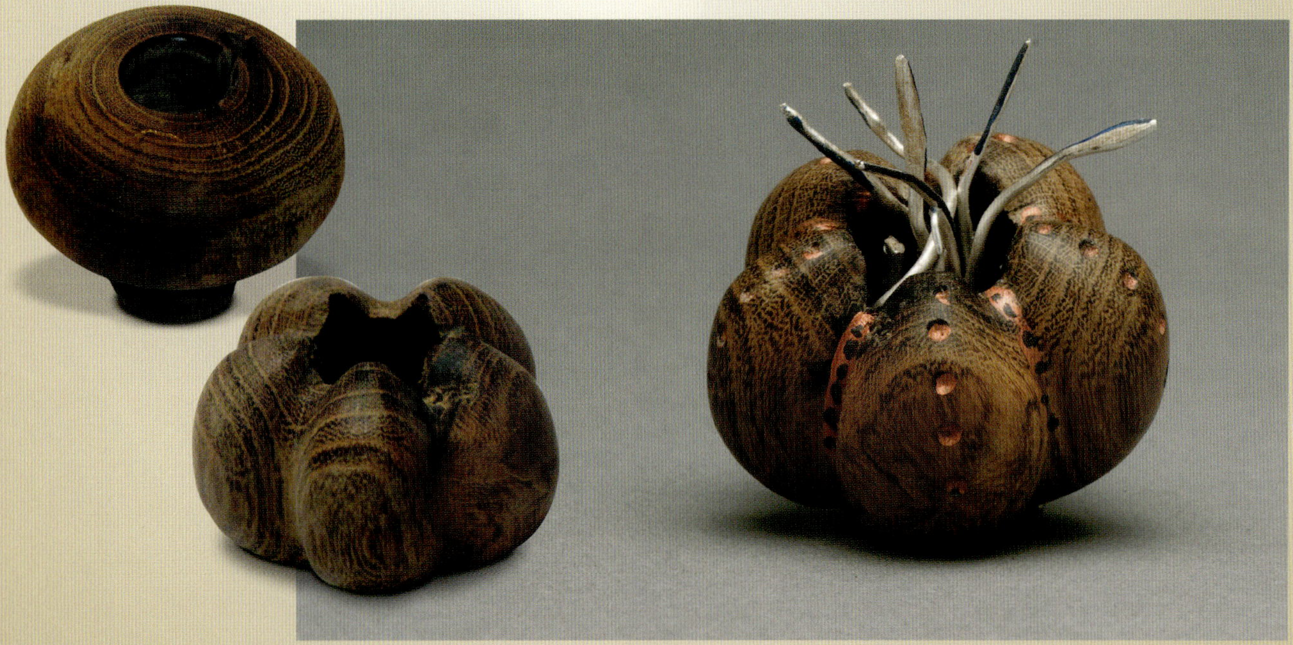

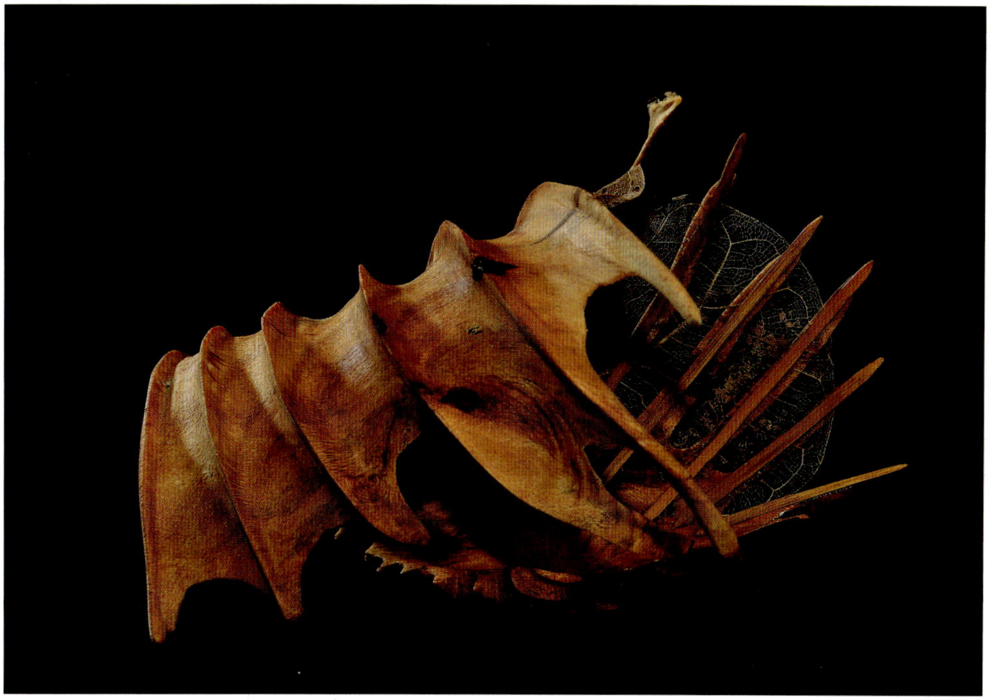

Spinose III, 2013

Swan Valley woollybush, fiddle leaf, wax
7" x 8" x 5"

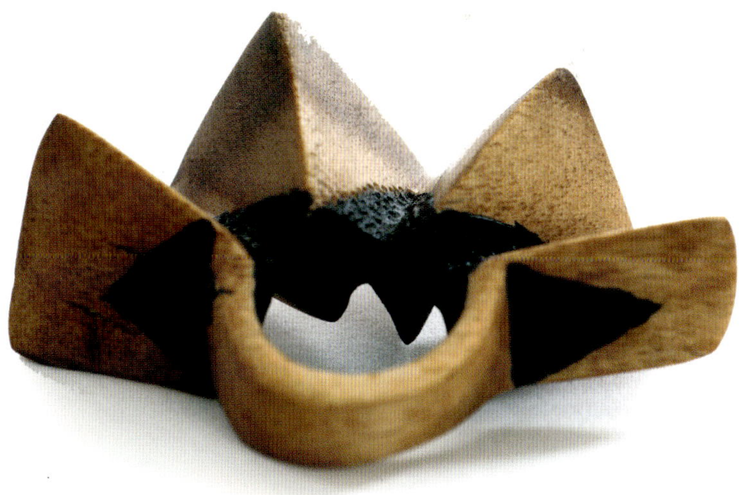

Art Deco – Architectural ring series, 2013

Eucalyptus obliqua, black paint, wax finish
2" x ½" x 2"

Gabriel Romeu

UNITED STATES

Core Intersection Wall Lamp, 2012
Core, oak, purpleheart, aluminum, copper leaf, acrylic, ABS plastic, halogen lamp
32" x 16" x 32"

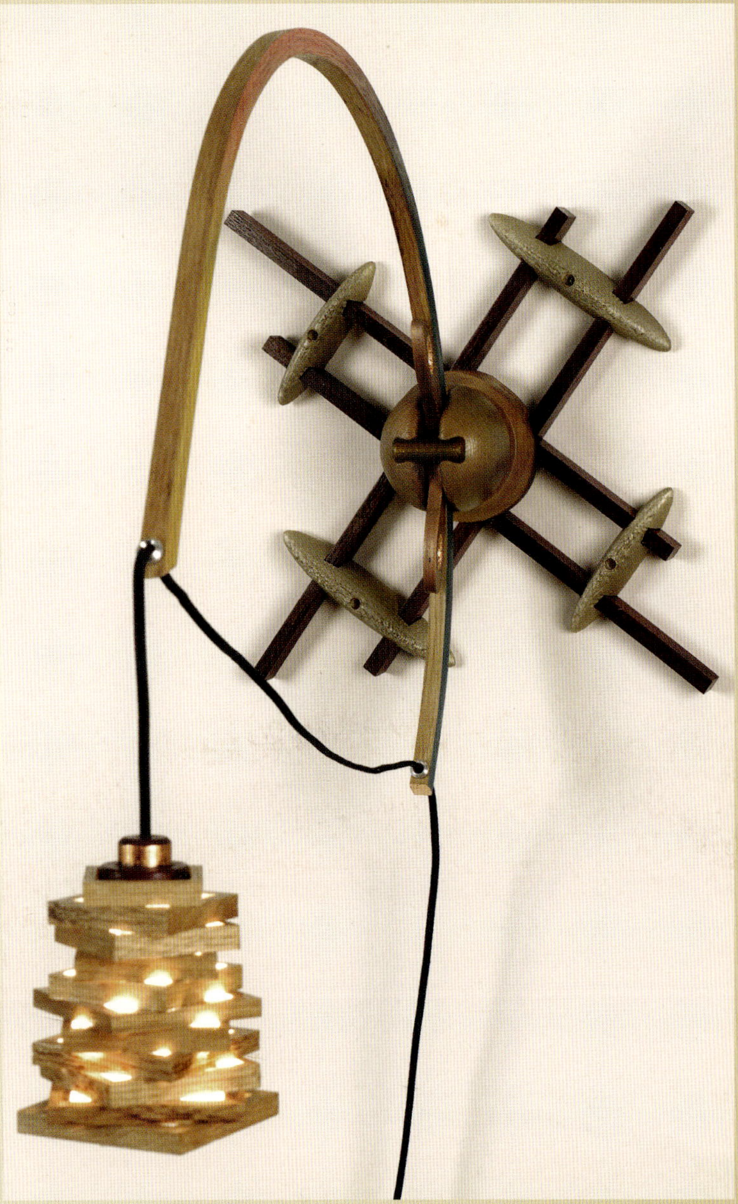

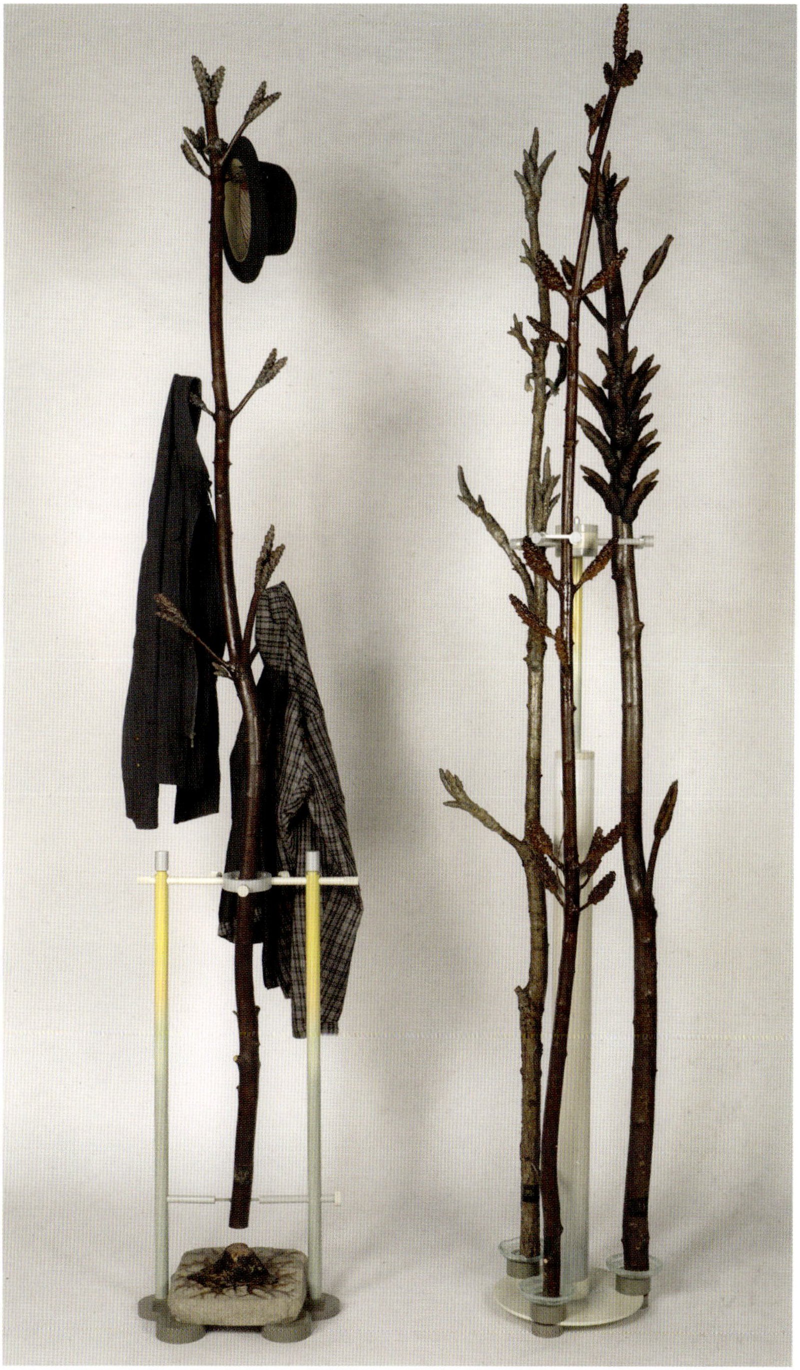

Personal Hangups, all natural, 2011–12

Aluminum, tree, ABS, limestone, steel, glass, silver leaf, fiberglass
96" × 18–22" × 14–22"

Randall Rosenthal

UNITED STATES

Match Book + Box, 2012
Core, acrylic paint | 1 ¾" x 3 ¼" x 2 ¾"

The piece is one of a series of small sculptures I've done involving boxes (usually cigar) and match books.

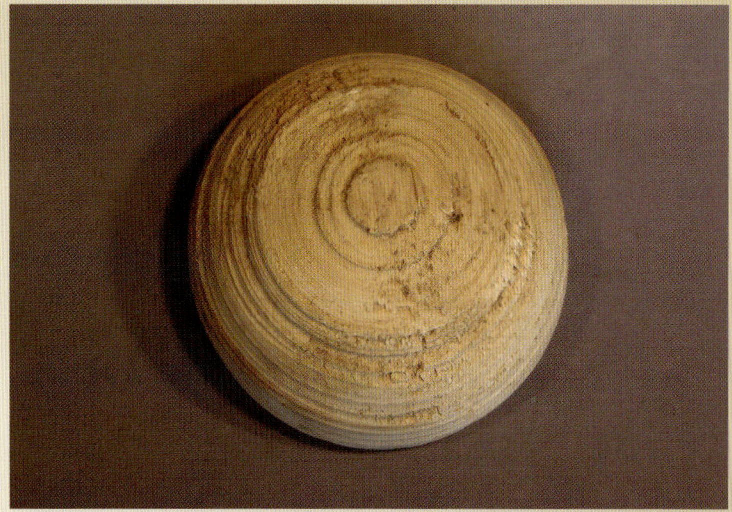

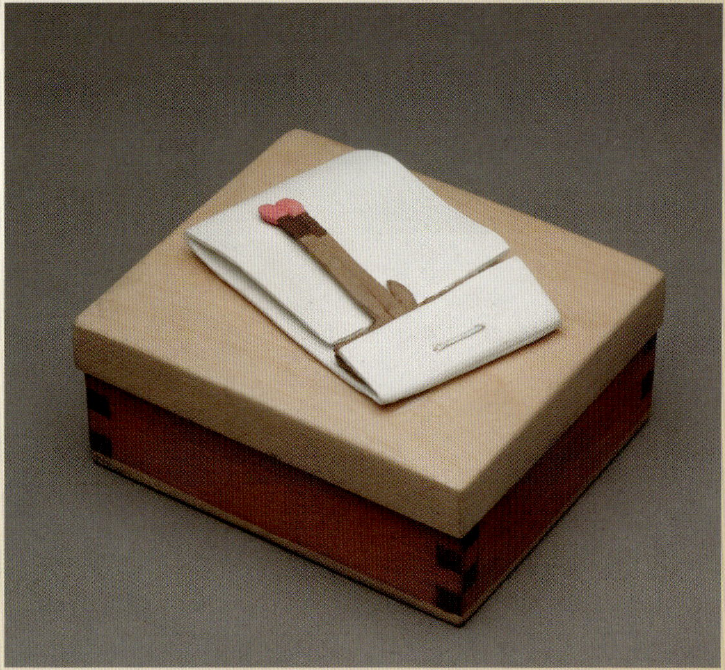

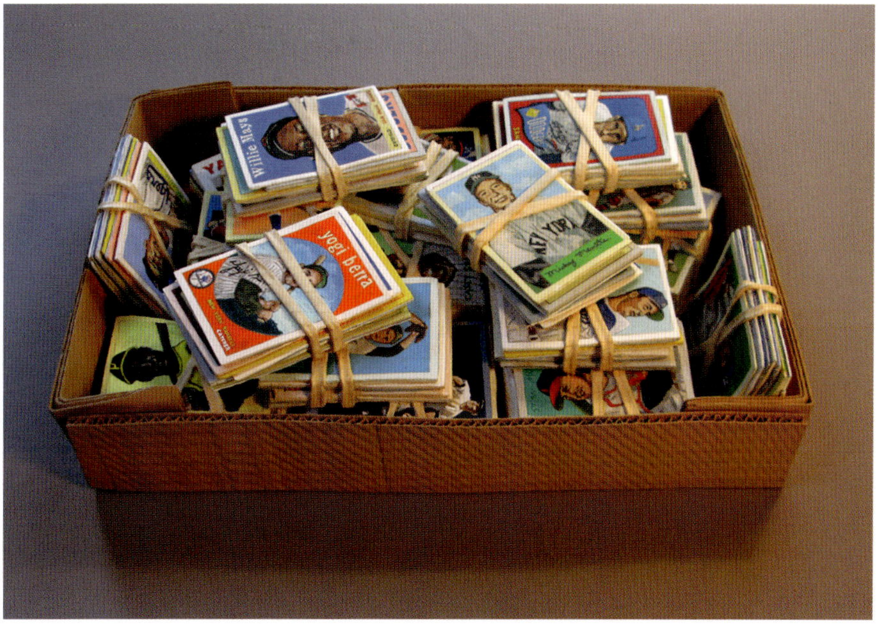

Cardbox, 2009

Wood, ink, acrylic
3 ½" x 14" x 11"

Cutting board, 2009

Wood, ink, acrylic | 3" x 18" x 14"

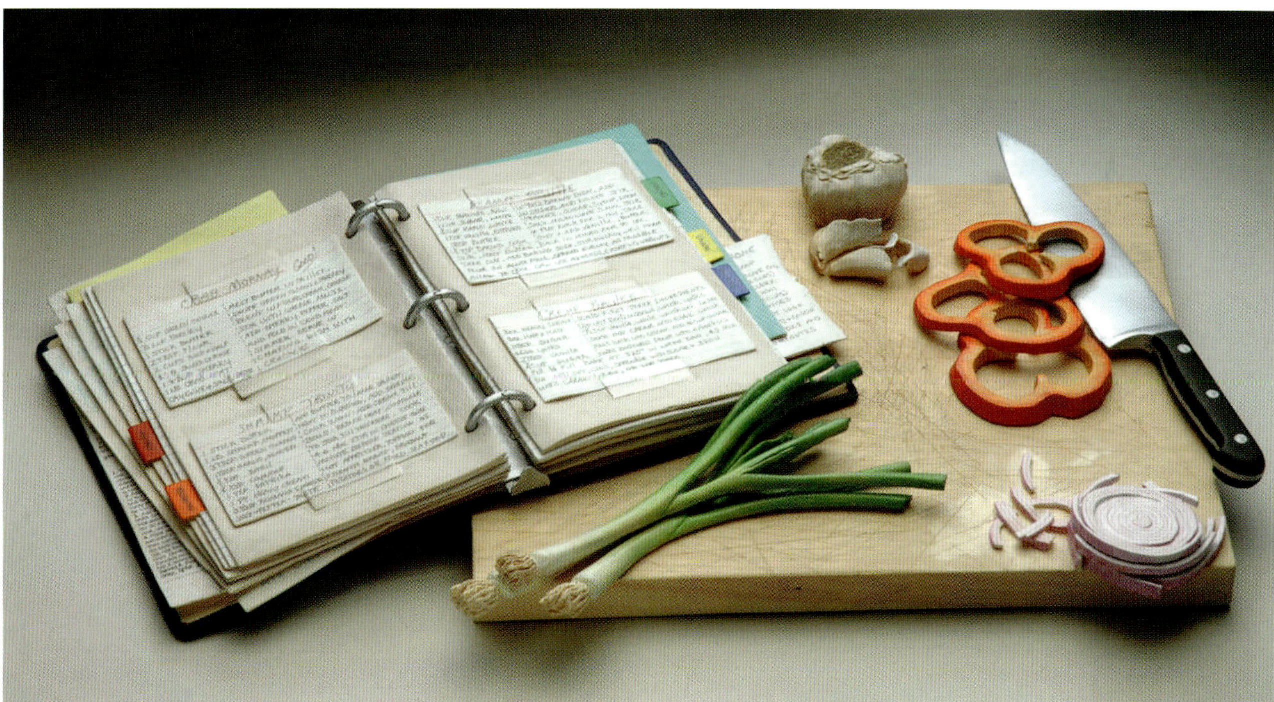

Jamie Russell

CANADA

Rockabye Birdies, 2012
Core, padouk | 2 ⅛" x 5" x 3 ⅝"

I've always wanted to play with cutting apart and re-assembling turned pieces to make something entirely new. As soon as I saw the blanks for the CORES project, I flashed on a series of bowls and small tables I've done using paired birds in a courtship pose. This piece is the joining of those two ideas.

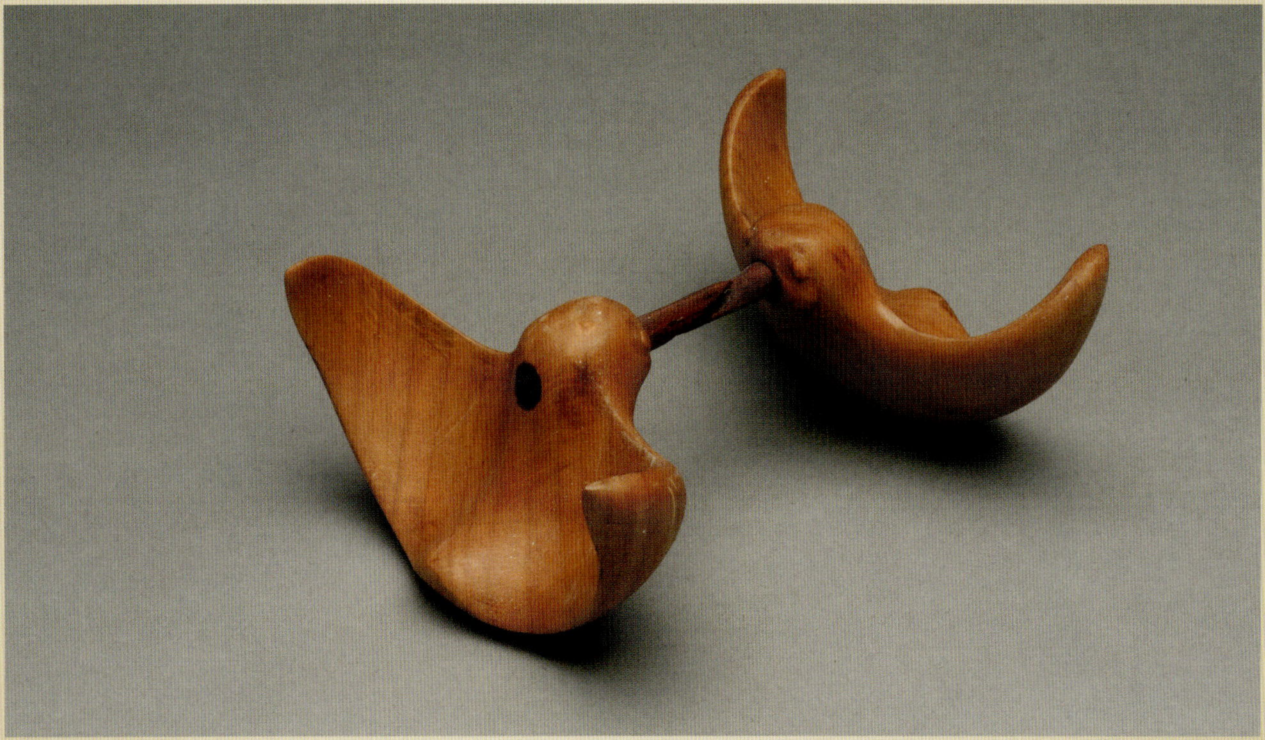

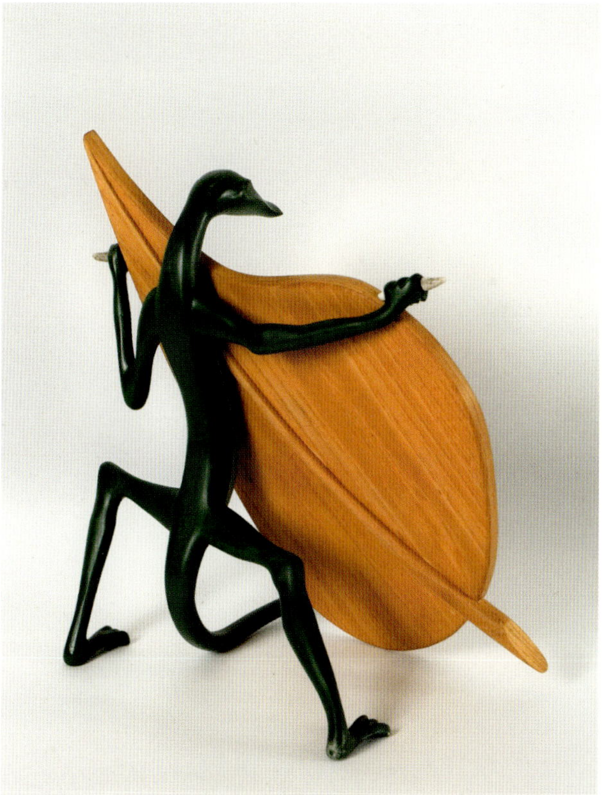

Little Luke, 1993

Ash, bent laminated ash veneer, colored lacquer, mirror | 15" x 13 ½" x 10 ½"

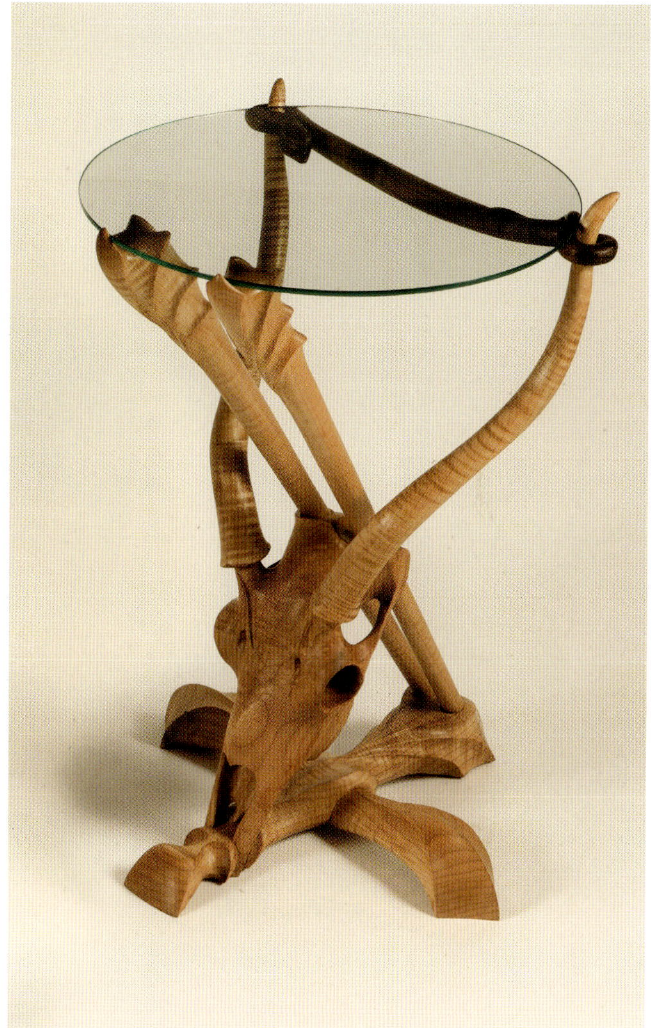

Ghost Table, 2004

Western big leaf maple, glass | 26" x 18"
Photo by Jamie Russell

Joshua Salesin

UNITED STATES

Core-upted, 2012
Core, African blackwood | 3" x 6" x 4"

Core-upted creates a lineage of turning expression as I've preserved part of the visual history of Robin Wood's "core" waste product (located in the center of the work) and then "upted" it by adding another layer to the archeological history of the turning, so perhaps 1,000 years from now one could reconstruct our activities—from Robin's turning on an ancient pole lathe (a technique that dates back 2,000 years) to my turning on a rose-engine lathe (a technique that dates back 500 years).

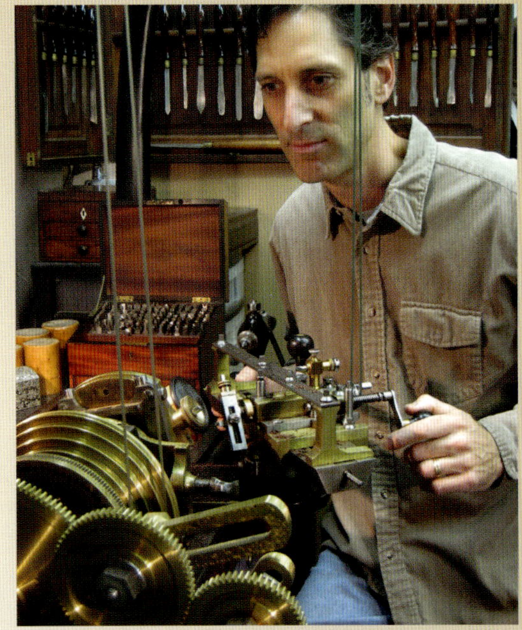

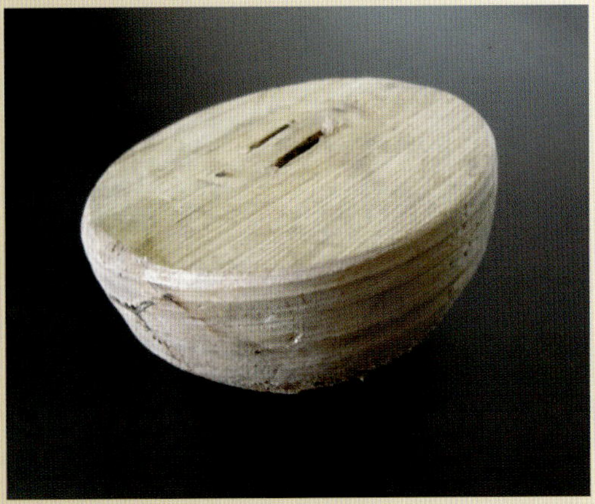

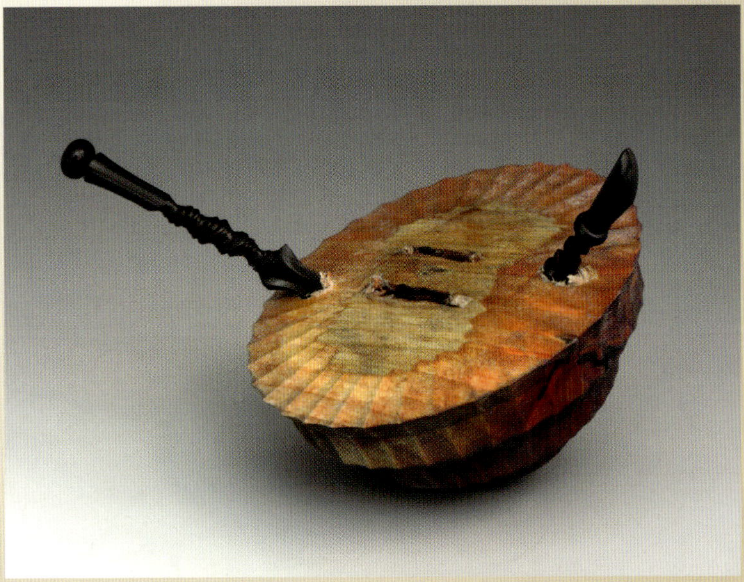

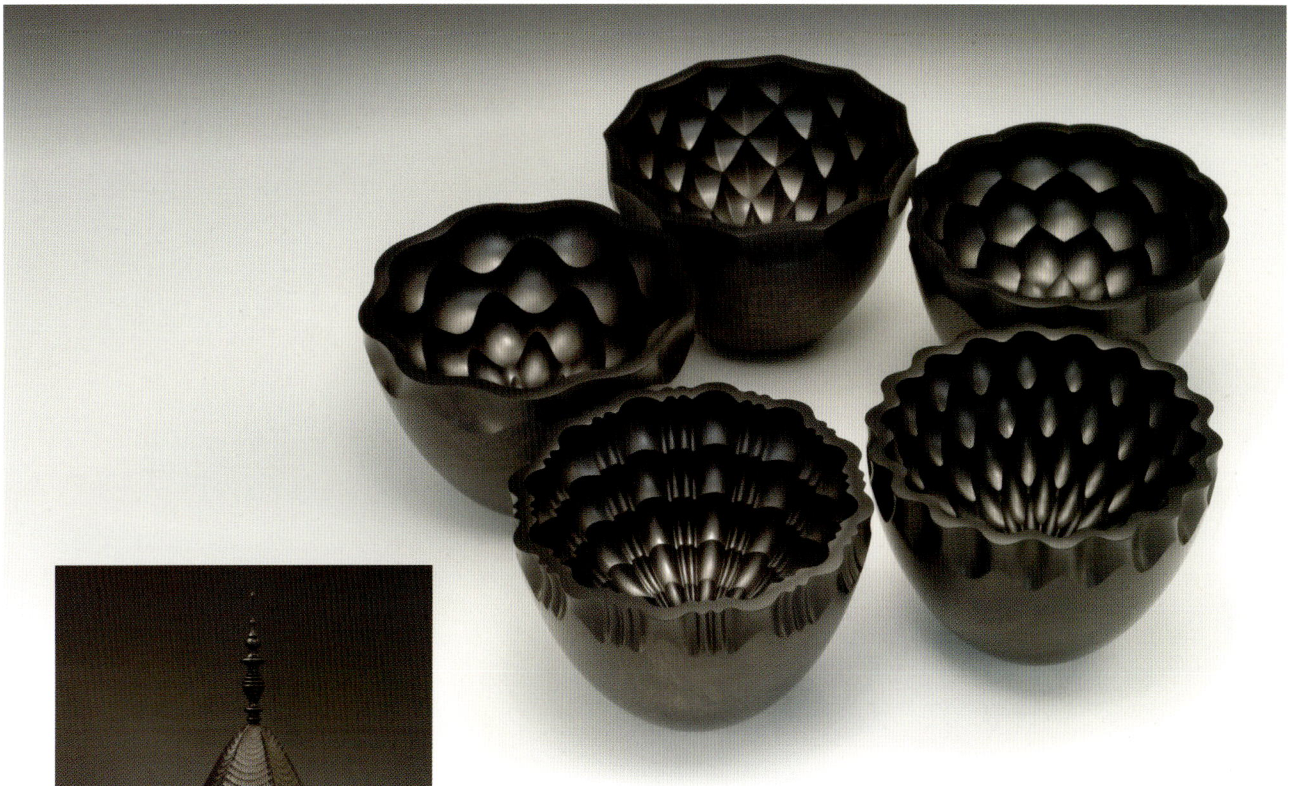

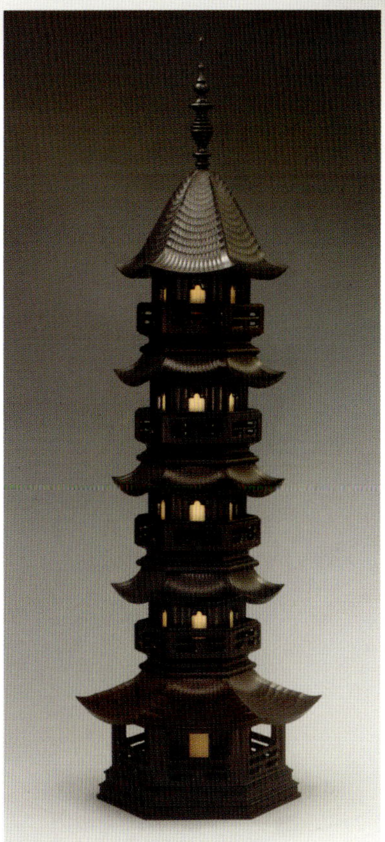

Mandala Cup Series, 2003
African blackwood | 2" x Dia. 2 ¾" each

Pagoda Box, 2010
African blackwood, European boxwood | 11" x Dia. 3 ¾"

Norm Sartorius

UNITED STATES

Plum Spoon, 2012
Core (plum wood) | ¾" x 2 ½" x 2 ½"
Photo by Jim Osborn

Spoon is a category, similar to bowl, plate, or teapot. Within each are infinite varieties of form, size, texture, abstraction, color, and emotion. This shape (the spoon) has a rich inherent symbolism through which the most ordinary aspects of our life are transfigured into something timeless. My goal is to explore that reservoir of form and idea and to carve sculptures that people will view as treasured objects. Carved from unique and unusual woods, my spoons are sculptures, and my sculptures are spoons

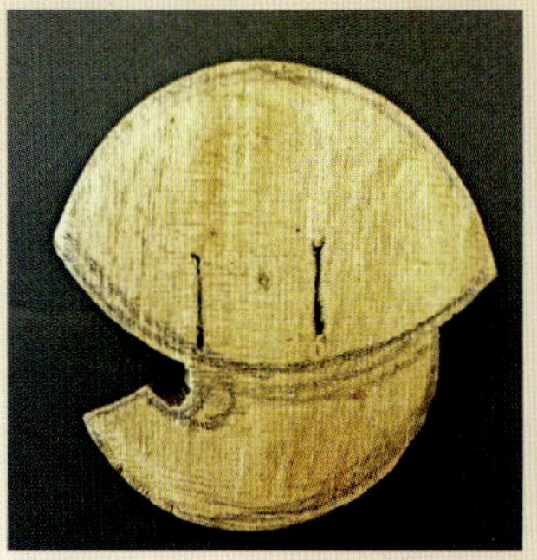

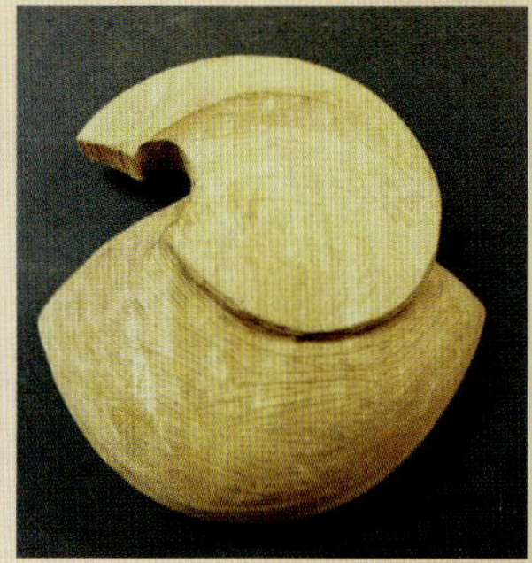

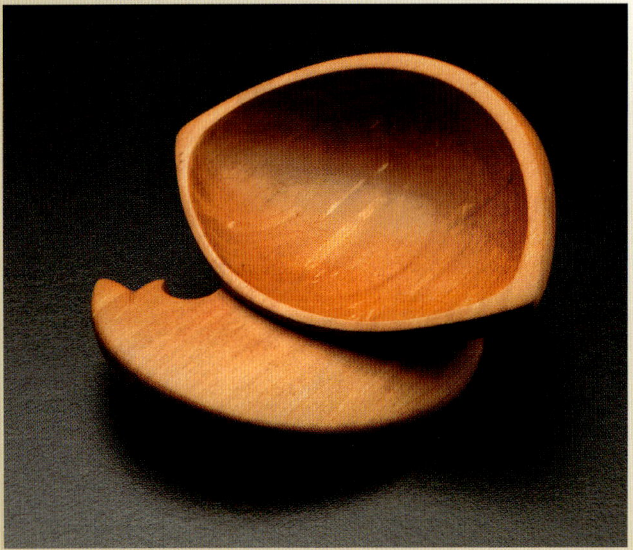

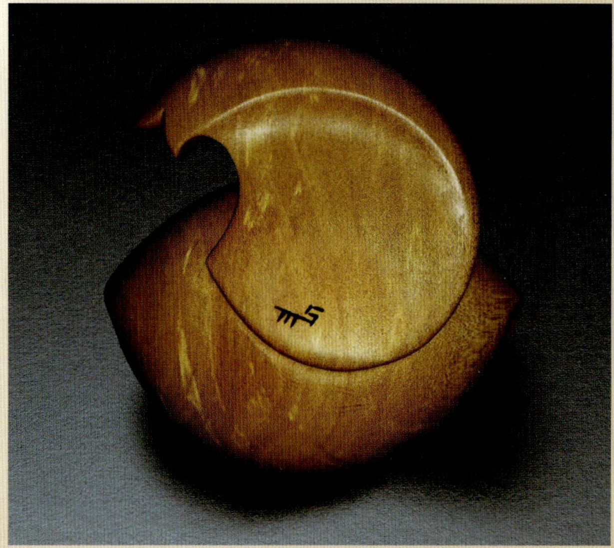

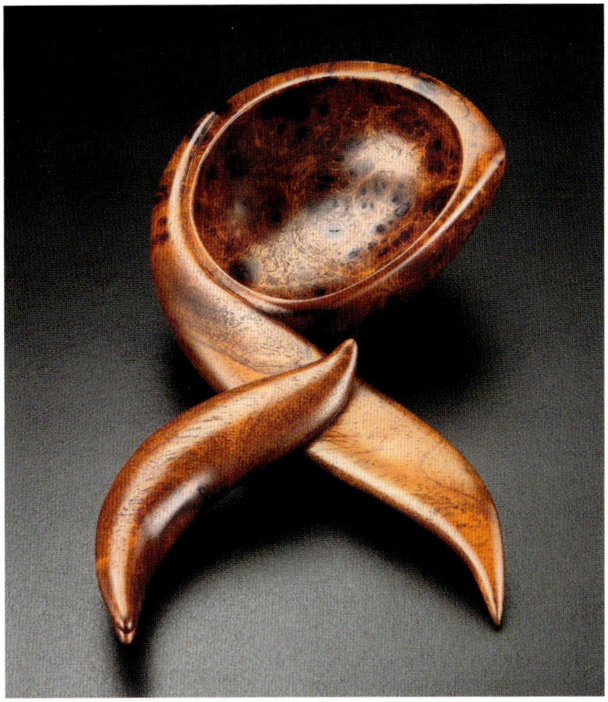

Dancer, 2012
Honduras mahogany | 2 ¼" x 4" x 8"

Algerita, 2012
Algerita | 2" x 7" x 1"

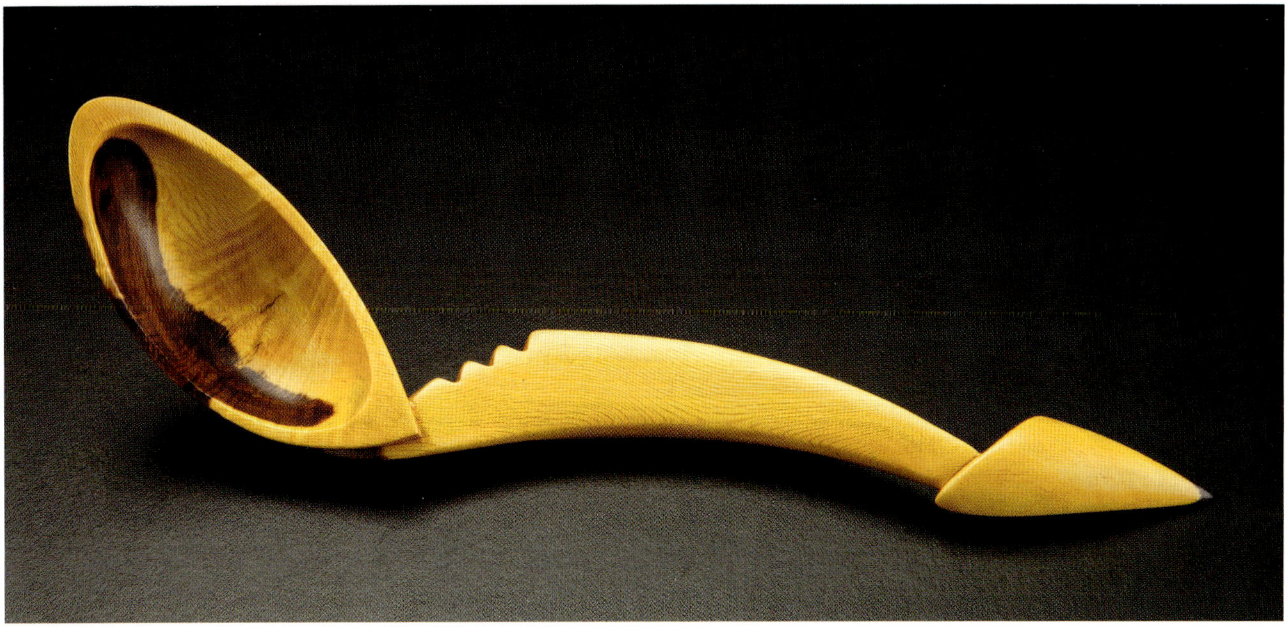

Merryll Saylan

UNITED STATES

Core Ore, 2012
Core, poplar, milk paint, acrylic
5" x 5" x 4"

I have always admired Robin Wood, so when I was given the opportunity to participate in this project using one of Robin's cores, I accepted. The piece of wood/ core I received was smaller and rougher than I had anticipated. There were four blackish slots on the bottom that I wasn't quite sure remained from the technique Robin used to mount his block. The piece was quite rough and showed tool marks, grooves, tears, shredded wood; additionally, because it had been turned from green wood, it had warped into an elliptical shape.

I originally intended to turn the core into a small bowl. I do not turn miniatures and thought the piece a bit small. I mentioned it to someone at The Center for Art in Wood and they said they could send me a second one that was one of the larger cores. When it arrived, it was smaller than the one I already had. Now I had two. I felt embarrassed and decided I would need to use both pieces.

Many of my pieces are housed in boxes; not only to contain them, but to focus on their shapes and forms, to highlight the colors or textures on them. I've always used scraps to make small feelies or small sculptures. The corner waste blocks left from my larger disk pieces I use to make small bowls. I thought the cores interesting as they were, and I decided I wanted to keep the essence and texture of the pieces and of the tools that made them—to change them minimally. I cut up the second core and used the larger one to make a lid on a box. The box became a place to hide the small cut-up pieces. I made two small pieces that nestle in your hand, a talisman. The magic that comes from working on a pole lathe (which I use), without power, I hoped might be represented in this small object.

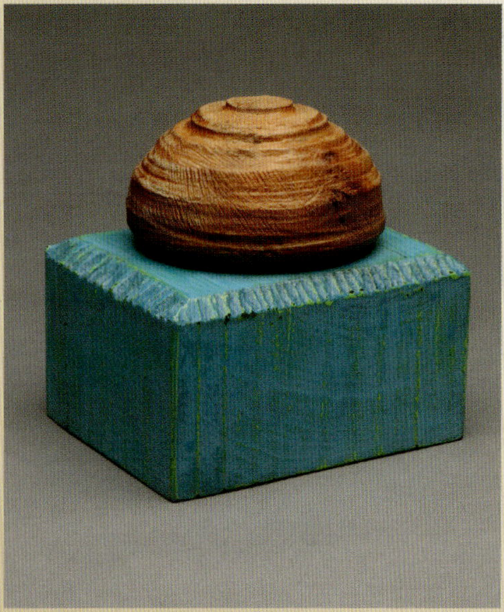

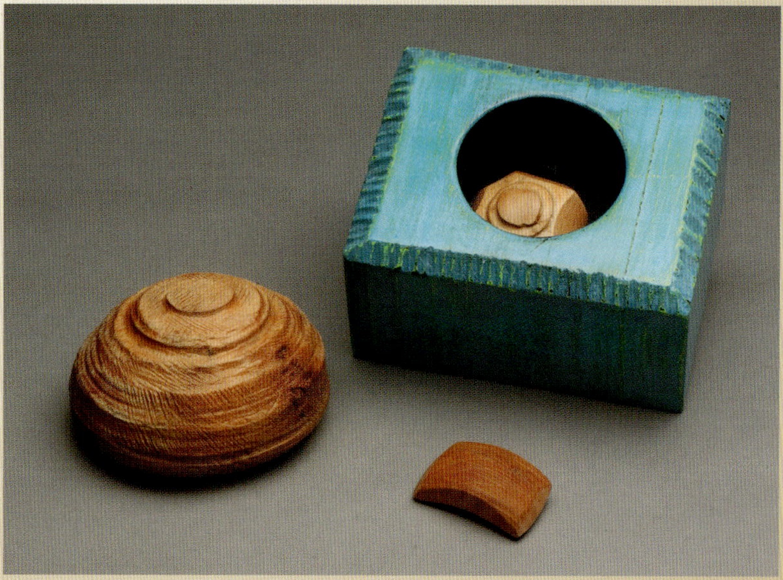

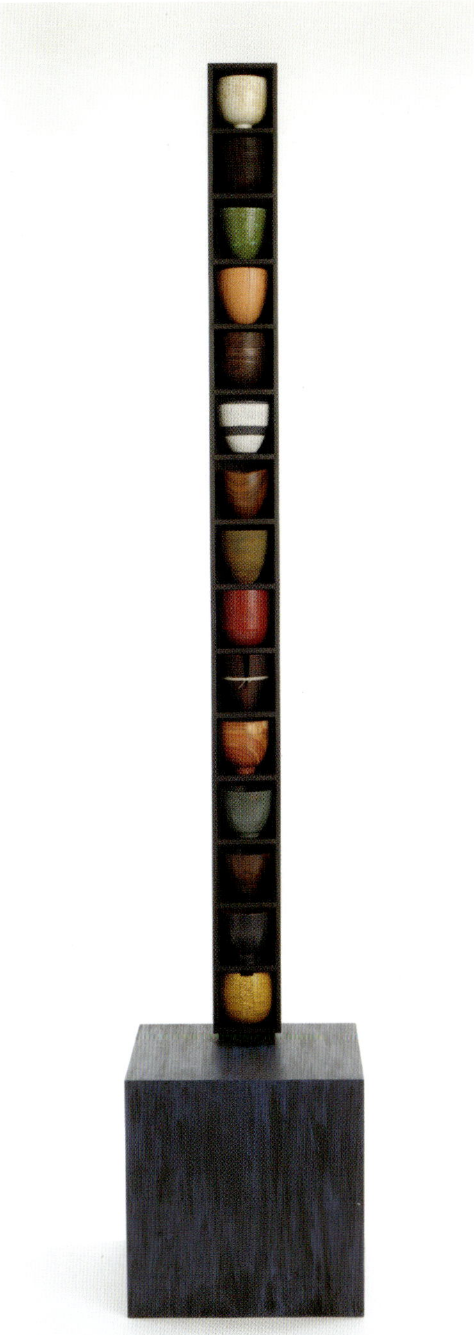

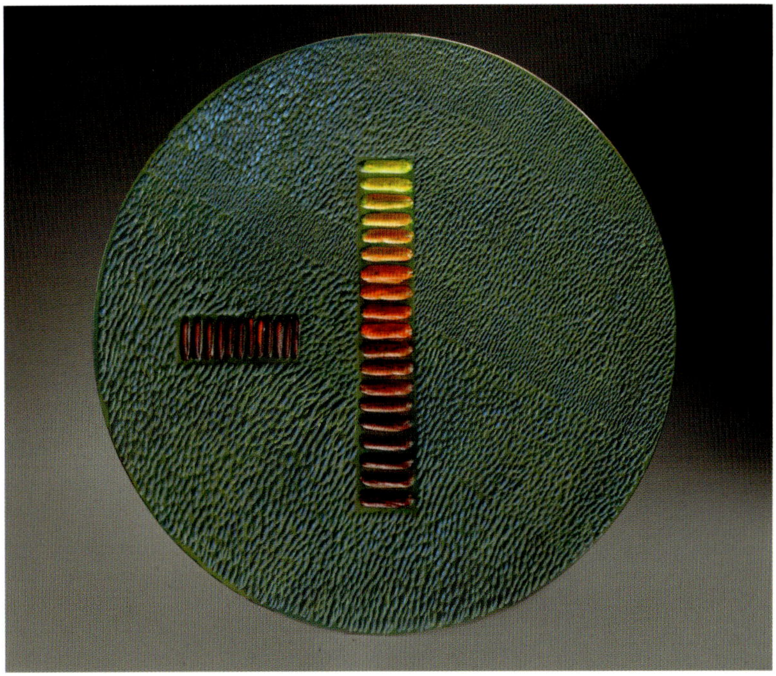

Boardwalk at St. Ives, 2006
Mahogany, milk paint, oil glaze
2" x Dia. 2

Tower of Bowls II, 2012/2013

Various woods, vertical grain fir for tower, ultralite MDF, polychromed (various paints) wire, linen thread
83" x 20 ⅜" x 20"

Michael Scarborough

UNITED STATES

Akai Maru (Red Circle), 2012
Core, paint, varnish, 23K gold leaf
1 ¾" x Dia. 4 ½"

My childhood years in Japan were the happiest of my youth. Despite spending twenty-five years singing opera internationally, I now find that creating lacquerware inspired by that time in Japan has made me more artistically fulfilled, and happier, than at any time in my adult life. It is a daily adventure in research, experimentation, discovery, and the meditation of a spinning lathe.

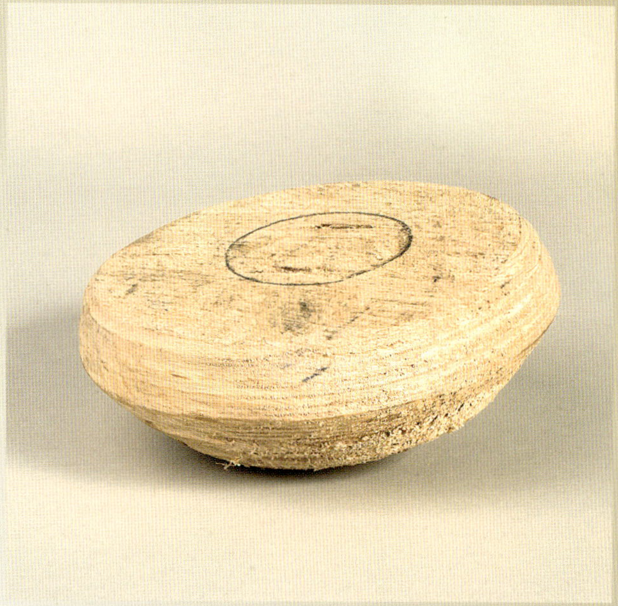

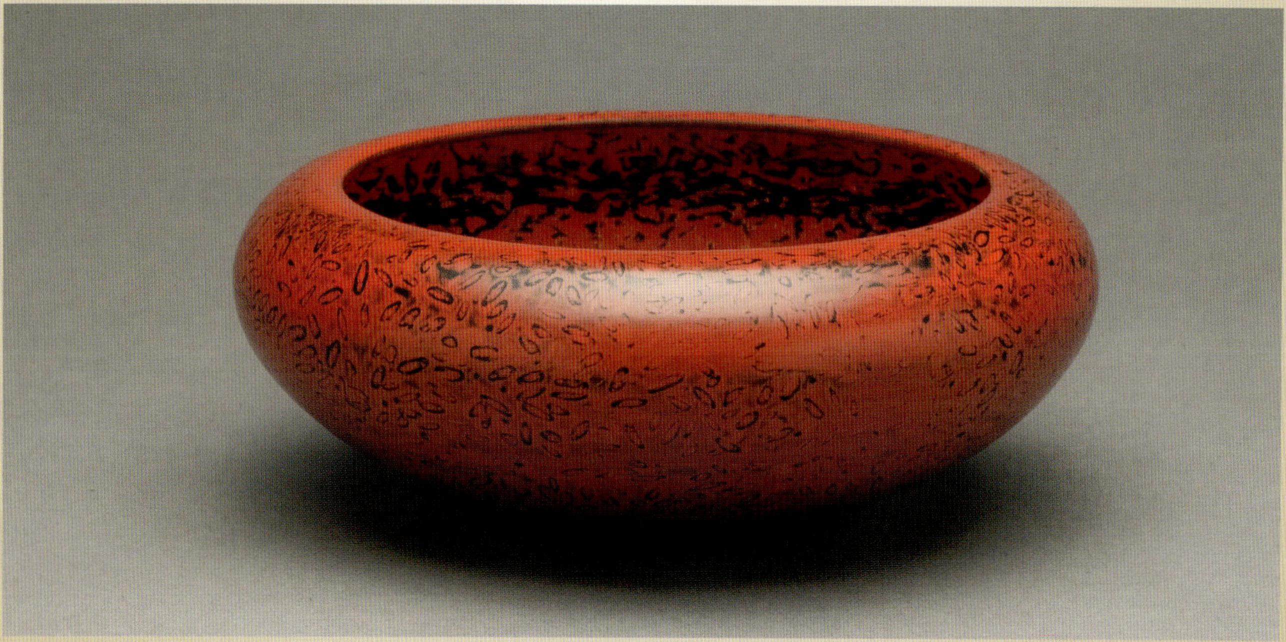

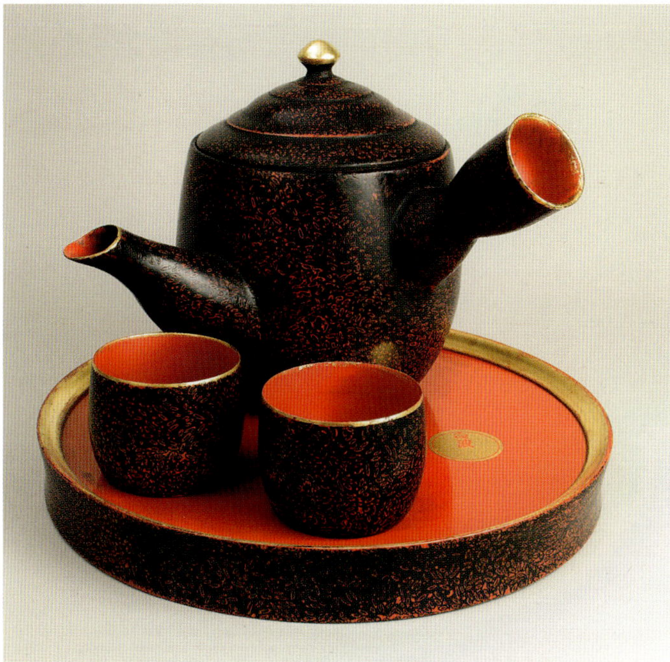

Winter Afternoon Tea, 2013

Sapele, paint, 23K gold leaf
7" x 9" x 6"

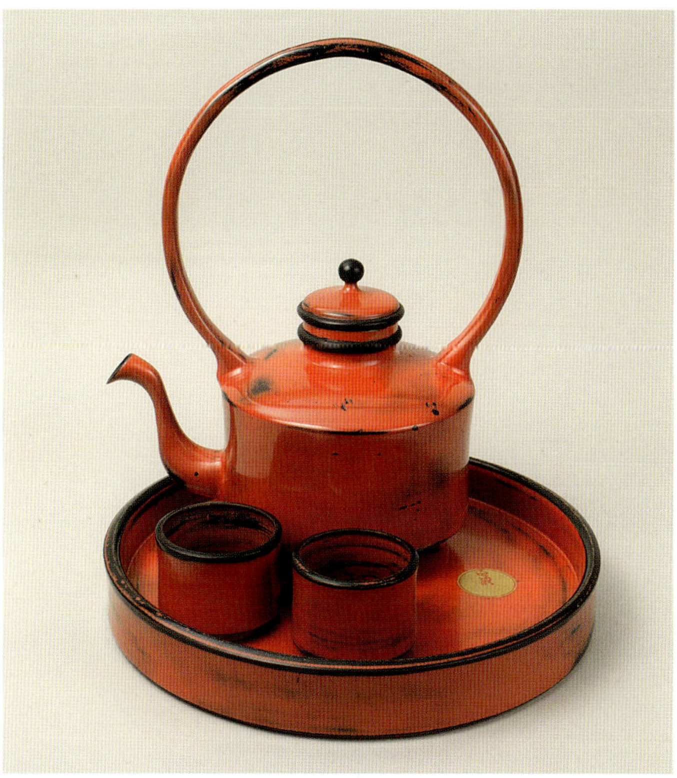

Akebono – Tea at Dawn, 2013

Maple, paint, 23K gold leaf
12" x Dia. 9½"
Photo by Michael Scarborough

David Sengel

UNITED STATES

My Grandfather Recycled Everything, 2012
Core, old wire, paint | 5" x Dia. 3"

My experience with object making began by using found objects, mostly metal and wood, and the process that uses or recycles material from some other time or place remains my favorite.

My grandfather in western Arkansas was a jack of all trades and a collector of objects that most would not value. When I cleaned out his garage after he died, I found sixty-three hammers. I decided to collect hammers. There were also many rolls of wire of various material and gauges. The core that was sent to me brought back images of that, and I went from there.

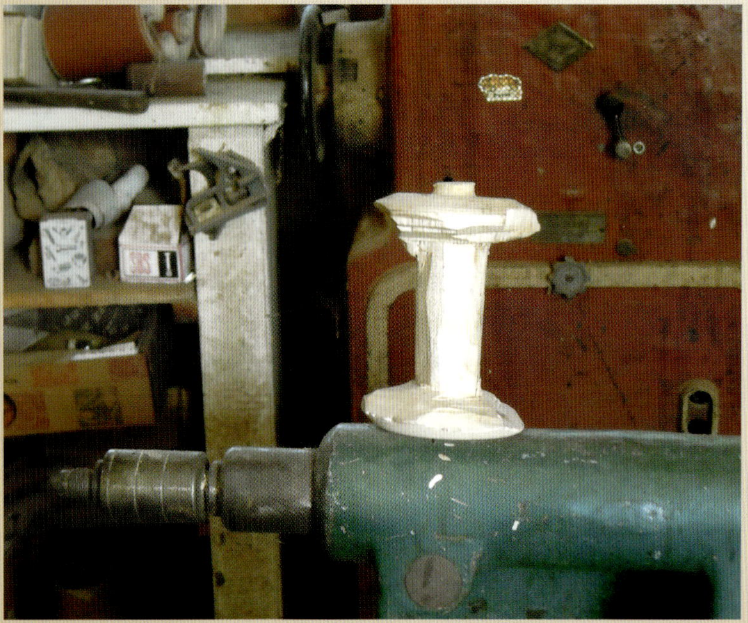

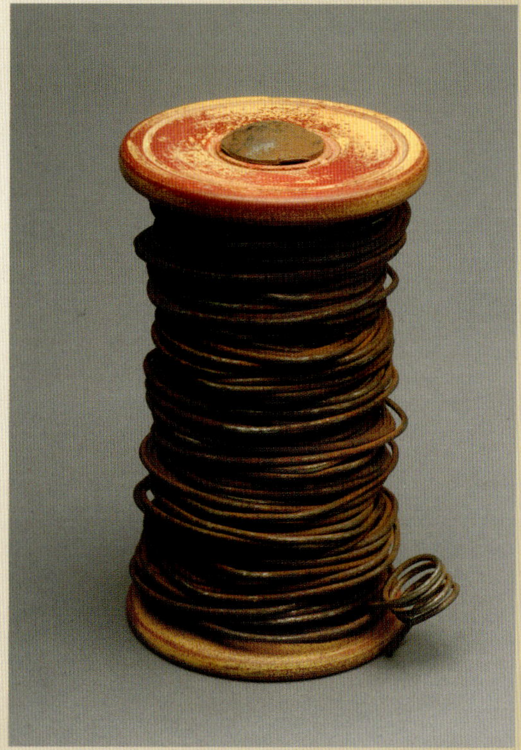

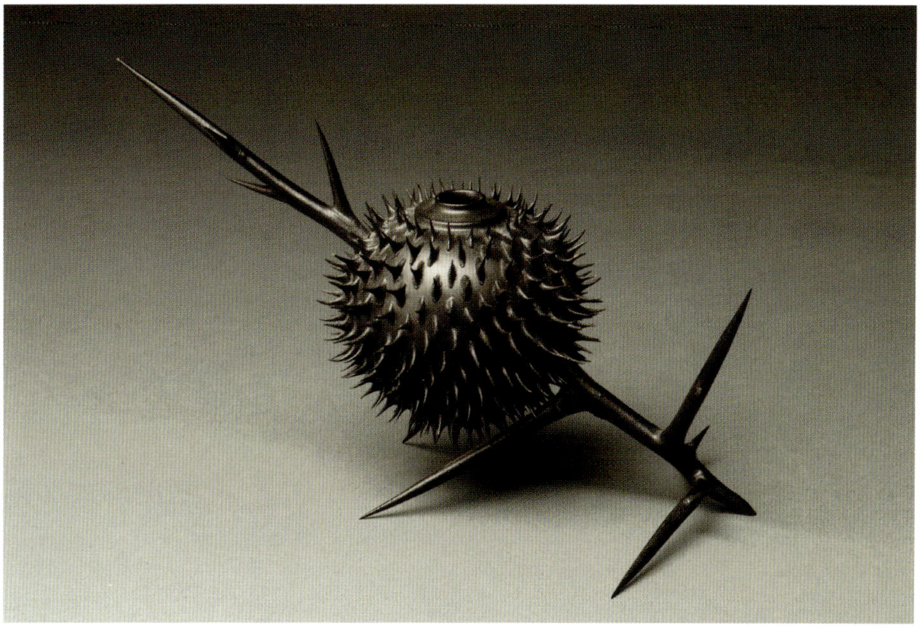

Thorned Vessel, 1993

Wood, paint, rose and locust thorns
4 ¼" x 4 ½" x 7 ½"
The Center for Art in Wood Museum Collection,
Donated by Bruce A. Kaiser.

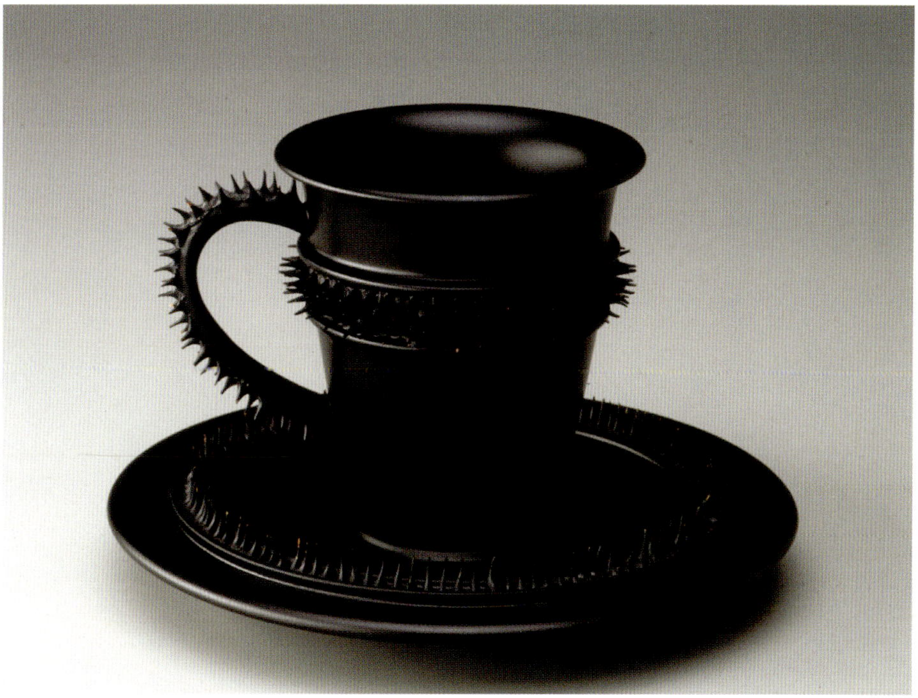

Teacup, 1996

Pear wood, black paint
3 ¼" x Dia. 5 ½"
The Center for Art in Wood Museum Collection,
Donated by the artist.

Jack Slentz

UNITED STATES

A Little Jack Slentz, 2012
Core | 1 ½" x 1 ½" x 1 ½"

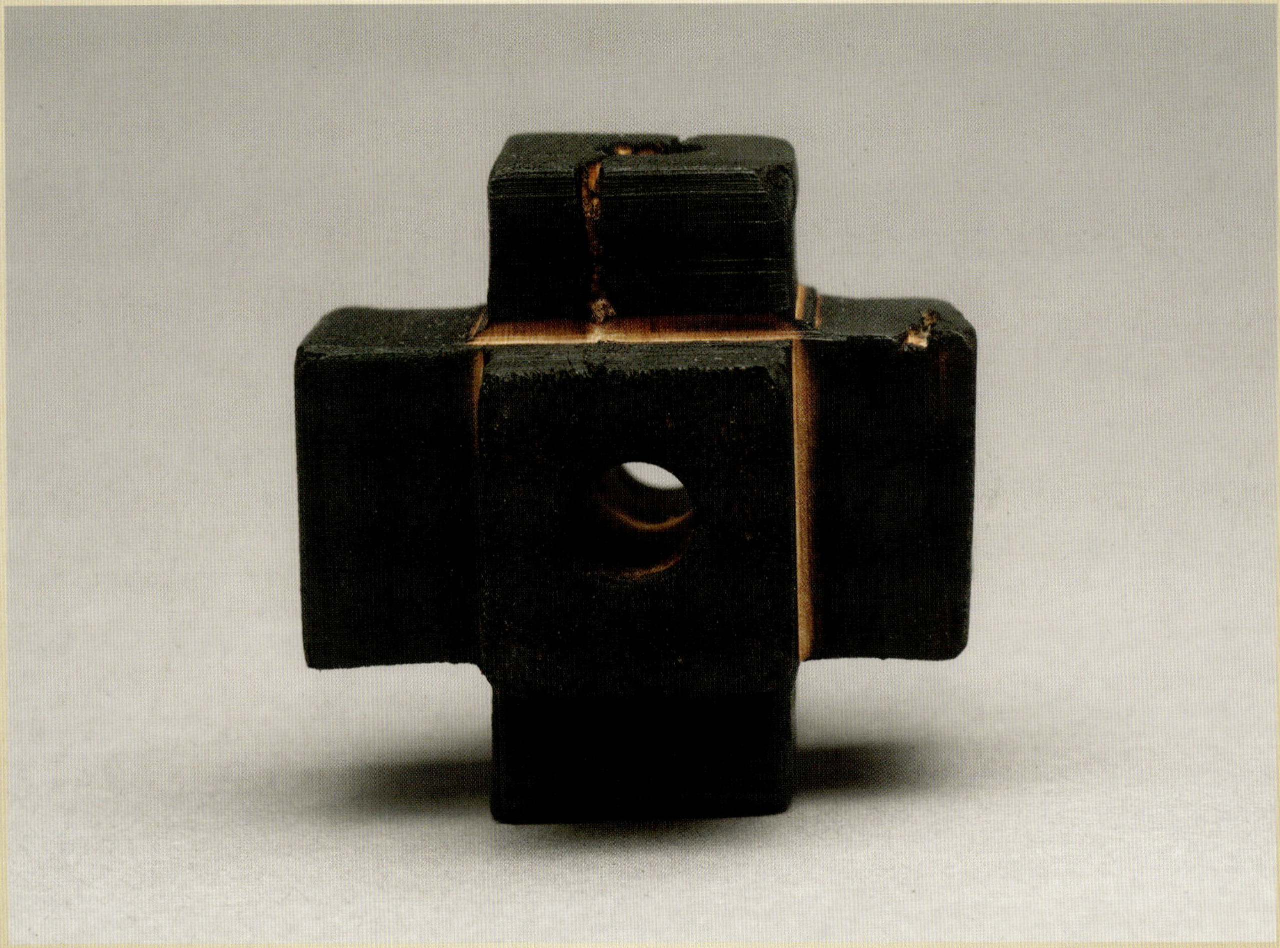

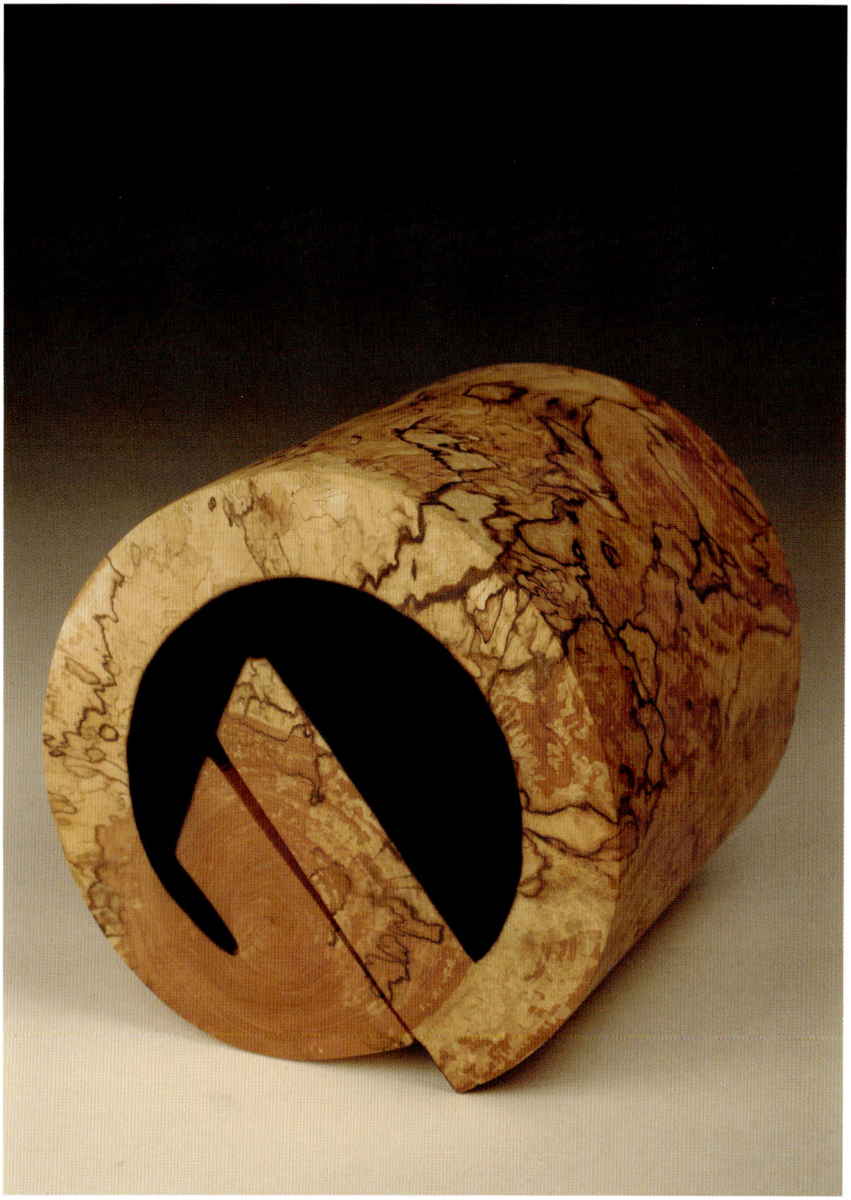

Circle in, 2012

Cherry burl | 8" x 8" x 9"

Brad Smith

UNITED STATES

165 Heels, 2012
Core, cherry, poplar, willow, ash, milk paint
34" x 13 ½" x 13 ½"
Photo by Joseph Kolasinski

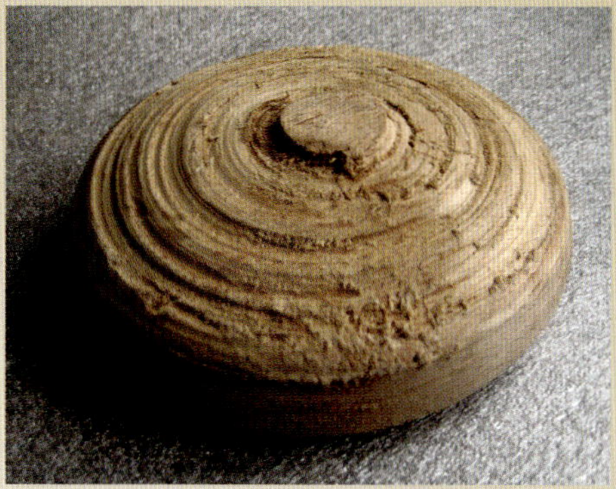

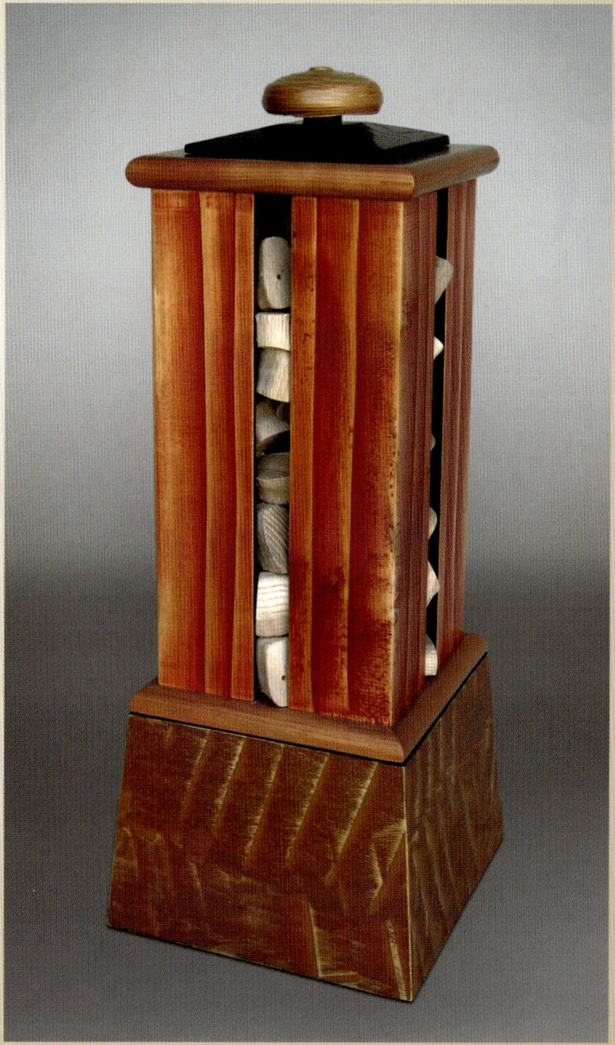

165 Heels is my interpretation for the CORES project. I've incorporated cut-offs from my own axe handle production. I call these pieces heels. I am having fun with the concept of using a scrap or discarded piece of wood as the focus for a new piece. I've used Robin Wood's core as a very functional handle to lift the lid of my piece and expose the heels.

I make furniture because I really enjoy the process. I like everything about it, from starting with a raw log to designing and building the piece to applying the finish.

I grew up on a farm, so I've used that as a theme in my work. It manifests itself in the use of farm-related parts in my furniture. I try to hide these parts in plain sight; it is not immediately obvious that they are axe handles or a pitchfork, but it becomes a fun discovering process as the new viewer sees what they are looking at.

My manufacturing process uses a century-old lathe, which I bought from a tool company when they were going out of business. At first, I bought handles in bulk from them, but now I can make my own in-house. Having this machine in my shop has given me the chance to push the creativity of what this old beauty is capable of. The spiraled texture from this unique lathe has become a foundation look throughout my furniture designs.

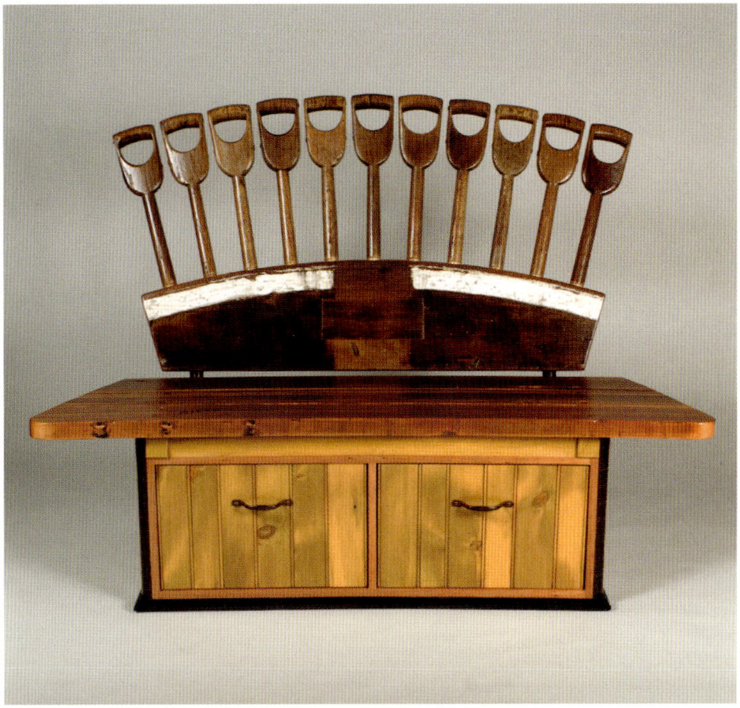

Shovel Handle Bench, 2012

Recycled laminated arched rafters, salvaged shovel handles, salvaged barn siding, cherry, charred ash
44" x 61" x 30"

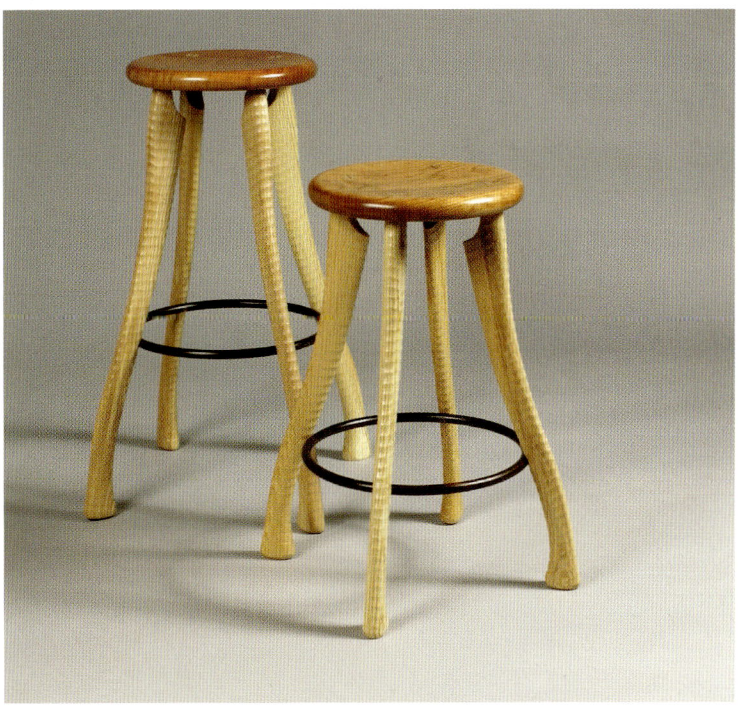

Ax Handle Stools, 2012

Turned ash ax handle legs, cherry seat, steel footrest
Counter height: 25" x 16" x 16";
Bar height: 30" x 17" x 17"

Alan Stirt

UNITED STATES

Textured Bowl, 2012
Core (oak), milk paint | 2 ½" x Dia. 3 ⅛"
Photo by Alan Stirt

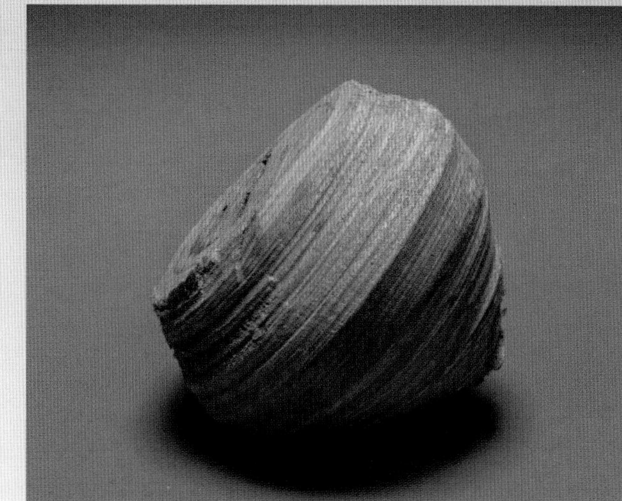

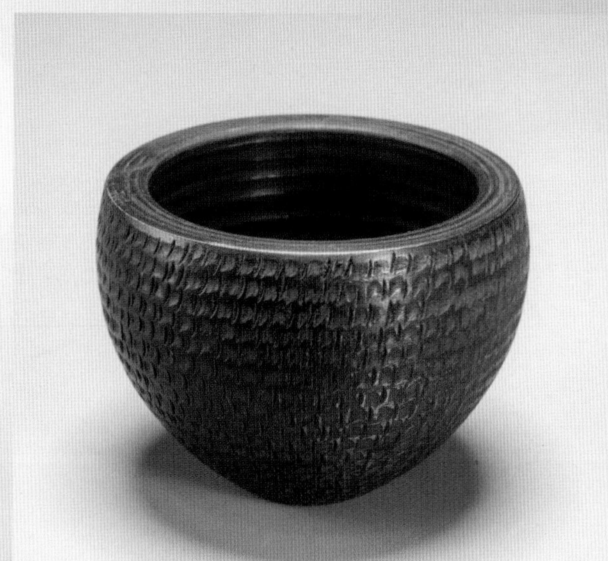

Like much of my recent work, this piece uses wood not for its grain patterns but for its structural and tactile properties.

With its patterns that are both orderly and irregular, this bowl echoes both ageless pottery forms and objects of the natural world.

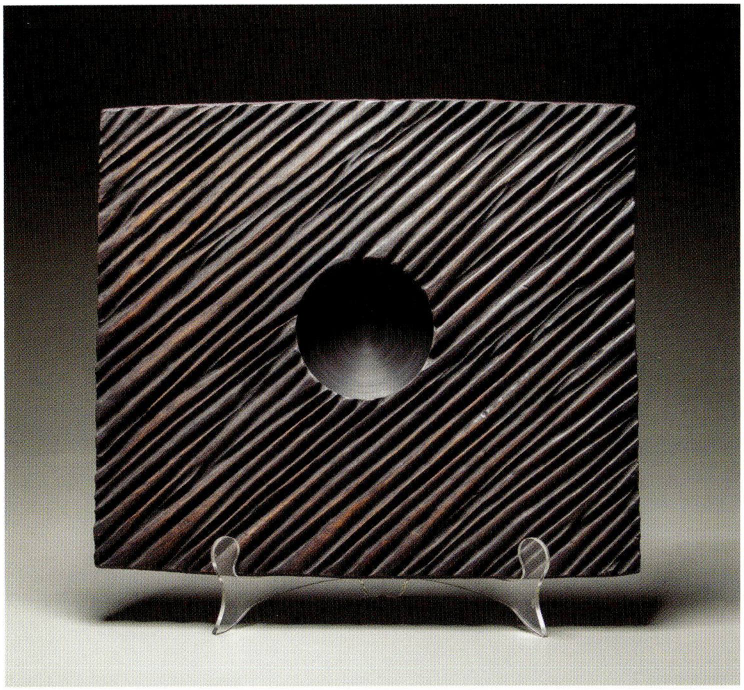

Crowded Square Bowl, 1998
Maple with black gesso
2 ½" x 14" x 14"

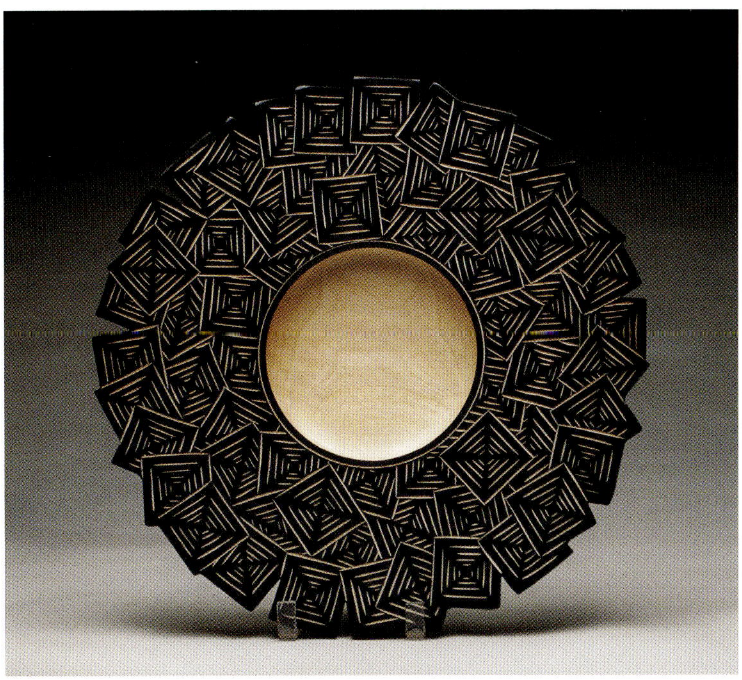

Erosion Series, 2011
Black cherry with milk paint
12 ¾" x 15" x 1 ½"

Holly Tornheim

UNITED STATES

Between Tides, 2012
Core | 1 ¼" x 4" x 4"

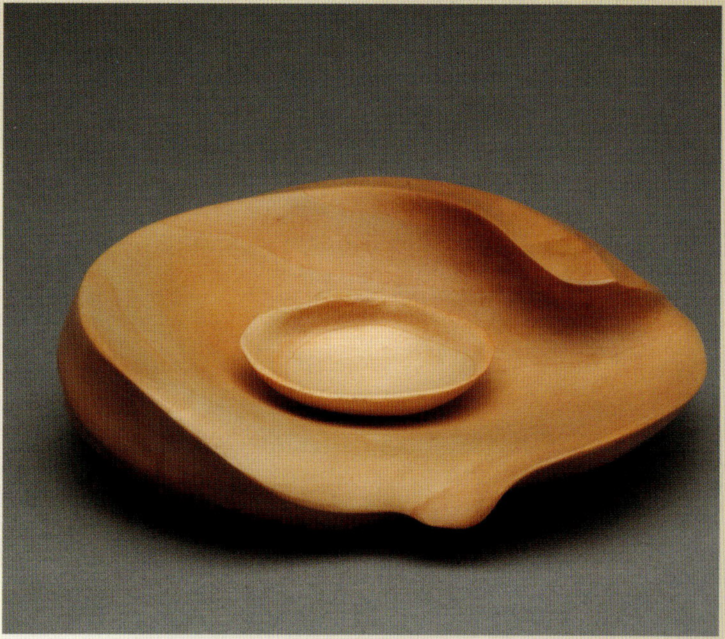

As an artist, I find the natural world—from the molecular to the human-scale to the cosmos—provides a continuous source of inspiration to me. As a carpenter, door and furniture maker, and carver of both sculpture and functional pieces, I value the versatility and the warm-to-the-touch feel and glow of polished wood. The whorls in the core that I was given brought to mind the movement of water and layers of growth in shells and led to the composition of this piece.

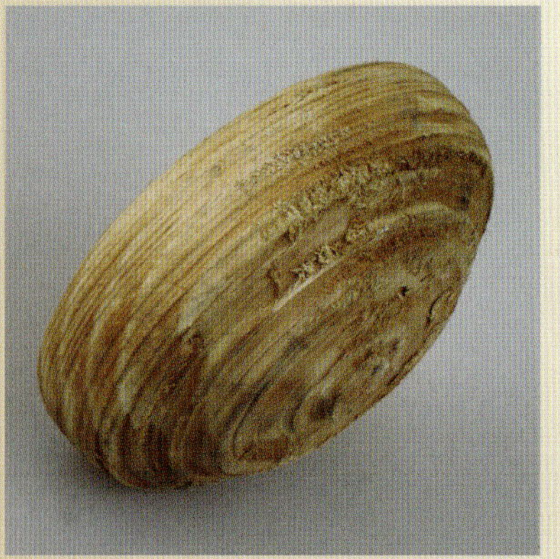

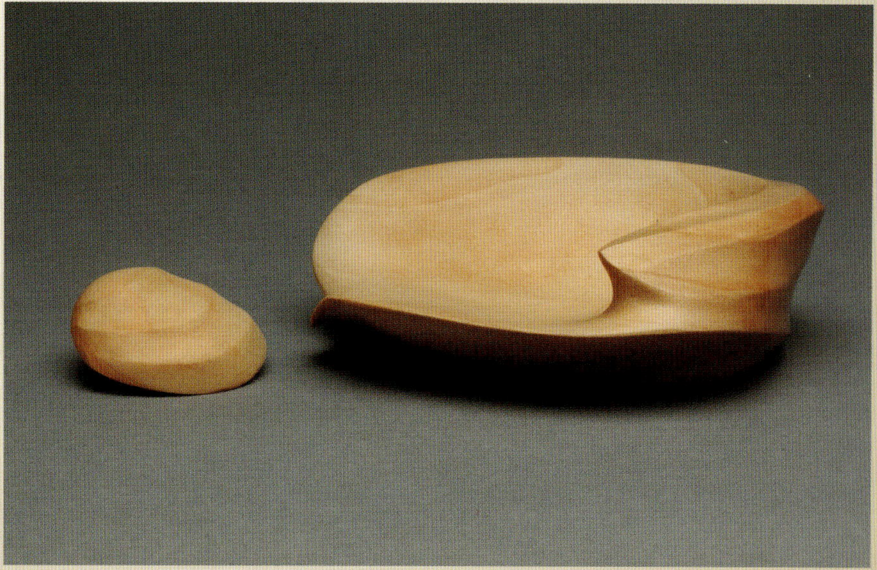

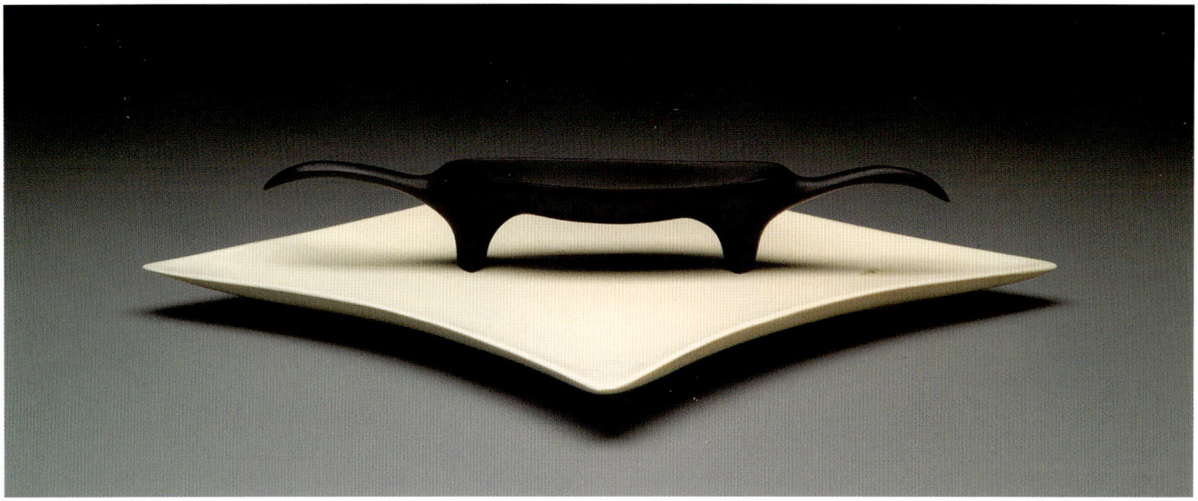

Black vessell, 2005 African blackwood, holly | 2" x 12" x 10"

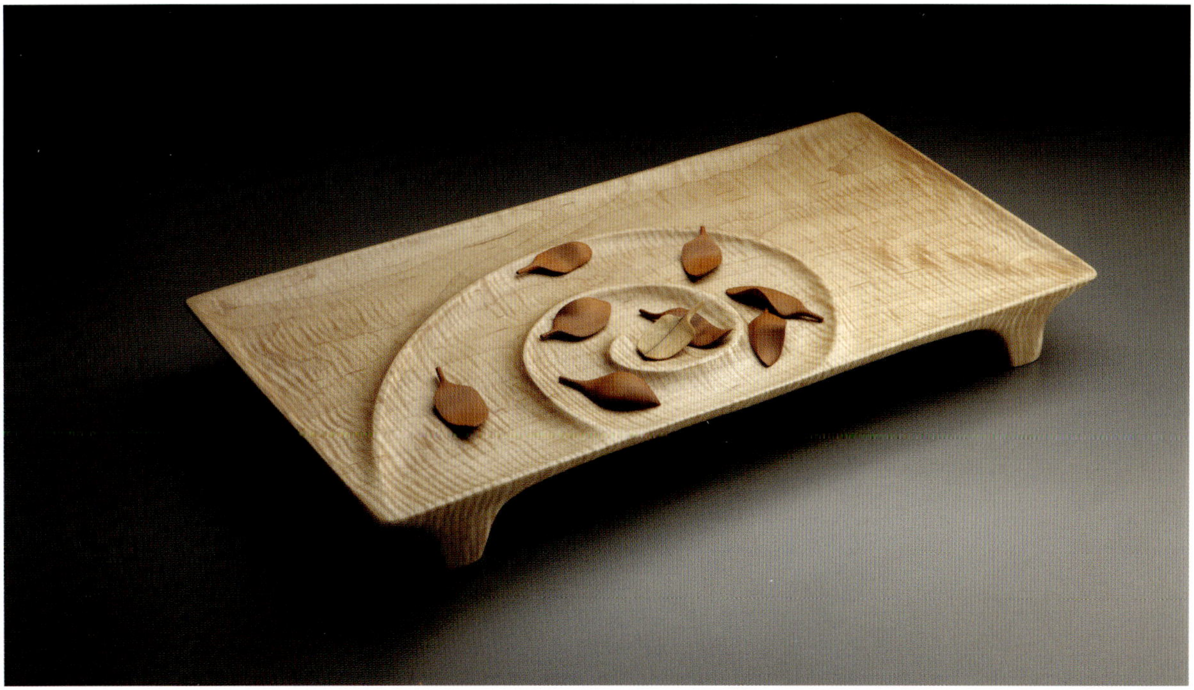

Gyre, 2011 Fiddleback maple, Pacific yew, spalted maple | 2 ¼" x 17 ¾" x 8 ½"

Neil Turner

WESTERN AUSTRALIA

Coral Core, 2012 | Core | 2 ⅝" x Dia. 4"
Photo by Suellen Turner

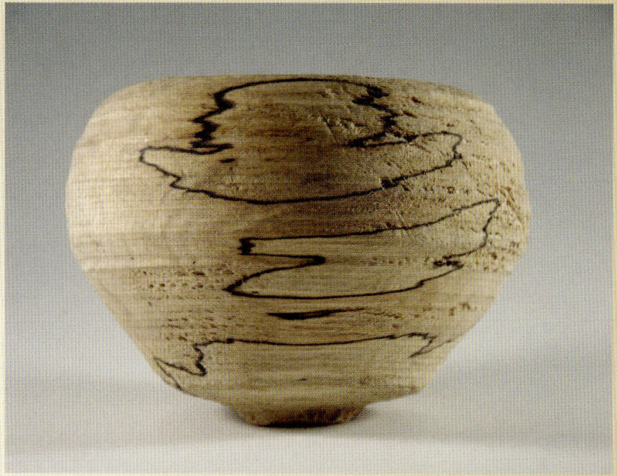

At the time, I was exploring a new texture that had been inspired by coral on my local beach. This seemed like an opportune time to explore the balance between a fragile form and intricate embellishment whilst using the spalting to frame the pieces I didn't embellish.

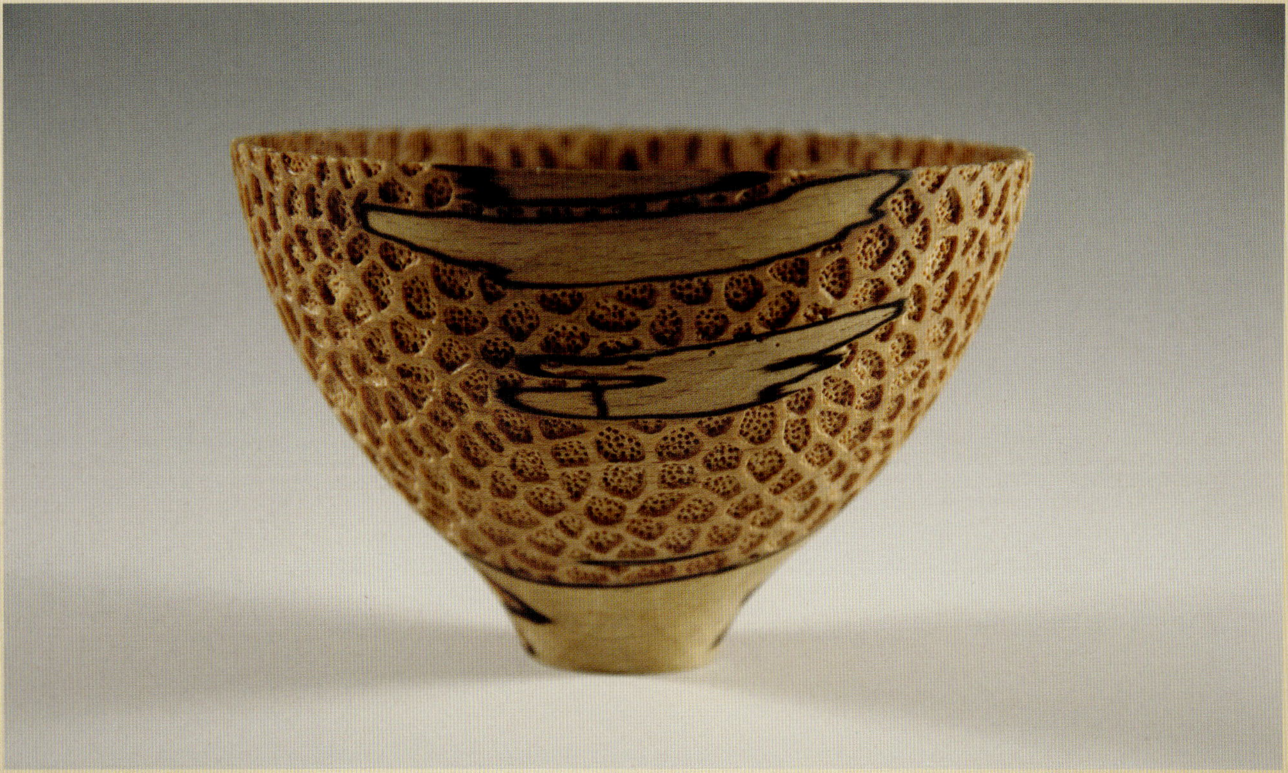

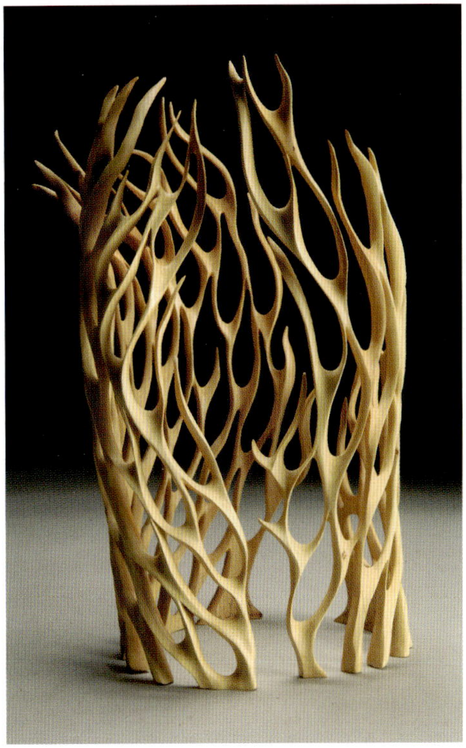

2 Piece Fire, 2005

Sandalwood | 11 ¾" x 13 ¾" x 7 ½"

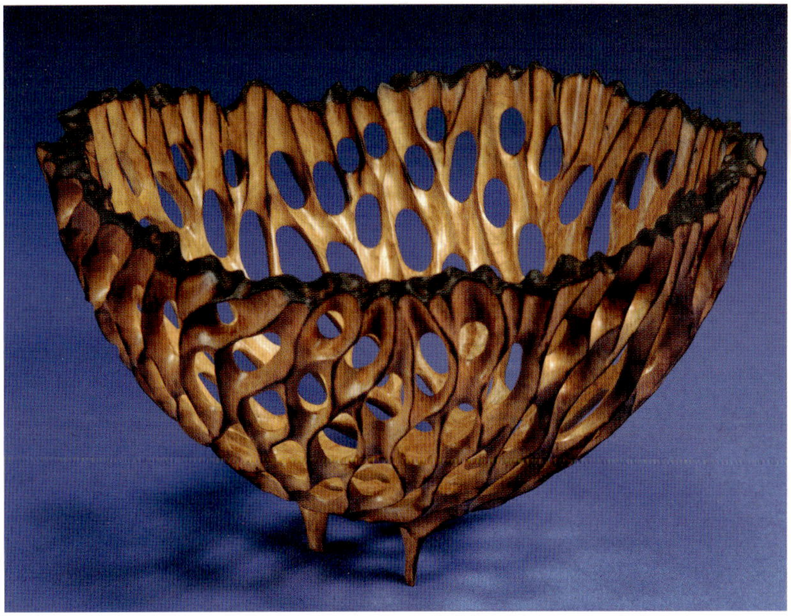

Spirit Dreaming, 2006

Yorkgum root burl | Dia. 6"

Joël Urruty

UNITED STATES

Casa, 2012
Core, 23K gold leaf | 6 ½" x 3 ½" x 2"
Photo by Joël Urruty

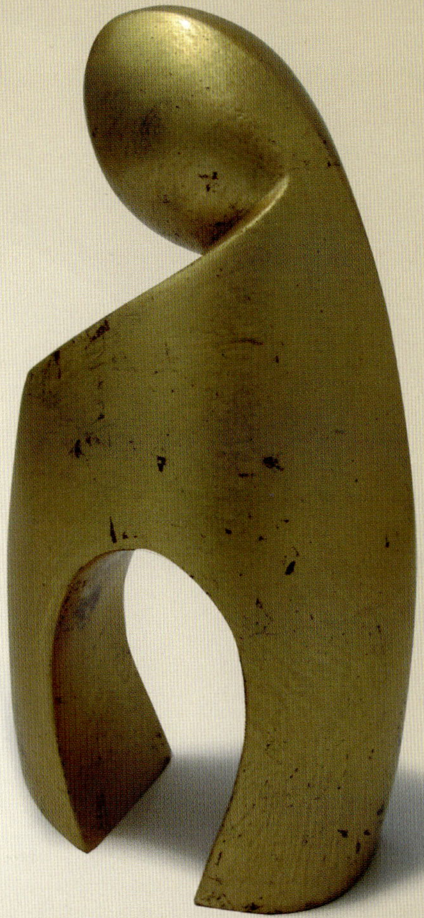

As an artist, I strive to create elegant sculptures that capture the true essence of the subject matter. Form, line, and surface are used as the visual language. The figure is abstracted to a minimalist form, void of any superfluous information. The primary material, wood, is often masked by paint to allow the form to take precedence over the material. Monochromatic colors, such as black or white, are often used on the sculptures, allowing light and shadow to play off the subtle shifting facets of the sculptures.

This is what I do. Why I do it, I don't really know. I do know that there is something deep inside that drives me to make these things—things I don't completely understand myself. But when a piece is finished and it feels right, I know I have done what it was I was supposed to do and move on to the next.

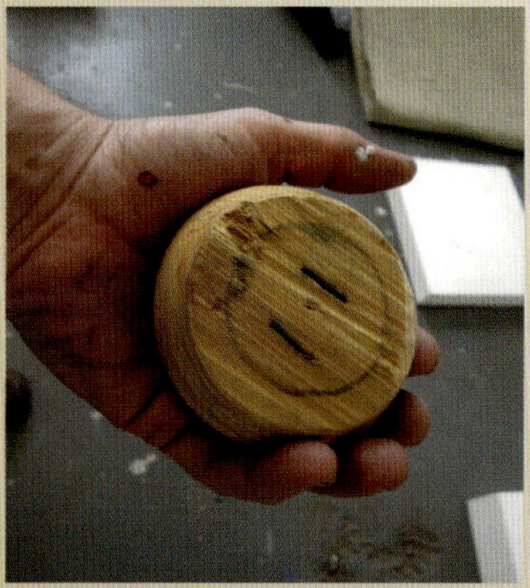

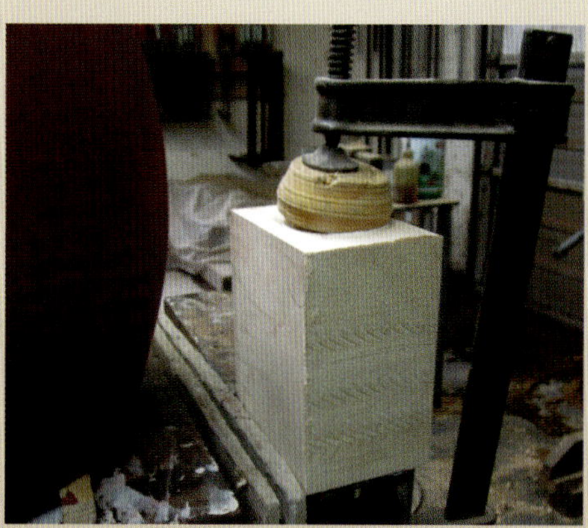

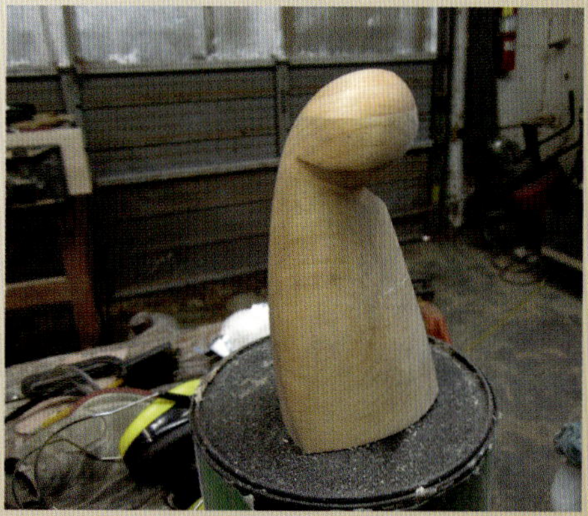

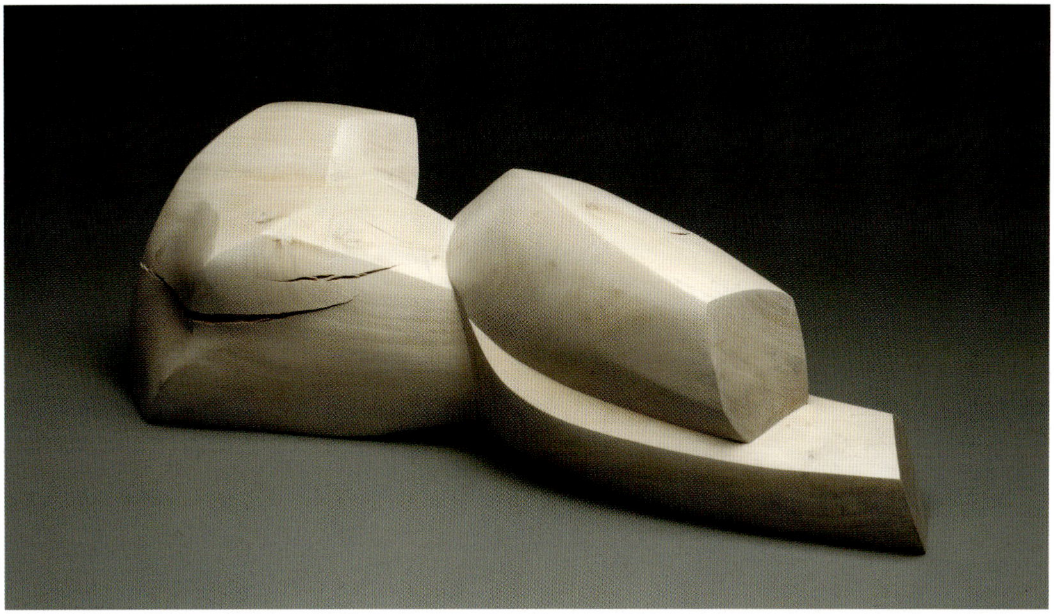

Reclining Nude, 2004

Wood | 9" x 20" x 7"

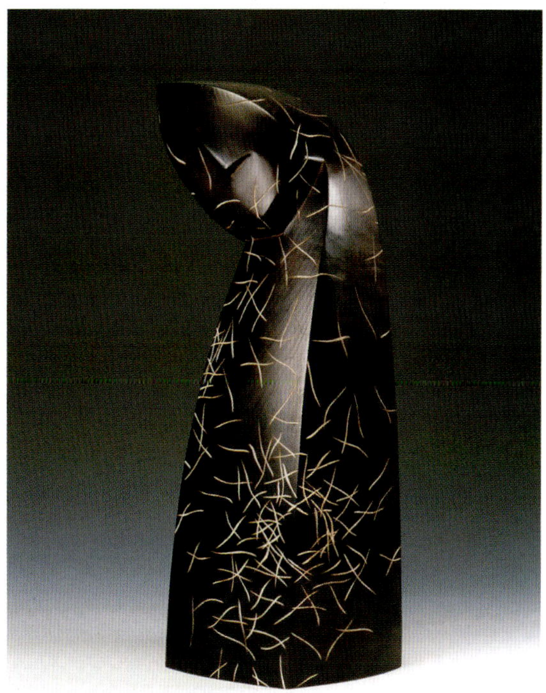

Head #3, 2004

Maple and paint | 22 ½" x 11" x 7"

Derek Weidman

UNITED STATES

Little World, 2012
Core, cherry, acrylic | 4" x 3" x 1"

This particular core was quite weathered, rotted almost, or at least eaten away, and reminded me somewhat of the outside of a bee/wasp nest. I find bees to be quite remarkable creatures, selfless and amazing in the way they work towards the betterment of their colony. There is a beauty to their civilization, their tiny world, and indeed contrasts so enormously at times with the wide range of beings engaged in our own human experience, with the tyrants and martyrs all under one roof. I am glad we humans are not mere drones, but the way of bees is inspiring nonetheless. For *Little World,* I thought bees' collective unity seems to fit nicely into the shape of a circle, a line connected perfectly to itself.

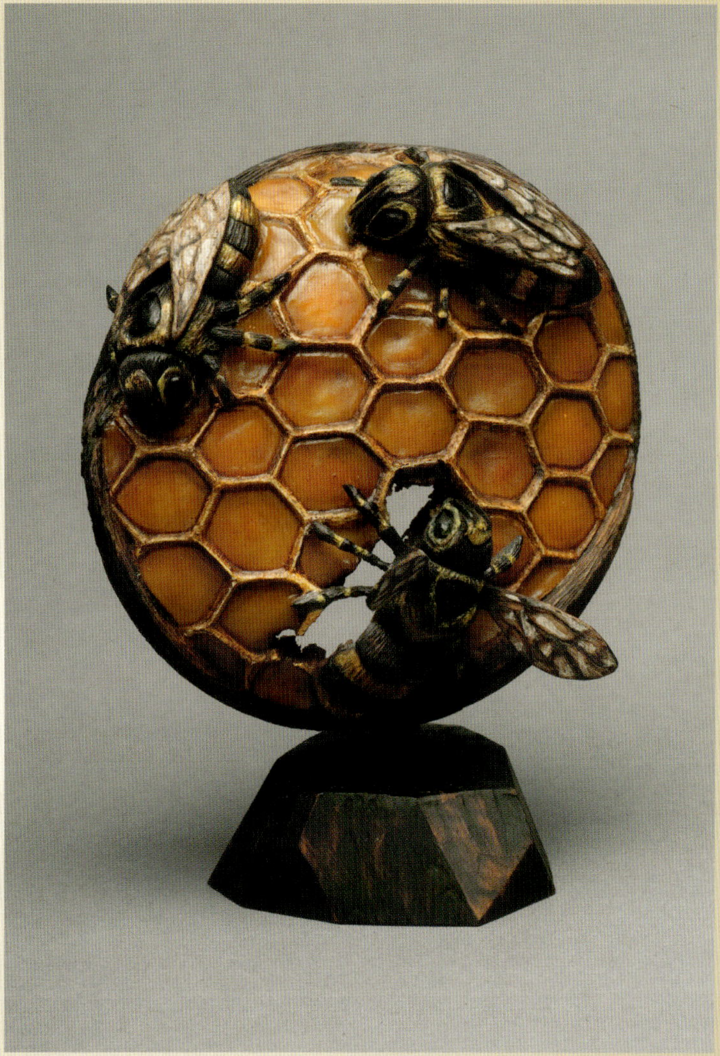

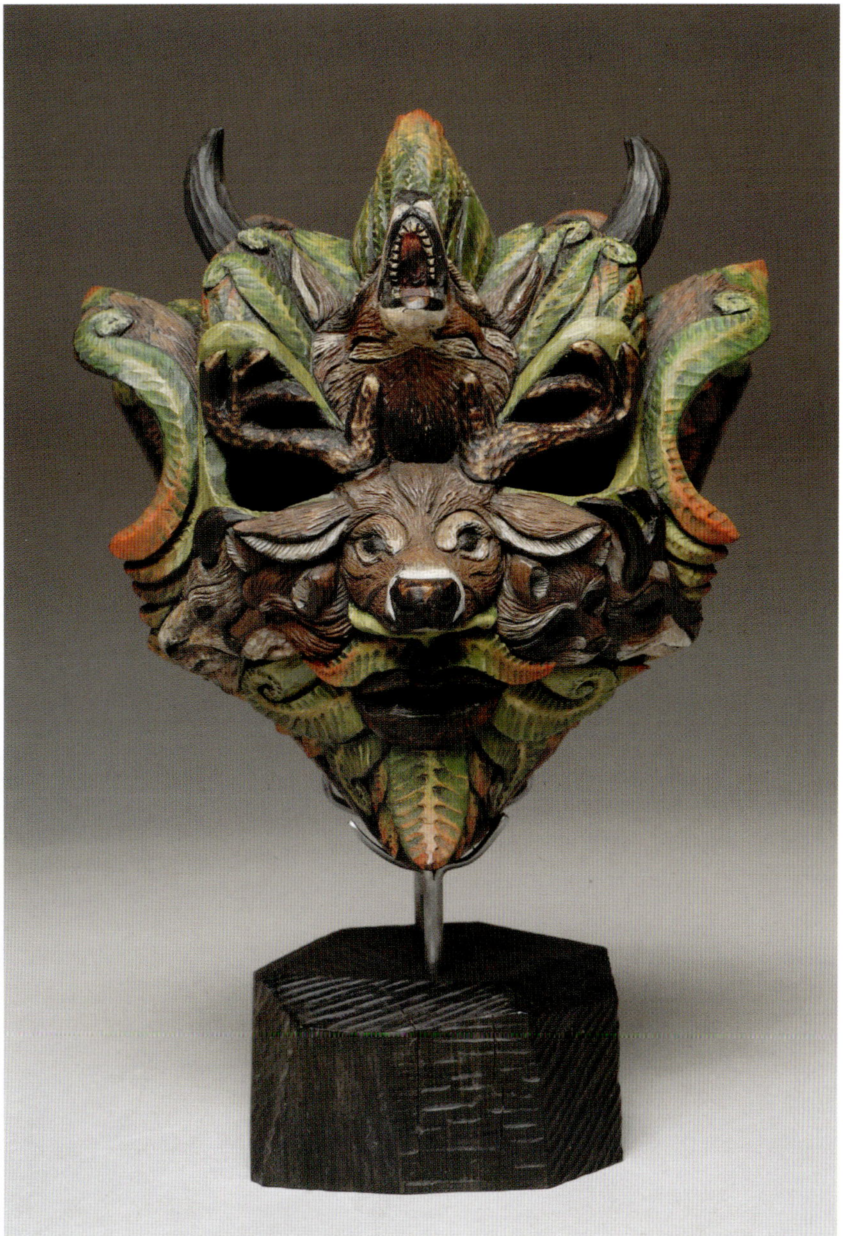

Pan, 2008 Holly, ebony, wood, acrylic paint | 8" x 5" x 6"

Christopher Weiland

UNITED STATES

Spin Top Series: Cast and Die, 2012
Core (beech), maple, cardboard | 5" x 4" x 4"
Photo by Roy Engelbrecht

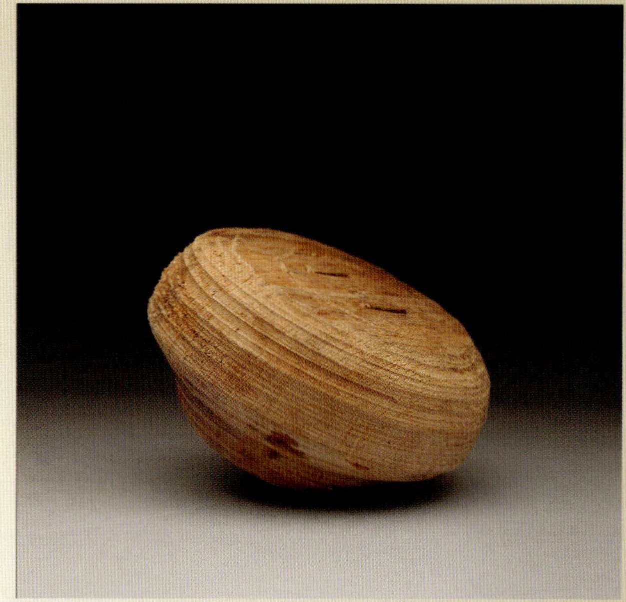

Being part of the *Robin Wood's CORES Recycled* exhibition and fundraiser gives me the opportunity to express my personal gratitude to The Center for Art in Wood for its continued contributions to the contemporary turning movement and to revisit my *Spin Top* series. The core remnant has been re-turned to one of my favorite top forms. It's classified as a palm spinner. Its performance/balance rating from 1 to 10 is a 10.

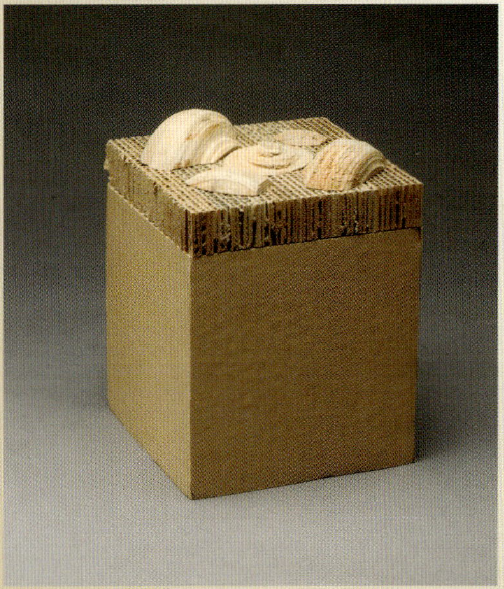

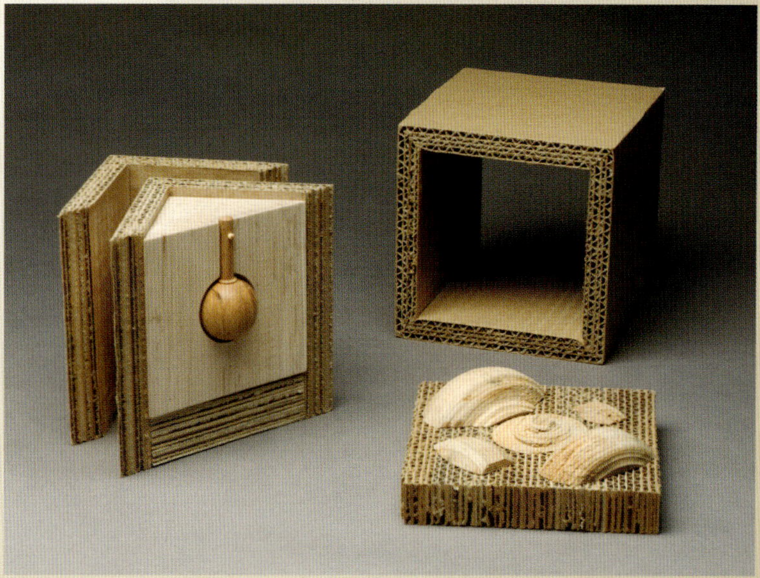

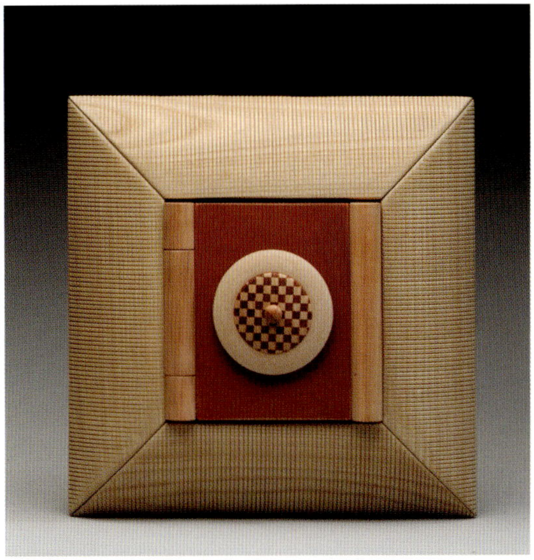

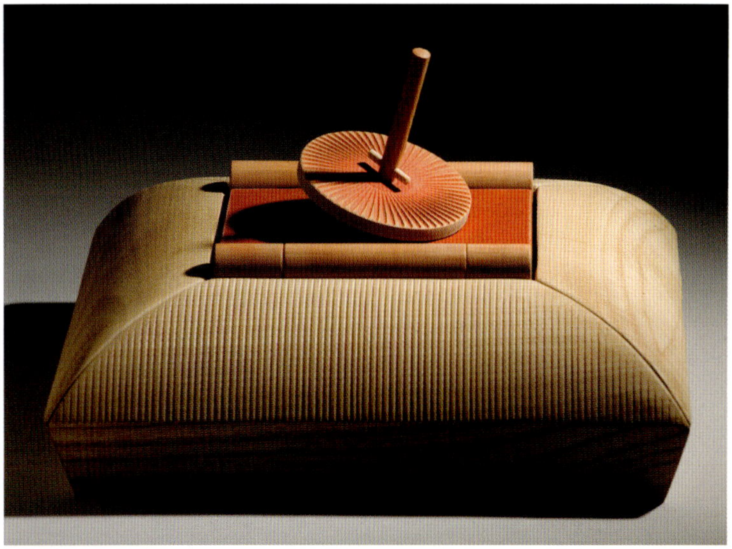

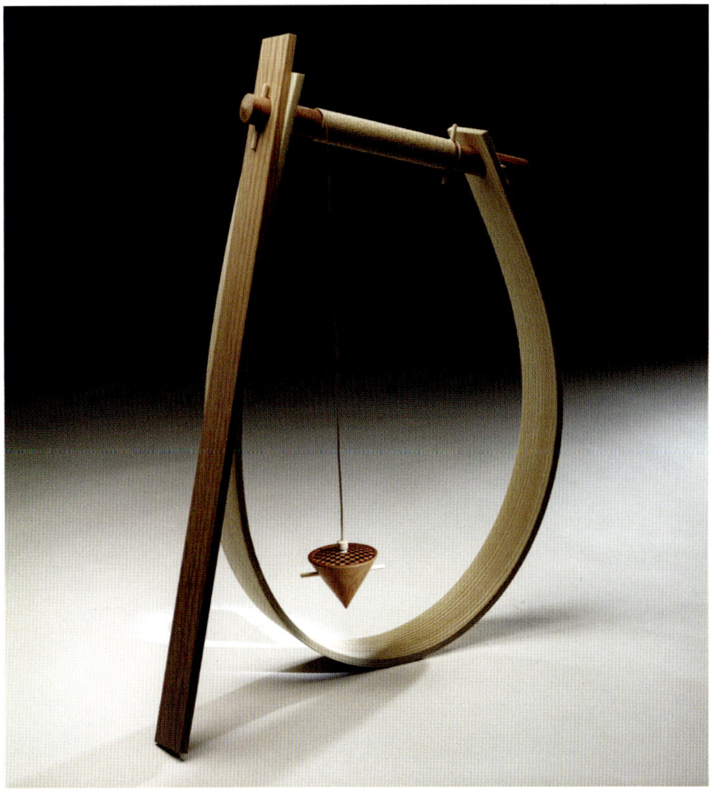

Two images above:
Pennsylvania Governor's Award, 2006

Catalpa, mahogany, maple, pear, MDF | 4" x 12" x 12"

Study #1: Centered Series, 2004

Elm, ash, maple, pear, mahogany, rush | 26" x 20" x 6"

Kim Winkle

UNITED STATES

Hub, 2012
Core, milk paint, wire, thread | 10" x 10" x 20"
Photo by Dan Carothers

Employing traditional furniture making techniques and materials, I build forms and structures with results that are, oftentimes, untraditional. I use hardwood, paint, and graphite to create my works. The forms are generally streamlined in order to better play the role of an empty canvas for color and line. I activate the wood by painting and drawing onto its surface. This painting is not an act of irreverence for the material; instead I am interested in realizing its potential as something other than its naked self. My color palette is rich yet flat. I animate the painted surface with drawn marks consisting of varied arrangements of lines and dots; the combination of these marks results in an exciting, and somewhat quirky, dialogue of characters. These inscriptions serve as pattern, embellishment, and residual evidence of my hand. I strive to create an apparent sense of spontaneity, chaos with order, rhythm and gesture with these marks; all working in concert to imbue the object with individuality and charm.

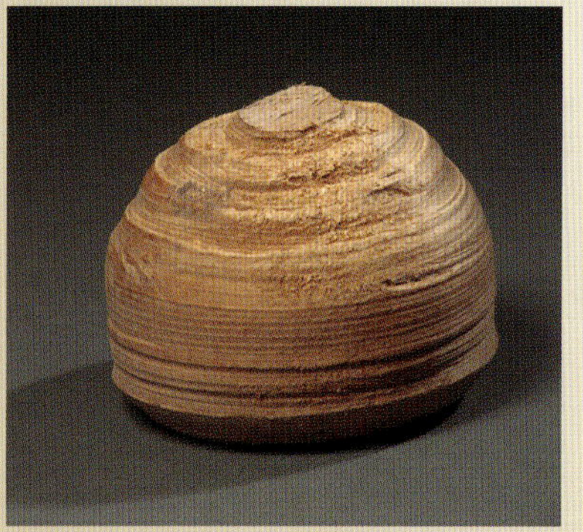

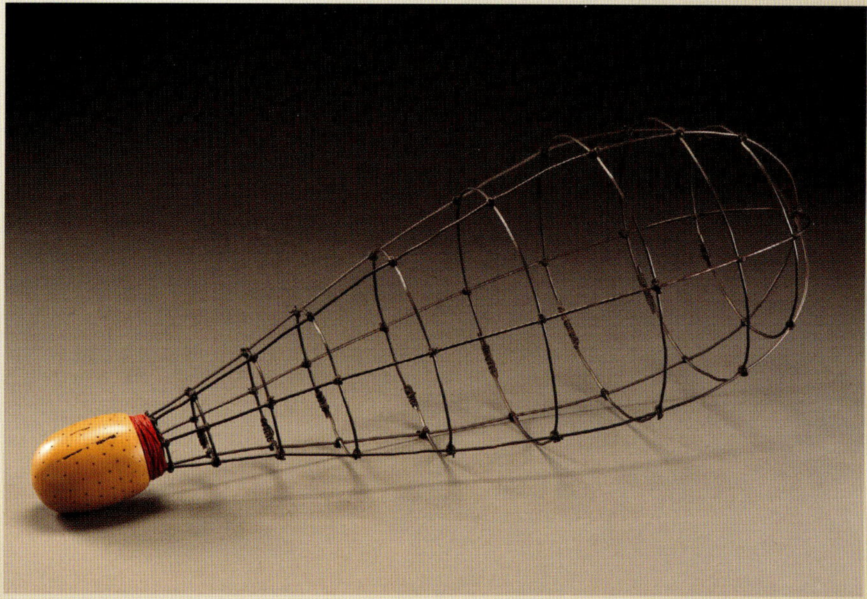

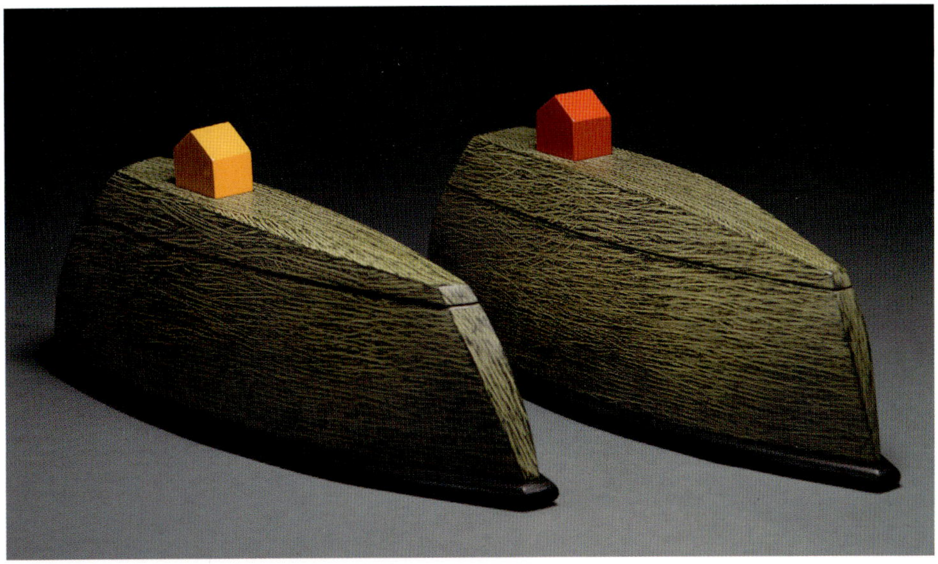

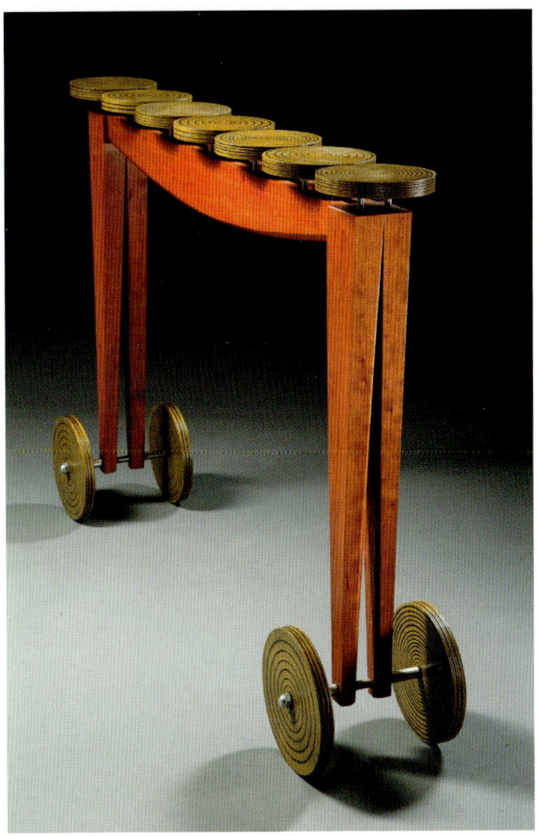

House on a Hill Boxes, 2012

Polychrome poplar | 10" x 20" x 8

Spinner Table, 2003

Cherry, aluminum, polychrome fiberboard | 36" x 48" x 14"

Robin Wood

DERBYSHIRE, ENGLAND

Art, 2012
Core, digital media (with a personal message from Robin Wood) | 2 ¼" x Dia. 2 ½"

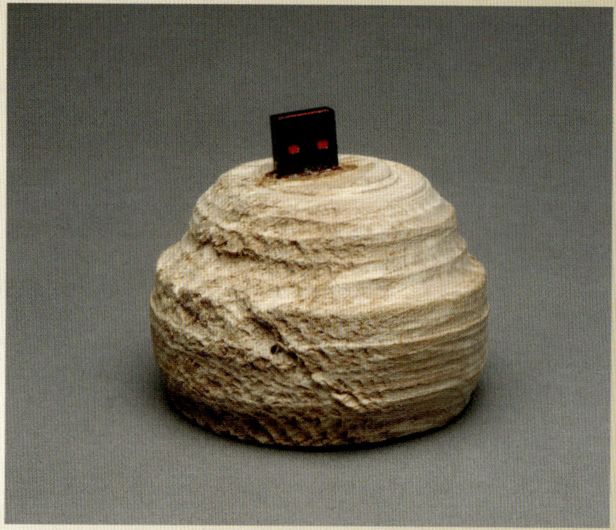

My original piece *Cor Blimey* was part video, part installation, part comment on the useful vs. the useless and part homage to turners past. I am passionate about the value of making things by hand in the twenty-first century, not only "art" but functional objects to enrich daily lives. I find it difficult to show this work in a critical context; mostly the art world does not accept it as having meaning. I personally think that we live in a time of mass consumption where few folk have any idea of how the stuff they consume is made. I believe questioning how that stuff is made and making viable alternatives by hand has more meaning than most "artwork." Not only that but because these functional objects get used every day they tend to work their way into people's lives and create a real and intimate bond between maker and user.

My core contained a USB memory stick; the purchaser had to take a punt on what he or she was getting, and I didn't know whether they were going to like it or not. It was another video, offering a bowl and spoon, but it was a conditional offer. I would keep my part of the deal if the purchaser promised to use the bowl and spoon regularly at home; I didn't want it to be an artwork on the shelf. I could not have been more pleased than to find that Albert LeCoff, executive director of The Center for Art in Wood, bought my core and now joins a growing band of folk around the world who use my bowls and spoons.

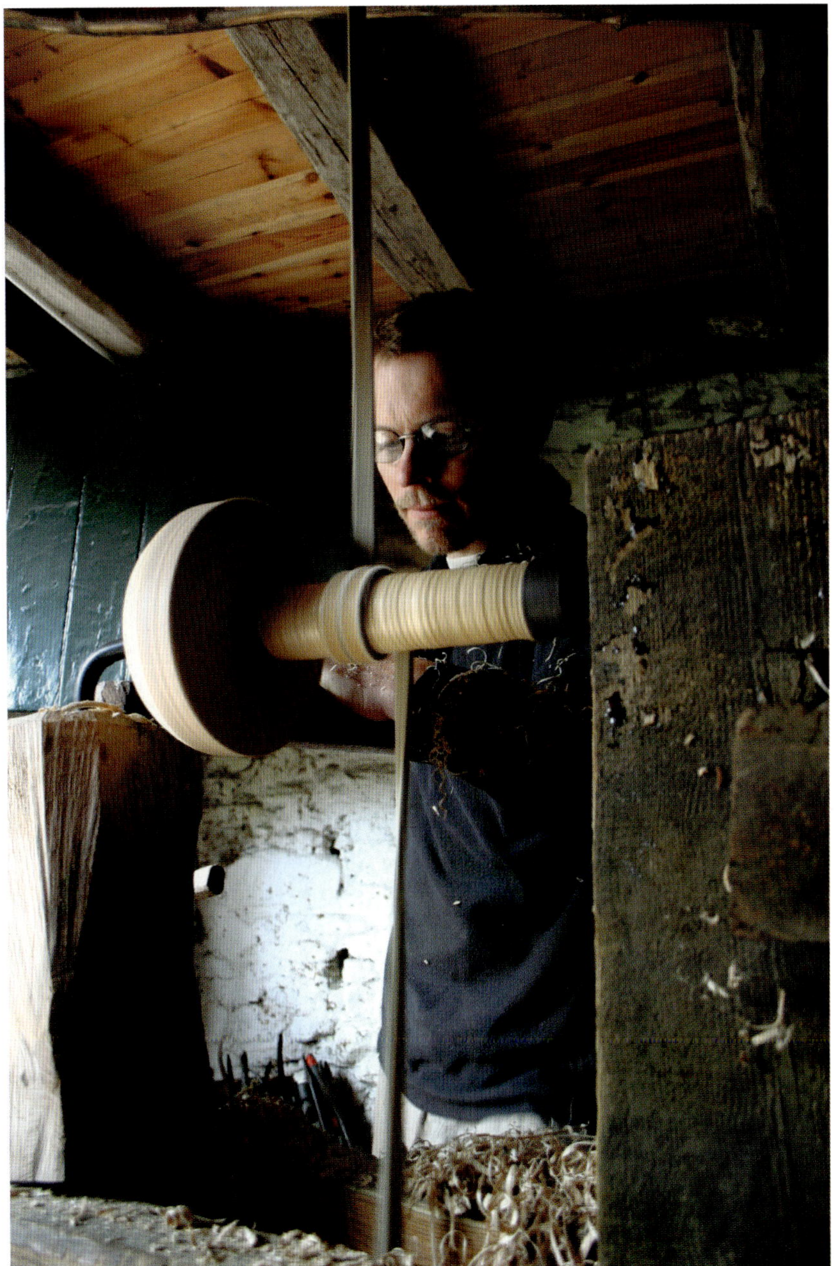

Robin Wood, an expert on medieval woodworking, turns a bowl on his pole lathe, using the oscillating turning caused by the strap attached to a foot treadle and a bending pole above.

Index

Laurent Guillot, France
Core than precious, 2012 | Core | 2" x Dia. 5"
page 62

Peter Harrison, United States
Rotary, 2012 | Core, sapele, stainless steel
7" x Dia. 10 ½"| page 64

Doug Haslam, Canada
Adamski Call Home!, 2012 | Core, pernambuco, mixed media | 6" x 4 ½" x 5 ½" | page 66

Michelle Holzapfel, United States
Cores Collage Arranged According to the Laws of Chance, 2012 | Core, mixed woods, found objects
32" x 18" x 6" Photo by David Holzapfel | page 68

Richard Hooper, United Kingdom
Reactor Core, 2012 | Core, glass, metal
4 ½" x 23" x 5" | page 70

Beth Ireland, United States | ***Metamorph, 2012***
Core, milk paint | 2" x 11" x ¾" | page 74

Michael Kehs, United States
Hint of Flight, 2012 | Core (maple) | 3" x Dia. 4 ½"
page 76

Max Krimmel, United States
CORE Dreams, 2012 | Core, color photography
9" x 5" x 5" Photo by Max Krimmel| page 78

Simon Levy, United States
Night Owl, 2012 | Core, metal | 2 ¼" x 2 ¼" x 2 ½"
Photo by Simon Levy| page 80

Yoav Liberman, United States
Artifact, 2012 | Core, mahogany, canvas, steel, cardboard | 6 ½" x 5" x 3" Photo by Yoav Liberman
page 82

Robert Lyon, United States
The Doodler's Dream, 2012 | Core, pencils, erasers
8" x Dia. 4 ¾" | page 84

Gord Peteran, Canada
"Before" and "After", 2012 | Color photography
18" x 21" | page 86

Michael Peterson, United States
Untitled, 2012 | Core (oak) | 2 ½" x 3 ½" x 3 ⅛"
Photo by Jean Peterson | page 88

Hilary Pfeifer, United States
Have Nothing In Your House That You Do Not Know To Be Useful And Believe To Be Beautiful (For Todd Akin), 2012 | Core, mixed media | 17" x 5" x 4"
Photo by Hilary Pfeifer| page 90

Carl Pittman, United States
From Earth to Oxygen, 2012 | Core (pear tree), copper wire, ammonite, book pages from ***Turning to Art in Wood*** | 2" x 3 ½" x 1 ⅜" | page 92

Jeannette Rein, Western Australia
Sea Urchin, 2012 | Core (walnut), silver, acrylic paint, carnauba wax | 1 ¼" x 1 ¼" x 1 ¾" | page 94

Gabriel Romeu, United States
Core Intersection Wall Lamp, 2012 | Core, oak, purpleheart, aluminum, copper leaf, acrylic, ABS plastic, halogen lamp | 32" x 16" x 32" | page 96

Randall Rosenthal, United States
Match Book + Box, 2012 | Core, acrylic paint
1 ¾" x 3 ¼" x 2 ¾" | page 98

Jamie Russell, Canada
Rockabye Birdies, 2012 | Core, padouk
2 ⅛" x 5" x 3 ⅝" | page 100

Joshua Salesin, United States
Core-upted, 2012 | Core, African blackwood
3" x 6" x 4" | page 102

Norm Sartorius, United States
Plum Spoon, 2012 | Core (plum wood)
¾" x 2 ½" x 2 ½" Photo by Jim Osborn| page 104

Merryll Saylan, United States
Core Ore, 2012 | Core, poplar, milk paint, acrylic
5" x 5" x 4" | page 106

Michael Scarborough, United States
Akai Maru (Red Circle), 2012 | Core, paint, varnish, 23K gold leaf | 1 ¾" x Dia. 4 ½" | page 108

David Sengel, United States
My Grandfather Recycled Everything, 2012
Core, old wire, paint | 5" x 3" | page 110

Jack Slentz, United States
A Little Jack Slentz, 2012 | Core
1 ½" x 1 ½" x 1 ½" | page 112

Brad Smith, United States
165 Heels, 2012 | Core, cherry, poplar, willow, ash, milk paint | 34" x 13 ½" x 13 ½"
Photo by Joseph Kolasinski | page 114

Alan Stirt, United States
Textured Bowl, 2012 | Core (oak), milk paint
2 ½" x Dia. 3 ⅛" Photo by Alan Stirt | page 116

Holly Tornheim, United States
Between Tides, 2012 | Core | 1 ¼" x 4" x 4"
page 118

Neil Turner, Western Australia
Coral Core, 2012 | Core | 2 ⅝" x Dia. 4"
Photo by Suellen Turner | page 120

Joël Urruty, United States
Casa, 2012 | Core, 23K gold leaf
6 ½" x 3 ½" x 2" Photo by Joël Urruty
page 122

Derek Weidman, United States
Little World, 2012 | Core, cherry, acrylic
4" x 3" x 1" | page 124

Christopher Weiland, United States
Spin Top Series: Cast and Die, 2012 | Core (beech), maple, cardboard | 5" x 4" x 4"
Photo by Roy Engelbrecht | page 126

Kim Winkle, United States
Hub, 2012 | Core, milk paint, wire, thread
10" x 10" x 20" Photo by Dan Carothers | page 128

Robin Wood, Derbyshire, England
Art, 2012 | Core, digital media (with a personal message from Robin Wood) | 2 ¼" x 2 ½"
page 130

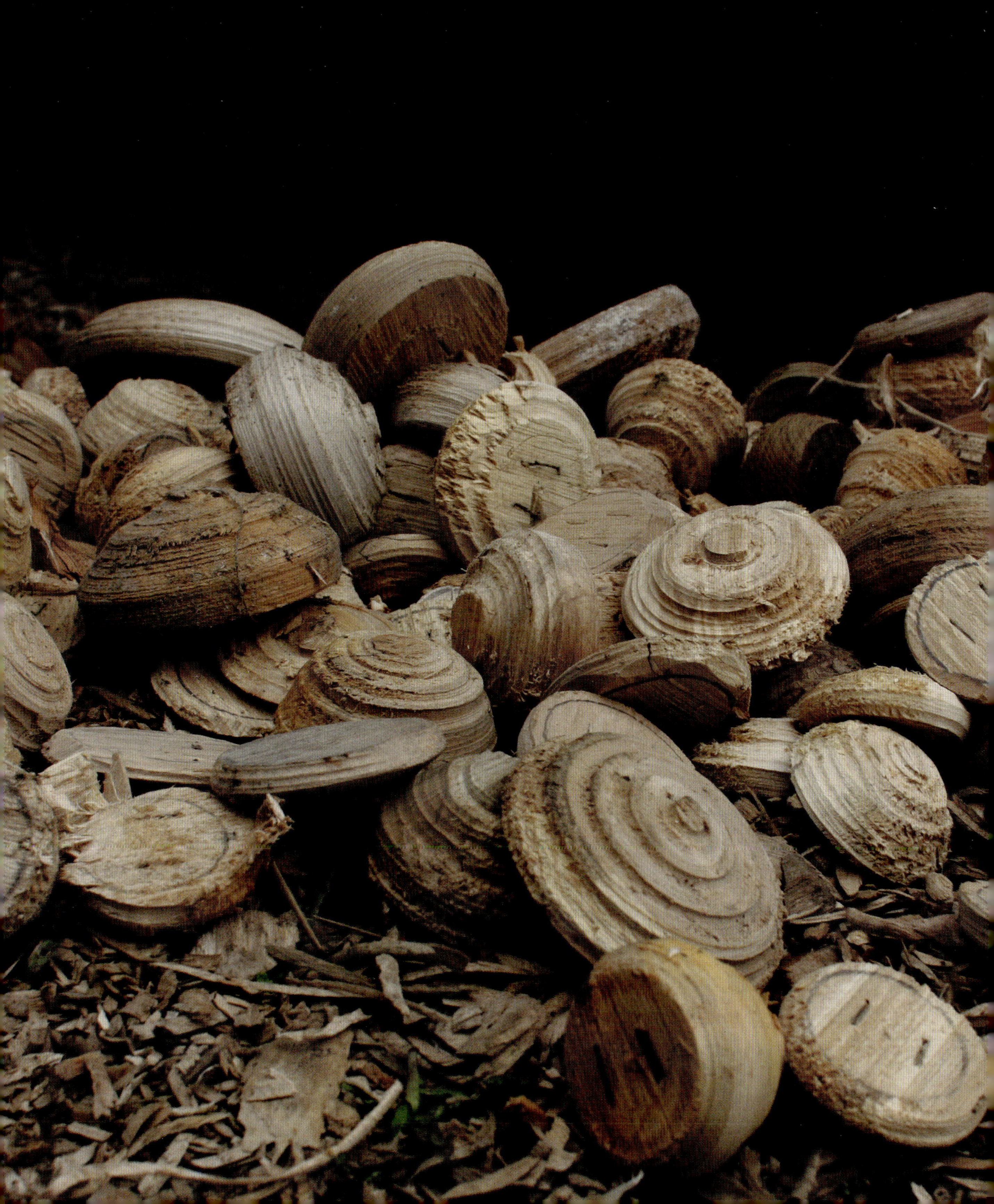

Other Schiffer Books by the Author:

Turning to Art in Wood: A Creative Journey, 978-0-7643-4204-2

Bartram's Boxes Remix, 978-0-7643-4736-8

Other Schiffer Books on Related Subjects:

Studio Furniture: Today's Leading Woodworkers, by Tina Skinner, 978-0-7643-3287-6

Turning Bowls, By Dick Sing, 978-0-7643-1795-8

Library of Congress Control Number: 2014853788

Editor: Judson Randall, Portland, Oregon

Designer: Brenda McCallum
Cover Design: Justin Watkinson

Photographer: Except where specifically noted, John Carlano, Philadelphia, Pennsylvania

ISBN: 978-0-7643-4783-2
Printed in China

The Center for Art in Wood
The Fleur Bresler Publication Fund

141 N. 3rd Street, Philadelphia, PA 19106
215-923-8000
www.centerforartinwood.org

Published by Schiffer Publishing, Ltd.
4880 Lower Valley Road
Atglen, PA 19310
Phone: (610) 593-1777; Fax: (610) 593-2002
E-mail: Info@schifferbooks.com

Front cover: Top: Luc Deroo, *Butterfly*;
Bottom: Robin Wood, Cores

Back cover: Clockwise from top right: Beth Ireland, *Metamorph*; Neil Turner, *Coral Core;* Derek Weidman, *Little World*; Peter Harrison, *Rotary*: Robin Wood, Cores

COLOPHON

Typset in Futura/Helevtica